the Adobe® photoshop® CS3 book

for digital photographers

Scott Kelby

THE ADOBE PHOTOSHOP CS3 BOOK FOR DIGITAL PHOTOGRAPHERS

The Adobe Photoshop CS3 Book for Digital Photographers Team

CREATIVE DIRECTOR
Felix Nelson

TECHNICAL EDITORS
Kim Doty
Cindy Snyder

TRAFFIC DIRECTOR
Kim Gabriel

PRODUCTION MANAGER
Dave Damstra

DESIGNER
Jessica Maldonado

COVER PHOTOS BY
Scott Kelby
Dave Gales

STOCK IMAGES
The royalty-free stock images
used in this book are courtesy of
iStockphoto.com

Published by
New Riders

Composed in Cronos and Helvetica by Kelby Publishing

ISBN 13: 978-0-321-50191-2
ISBN 10:   0-321-50191-8

9 8 7 6 5 4 3 2

www.newriders.com
www.scottkelbybooks.com

For three people
who I absolutely adore:
Kalebra, Jordan, and Kira.
You make my life a joy.

ACKNOWLEDGMENTS

First, I want to thank my amazing wife Kalebra. We've been married nearly 18 years now, and just looking at her still makes my heart skip a beat, and again reminds me how much I adore her, how genuinely beautiful she is, and how I couldn't live without her. She's the type of woman love songs are written for, and I am, without a doubt, the luckiest man alive to have her as my wife.

Secondly, I want to thank my 10-year-old son Jordan, who spent many afternoons pulling me away from writing this book so we could play *Dragon Ball Z: Budokai Tenkaichi 2* or *Guitar Hero II* (a game I'm finally decent at). God has blessed our family with so many wonderful gifts, and I can see them all reflected in his eyes. I'm so proud of him, so thrilled to be his dad, and I dearly love watching him grow to be such a wonderful little guy, with such a tender and loving heart. (You're the greatest, little buddy.)

I also want to thank my daughter Kira Nicole Kelby for being such a little sweetie. My wife and I knew we were having a baby girl, we just didn't realize that she would in fact be "the cutest little baby in the whole wide world."

I also want to thank my brother Jeffrey for being such a positive influence in my life, for always taking the high road, for always knowing the right thing to say, and just the right time to say it, and for having so much of our dad in you. I'm honored to have you as my brother and my friend.

My heartfelt thanks go to the entire team at KW Media Group, who every day redefine what teamwork and dedication are all about. They are truly a special group of people, who come together to do some really amazing things (on really scary deadlines), and they do it with class, poise, and a can-do attitude that is truly inspiring. I'm so proud to be working with you all.

Thanks to my layout and production crew. In particular, I want to thank my friend and Creative Director Felix Nelson for his limitless talent, creativity, input, and just for his flat-out great ideas.

A heartfelt thanks goes to my Tech Editor Kim Doty, who did an amazing job keeping this project on track and organized (while making sure I was organized, too, which is not easy to do). I am just so tickled to have you on our team, and working with you is really just a joy. Besides all your editing and management skills—you're going to make one really great mommy!

Also, a big, big thanks to Cindy Snyder, who helps test all the techniques in the book and, as always, she caught lots of little things that others would have missed.

My thanks to "The Michigan Layout Machine" Dave Damstra and his amazing crew for giving the book such a tight, clean layout. We got truly lucky when we found you!

Thanks to my best buddy Dave Moser (Hey You!), who makes darn sure everything we do is better than what we did last. Thanks to Jean A. Kendra for all her support, and for keeping a lot of plates in the air while I'm writing these books. A very special thanks to my Executive

Assistant Kathy Siler for all her hard work and dedication, and for keeping the rest of business running like clockwork so I have time to work on books like this. I don't know what I'd do without you. (Oh, and thanks for the meatballs. Mmmm. Meatballs.)

Thanks to my Publisher Nancy Ruenzel, and the incredibly dedicated team at Peachpit/New Riders. You are very special people doing very special things, and it's a real honor to get to work with people who really just want to make great books. Also many thanks to the awesome Ted "The L Shirt Connection" Waitt, Glenn Bisignani, and to marketing maverick Scott Cowlin.

Thanks to Kevin Connor and John Nack at Adobe for their help, and for hearing my pleas, and to the wonderful Deb Whitman, Mala Sharma, and John Loiacono for all your continued support and great ideas.

Thanks to my friends at Adobe Systems, including: Terry White, Addy Roff, Cari Gushiken, Russell Brady, Julieanne Kost, Tom Hogarty, Jennifer Stern, George Jardine, Dave Story, and Russell Preston Brown, and the amazing engineering team at Adobe (I don't know how you all do it). Gone but not forgotten: Barbara Rice, Rye Livingston, Bryan Lamkin, and Karen Gauthier.

Thanks to my "Photoshop Guys" Dave Cross and Matt Kloskowski, for being such excellent sounding boards for the development of this book. You guys are the best! Also, thanks to Corey Barker (The Photoshop Lad), and to RC (El Bandito de Photoshop) for coming on board and making my life easier and more fun.

I want to thank all the talented and gifted photographers who've taught me so much over the years, including: Bill Fortney, Moose Peterson, Joe McNally, Anne Cahill, Vincent Versace, David Ziser, Helene Glassman, and Jim DiVitale.

My personal thanks to Susan Hill, Matt Kloskowski, Ashley Gellar, Sarah Crist, Susan Thelwell, Miguel Cairo, Jenna and Debbie Stephenson, Kalebra Kelby, Jordan Kelby, Lani Anderson, Tony Llanes, "Fiddles," Thomas, and Frank for lending me their wonderful faces for the book.

I would like to dedicate the "How to Show Your Work" chapter of this book to legendary wedding and portrait photographer, and gifted photography instructor, Monte Zucker who passed away earlier this year after battling pancreatic cancer. He truly was a remarkable person whose passion for sharing, and genuine love of people, could be seen by the twinkle in his eye, his warm caring smile, and the magical images he created. Our industry lost a true icon with his passing. He will be missed. Thanks to my mentors whose wisdom and whip-cracking have helped me immeasurably, including John Graden, Jack Lee, Dave Gales, Judy Farmer, and Douglas Poole.

Most importantly, I want to thank God, and His son Jesus Christ, for leading me to the woman of my dreams, for blessing us with two amazing children, for allowing me to make a living doing something I truly love, for always being there when I need Him, for blessing me with a wonderful, fulfilling, and happy life, and such a warm, loving family to share it with.

OTHER BOOKS BY SCOTT KELBY

ABOUT THE AUTHOR

Scott Kelby

Scott is Editor, Publisher, and co-founder of *Photoshop User* magazine, Editor and Publisher of *Layers* magazine (the how-to magazine for everything Adobe), and is the host of the top-rated weekly video podcast *NAPP TV*.

Scott is President and co-founder of the National Association of Photoshop Professionals (NAPP), the trade association for Adobe® Photoshop® users, and he's President of the software training, education, and publishing firm KW Media Group.

Scott is a photographer, designer, and an award-winning author of more than 40 books, including *Photoshop Down & Dirty Tricks*, *The Adobe Photoshop Lightroom Book for Digital Photographers*, *The Photoshop Channels Book*, *Photoshop Classic Effects*, and *The Digital Photography Book*.

Since 2004, Scott has been honored with the distinction of being the world's #1 best-selling author of all computer and technology books, across all categories. His books have been translated into dozens of different languages, including Chinese, Russian, Spanish, Korean, Polish, Taiwanese, French, German, Italian, Japanese, Dutch, Swedish, Turkish, and Portuguese, among others, and he is a recipient of the prestigious Benjamin Franklin Award.

Scott is Training Director for the Adobe Photoshop Seminar Tour and Conference Technical Chair for the Photoshop World Conference & Expo. He's featured in a series of Adobe Photoshop training DVDs and has been training Adobe Photoshop users since 1993.

For more information on Scott, visit scottkelby.com.

TABLE OF CONTENTS www.scottkelbybooks.com

AN UNEXPECTED Q&A SECTION

Q. I didn't expect to see the book start with a Q&A section. Don't Q&A sections normally come after a chapter, rather than before the first chapter?

A. Normally they do. That's why this one is so unexpected. Back in the CS2 edition of this book, rather than an unexpected Q&A here, instead I interviewed myself. Basically, I asked myself questions about the book and then I answered them. (Luckily, I knew most of the answers. Well, except for two, but they were really hard.)

Q. So how did the interview with yourself go?

A. I have to tell you—I found me absolutely fascinating. But as engaging as I found myself, this time I thought I'd go with something different, and incorporate an idea from my book *The Adobe Photoshop Lightroom Book for Digital Photographers*, which is the "Unexpected Q&A" you're reading now. I've received a lot of great emails from readers who told me they liked this "Unexpected Q&A" because: (a) it was unexpected, (b) it wasn't me interviewing myself (apparently, they don't find me nearly as riveting as I do), and (c) they were just so happy to read anything up front that wasn't the introduction of the book.

Q. So, do people not like reading the introduction section of books?

A. Are you kidding? They hate it. As best as I can tell, most people would rather endure an invasive, non-elective, medically unnecessary surgical procedure than take the few short minutes it takes to read a book's introduction.

Q. How do you know?

A. It's because each year a large number of people actually schedule, and pay in advance, for invasive, non-elective, medically unnecessary surgical procedures. Contrast that with the most recent figures gathered by the Mintz/Lawler Data Group (the leading book publishing industry statistical research firm), which shows that between the years 2005 and 2007, only 14 people in the U.S. (15 if you include data collected in the U.K.) have actually read a computer book's introduction.

Q. Are you serious?

A. Of course not. It's more like 16 people.

Q. So why don't people read the introductions?

A. I think it's because these days a lot of book introductions just try to convince you to buy the book, so they think "Oh, that's another one of those," and they skip it. But my introductions are nothing like that.

Q. Why not?

A. It's because I figure if you're reading this, you've already bought the book, right? Here's the thing: if we (as authors) can't get people who've actually bought the book to read the introduction, imagine how few people read it that haven't bought the book. The number has to be next to nil. Actually, thanks to years and years of made up analytical studies, we in fact know the exact number. It's two (but only one of them is still living).

Continued

AN UNEXPECTED Q&A SECTION (continued)

Q. So, are you saying what I think you're saying?

A. Yes, that's what I'm saying. Look, I'm not going to lie to you. We've been through too much together for that, so I'm going to be straight with you. You're reading the book's introduction right now. Oh sure, it's called "An Unexpected Q&A Section" but come on, have you ever heard of an unexpected Q&A section? Especially one that comes before the first chapter? The sad part is— you knew this was just a ruse to get you to read the introduction, but yet you kept on going. A lot of people would have bolted for the first chapter as soon as they realized what was going on, but not you. You're different. You're special. People like you. I like you. (Buy this book.) Strangers find you attractive. (Buy this book.) Deer and other small animals in the woods are drawn to you. (Buy this book.) You are successful and energetic. (Buy this book.) Buy this book. (Whoops!)

Q. Ah ha—so you were trying to sell me on this book all along!

A. Absolutely not. But it's only because if you're reading this, concocted industry statistics clearly show that you've already bought the book.

Q. Rats!

A. That's not a question.

Q. Is the rest of the book like this?

A. Thankfully, no. The rest of the book is pretty straightforward, and pretty much just step-by-step instructions, without the powerful lure of these extraneous comments (my friend and editor Chris Main calls it stream-of-consciousness writing. Remind me to fire him). Here's the thing: when you write step-by-step books like this, there's no room for your own writing style to come through. It's pretty much: "Go under this menu for this" and "click on that button for that." So, in a step-by-step book like this, I only get two spots where I can inject any of my own personality and style (or lack thereof) into the book. They are (1) this unexpected Q&A, and (2) the chapter intros that start each chapter, which by the way, have little if anything to do with what's actually in said chapter.

Q. So, this "silly" stuff, this "stream-of-consciousness" stuff is pretty much limited to this intro and the chapter intros, right?

A. Right! Here's the thing: I've been trying different devices, different tricks, and unique ways to somehow fool my readers into reading these introductions for years now. That's because (in my books anyway) there is a real value in reading the introductions. (Buy this book.) For one thing, this is the only place in the book where I give the Web address where you can download the same photos I used in the book, so you can do the lessons, and try them right along with me. But there's a bigger issue. I genuinely want you to get the most out of this book, or any book I write, so in the introduction I try to give you some tips to help steer you in the right direction. To me, that's important, and since you've invested your time and money in this book, I hope it would be to you too. (Right about now you're probably missing that stream-of-consciousness stuff, aren't you?) That's why I keep coming up with these devices, like interviewing myself, and the unexpected Q&A. In one book I actually made the introduction look like a chapter (I even named it "Chapter 0"), complete with fake screen captures that didn't relate to the introduction in any way—but it worked. I got loads of emails from people who read the whole thing, and got a lot out of it. I also got some really angry email, too.

Q. Seriously—angry email?

A. Apparently, if you don't like my offbeat sense of humor, you don't like it in a big, big way. You hate it with a burning fire that knows no bounds. In fact, so much so that these folks (not you, of course) will either email me, or my publisher, or they'll write an exhaustive review online about just how much they hate it. And me. They'll sometimes mention my mother. My upbringing. My lineage. It gets pretty brutal sometimes, but I've learned to deal with it by drinking very heavily. I'm kidding. (See, if you're one of those people, you really, really hated those last two lines, and you're filled with rage. I await your email.)

Q. So, this is now the fourth edition of this book. What are the key things that are new in this edition?

A. Actually, I'm surprised at how much new content there is in this edition, as opposed to earlier updates of the book, especially since most of the new CS3 features (for photographers anyway) are contained within five areas: (1) the new Bridge CS3, which is so different and vastly updated that I pretty much had to rewrite both chapters pertaining to it; (2) the amazing new Camera Raw, which I pretty much rewrote from scratch and you'll see why shortly; (3) the whole Panorama/Photomerge thing (including Auto-Blend Layers and Auto-Align Layers), which is now so easy and automated I actually wound up writing less for it; (4) the new Black & White conversion feature; and (5) and the new printing features (I wound up rewriting that chapter too).

Q. So you've added other new stuff besides covering the new features for photographers in CS3?

A. You betcha! I've added lots of new techniques, including new, faster, and easier ways to do some of the things that I showed back in the last edition of the book, plus I've included a number of brand new techniques that I've never shown anywhere. Also, I've made time for a lot more shooting since I wrote the last edition of this book and I've learned loads of new Photoshop techniques since the last edition too (which was published back in April 2005). So, basically I added lots of new stuff I've learned in the past two years or so, but I also added something totally different. At the end of the book, I added a special workflow chapter that shows my own personal Photoshop workflow (exactly what I do, in the exact order I do it). I felt it was needed because, although the rest of the book shows you how to use everything from Curves to sharpening to how to create your own custom Black & White conversions, I thought it needed one place where it "all comes together" and that workflow chapter is it. I hope you find it useful. Of course, like always, the entire book is riddled with new little tricks, new features, new tips, and some helpful shortcuts and workarounds I've learned since the last book. See, I care.

Q. If you keep adding all this new stuff, this book should be around 900 pages, right?

A. That's right, Timmy, it should be, but it's not phonebook-sized by design. In fact, the book you're holding is actually a bit longer than I'd like, but choosing which content stays and which goes is really, really hard. In fact, it's almost harder than writing it. Here's the problem: this is the fourth edition of the book. If every time Adobe came out with an update to Photoshop, I did nothing other than add the new features (and I left everything else alone), it would already be over 900 pages, and this book would cost around $79. The problem is that virtually nobody buys 900-page books anymore, especially if they cost $79. (Personally, I wouldn't buy a 900-page book on any topic. Well, maybe if it was an in-depth study of the lyrical stylings of The Backstreet Boys, but even then, I'd be hard-pressed to pay $79. $65 maybe, but $79…I dunno.) The good part is—by pruning the low-hanging fruit (so to speak), each edition of the book gets progressively better and better, without it getting bigger and bigger.

Q. So what happens to all that stuff you took out?

A. I let my hamster tear it into a million pieces (it was one of the happiest days of my life). Actually, I've posted those bonus chapters in PDF format just for readers of this book, and you can go and download them from the book's website at www .scottkelbybooks.com/cs3book. You'll find entire chapters that were in the old version of the book, but updated for CS3. So, you still get that content, but without the needless bulk, and more importantly—without the added cost. However, if you feel somewhat guilty and are then compelled to send me a check, that's totally fine by me—I just want you to feel comfortable.

Continued

(By the way—you wouldn't even know about these bonus chapters had you skipped this intro and gone straight to Chapter 1. I feel bad for those people who did. Those are also some of the same people who will read the stream-of-consciousness chapter opener to Chapter 1 and think, "I really, really hate this guy's sense of humor," and then they'll fire up their email and…well, you can see where this is going.)

Q. Isn't calling those chapters you took out "bonus chapters" just marketing hype concocted by big oil and the government to divert my attention from what's happening in the Middle East?
A. Yes.

Q. That's a surprisingly frank and honest answer from a guy who tricked me into reading this whole unexpected Q&A.
A. I've gotta tell ya—I'm just amazed you're still reading it.

Q. Do I need to read this book in order, starting with Chapter 1, then on to Chapter 2, and so on, or can I skip around?
A. I specifically designed this book to be in "jump in anywhere" book, and although the chapters are in the order of a professional's workflow, everything is spelled out in every chapter, so you can turn to the technique you want to learn first and start right there—you'll be able to follow along, no sweat.

Q. How did you develop the original content for this book?
A. Each year I'm fortunate enough to train literally thousands of professional digital photographers around the world at my live seminars, and although I'm doing the teaching, at every seminar I always learn something new. Photographers love to share their favorite techniques, and during the breaks between sessions, or at lunch, somebody's always showing me how they "get the job done." It's really an amazing way to learn. Plus, and perhaps most importantly, I hear right from their own lips the problems and challenges these photographers are facing in their own work in Photoshop, so I have a great insight into what photographers really want to learn next. Plus, I'm out there shooting myself, so I'm constantly dealing with my own problems in Photoshop and developing new ways to make my digital workflow faster, easier, and more fun. That's because (like you) I want to spend less time sitting behind a computer screen and more time doing what I love best—shooting! So, as soon as I come up with a new trick, or if I learn a slick new way of doing something, I just can't wait to share it with other photographers. It's a sickness. I know.

Q. So, what's not in this book?
A. I tried not to put things in this book that are already in every other Photoshop book out there. For example, I don't have a chapter on the Layers panel, or a chapter on the painting tools, or a chapter showing how each of Photoshop's 110 filters look when applied to the same photograph. I just focused on the most important, most asked-about, and most useful things for digital photographers. In short—it's the funk and not the junk.

Q. Does it matter whether I use Mac OS or Windows?
A. Not one little bit. That's because Photoshop is pretty much identical on a Windows PC and on a Mac, so the book is designed for both platforms. However, the keyboard on a PC is slightly different from the keyboard on a Mac, so anytime I give a keyboard shortcut in the book, I give both the PC and Mac keyboard shortcuts.

Q. What advice would you give to more advanced Photoshop users who read this book?

A. Actually, I would just tell them one thing to look out for. I wrote this book so anyone at any level of the Photoshop experience could jump right in, so if you've been using Photoshop for years, don't let it throw you that I spell everything out. For example, in the tutorials, rather than writing "Open Curves" (which a pro instinctively knows how to do), I usually write, "Go under the Image menu, under Adjustments, and choose Curves." That way, everybody can follow along, and this is particularly important for photographers who are just now switching to digital (there are more holdouts than you'd think). Many of these traditional film photographers are brilliant, talented, amazing photographers, but since they're just now "going digital," they may not know anything about Photoshop. I didn't want to leave them out or make it harder for them, so I spell everything out. I knew you'd understand.

Q. So where are the photos we can download?

A. You can download the photos from the book's companion website at www.scottkelbybooks.com/cs3book. Of course, the whole idea is that you'd use these techniques on your own photos, but if you want to practice on mine, I won't tell anybody. Although I shot most of the images you'll be downloading, I asked our friends over at iStockphoto.com to lend me some of their work, especially for the portrait retouching chapter (it's really hard to retouch photos of people you know and still be on speaking terms with them after the book is published). So, I'm very grateful to iStockphoto.com for lending me (us, you, we, etc.) their images (portraits of total strangers which I don't mind retouching at all), and I'm particularly thankful they let us (you) download low-res versions of their photos used here in the book, so you can practice on them as well. Please visit their site—they've got a really unique community going on there, and it wouldn't hurt if you gave them a great big sack of money while you're there. At the very least, make a stock shot of a big stack of money and upload that. It might turn into an actual big stack of money.

Q. Scott, I have to tell you—I was skeptical about this whole unexpected Q&A thing, but you were right—there really was valuable information in here, and if I had skipped over it, the book wouldn't have been as valuable to me.

A. Thanks for letting me know that. It really means a lot that you've taken this time out of your busy schedule to spend some quality time with me. I think we really bonded during this unexpected Q&A, and I hope that we'll reconnect at the beginning of every chapter for a few moments of stream-of-consciousness soup.

Q. OK, can I get to work now?

A. Absolutely. You've paid your dues. You've put your time in. You experienced the unexpected. Now go and make great images, my friend. Fly...fly...soar up to the sky... (oh crap. I really don't know how to end this in any meaningful kind of way, so please just quickly turn the page and I promise—we'll never discuss this again).

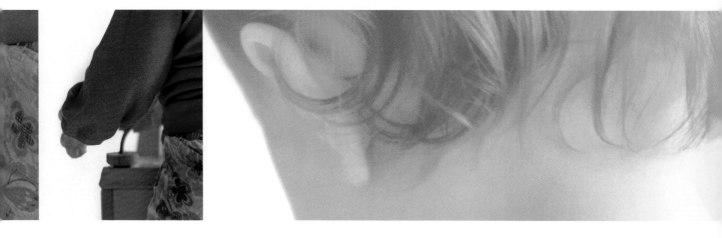

London Bridge
bridge essentials

This is the first chapter in the book (which is precisely why, against the wishes of my editor, I call it "Chapter 1"). Anyway, this is as good a time as any to let you know that I have always named the chapters in my books after songs, movies, or TV shows, so it's actually the subtitle that appears under the chapter title that really tells you what the chapter is about. If you looked at the chapter title above, you probably thought, "Oh, how cute. He named this chapter after a nursery rhyme." If you thought that, you are very old. At least 40. However, if you're much, much younger than that (like myself), and incurably cool (ditto), then you probably recognize the title not as a nursery rhyme, but as a tender, emotion-filled love song that includes the touching lyric "I'm Fergie Ferg and me love you long time." Ah ha (you loudly exclaim), that "love you long time" bit is a reference to the movie *Full Metal Jacket* (which came out in 1987. I was probably a toddler back then and definitely not already 27 years old, if that's what you're thinking). So now you're feeling all "Yeah, I knew that one," but then there's a single bead of sweat trickling down your forehead. It's there because you're afraid someone (me) is going to ask you who this Fergie is and the only Fergie you know (at your advanced age) is the Duchess of York, but you know darn well that she isn't likely to be quoting lines from *Full Metal Jacket* in her R&B songs, but now you're even more worried that the rest of the book you just bought is like this chapter intro. If you're worried about that, it can only mean one thing: you didn't read the "Unexpected Q&A" that came before this chapter. If I were you, I'd go back and read that now. Don't worry. I'll wait long time.

Getting Your Photos Into Bridge

So, you've finished your shoot, and now you're back at your computer and ready to look at your photos, see how you did, separate the keepers from the clunkers, etc. Of course, the very first step is to get the photos from your camera (or ideally, from your camera's memory card using a card reader) onto your computer and into Adobe Bridge. Luckily, in Bridge 2, Adobe included a built-in photo downloader, so the process is much easier than in the previous version. So, here's where it all starts—getting your photos into Adobe Bridge.

Step One:
To import photos from your digital camera, first launch Adobe Bridge (from here on out, I'll just call it Bridge for short), and then go under the File menu and choose Get Photos from Camera (as shown here).

TIP: The slowest, and most dangerous way to import photos is to connect your camera directly to your computer. A much faster and safer way is to use a memory card reader instead, and the faster the card reader the better (I recommend one that uses either a USB 2 or FireWire connection. I use a Lexar CompactFlash FireWire Card Reader, which is very fast and reliable. It's around $16.95 for the USB version, and $39.95 for the FireWire).

Step Two:
This brings up Bridge's Photo Down-loader. Before you do anything else, you'll want to click the Advanced Dialog button in the bottom-left corner (as shown here). While this does make some advanced options available, more importantly, it shows a preview of the photos you're about to import. If you ask me, that's not an "advanced" option—that's an "essential" option.

SCOTT KELBY

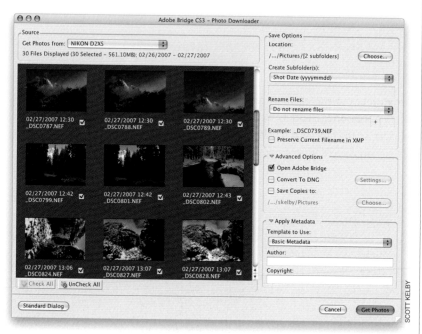

SCOTT KELBY

Step Three:

Here's the Advanced Photo Downloader, with the all-important thumbnail previews of what you're importing. By default, it imports every photo it finds on your memory card. If you see a photo you don't want imported, just turn off the checkbox to the right of its name (only checked photos will be imported). If you want just a few photos imported, first click the UnCheck All button (below the left side of the thumbnail preview area) to uncheck all the photos. Then press-and-hold the Command (PC: Ctrl) key and click on all the photos you want imported (as you do, each thumbnail is highlighted). Once you have all the photos you want to import selected, turn on the checkbox for any one of these selected photos, and they all become checked.

Step Four:

Once you've chosen which photos you want imported (it's probably all of them, but if not, at least you learned how to choose them back in Step Three), you get to choose where these photos will be saved to on your computer. By default, on a Mac it saves them in your Pictures folder, and on a PC it saves them in your My Pictures folder. If you want them saved to a different location, then click the Choose (PC: Browse) button (as shown here, where I've zoomed in on the Save Options section of the Photo Down-loader). This brings up a standard Open dialog, where you can choose the location where you'd like your imported photos stored. Pretty standard stuff—you've chosen which photos you want to import, and where you want to save them once they're imported.

Continued

Step Five:

By default, it's going to put your photos into subfolders named with the date you took them. So, let's say you have three different shoots, each taken a few days apart, on the same memory card. When they're imported, if you look in your Pictures (PC: My Pictures) folder, you'll see three new folders, each named with the dates the shots inside it were taken. If you'd prefer they were all in one folder with a custom name that you choose, then select Custom Name from the Create Subfolder(s) pop-up menu (as shown here), and type in the name you'd like in the field just below that pop-up menu (here, I named my single folder "Yosemite Winter").

Step Six:

Also by default, your photos will keep the same cryptic, non-descriptive, just-about-useless names your camera gave them when they were taken. (This stinks, because if you're trying to find a photo of Yosemite, you probably wouldn't search for a file named "_DSC0739.NEF." You'd probably search for something more like…oh, I dunno… Yosemite?) So, I recommend having the Photo Downloader rename your photos as they're imported with a descriptive name, which makes your life much easier down the road. To do this, click on the Rename Files pop-up menu, and choose which naming convention you'd like. Personally, I like to give each of my photos a descriptive custom name, followed by the year it was shot, the month, and day. So, from this pop-up menu I would choose Custom Name + Shot Date (yymmdd), as shown here.

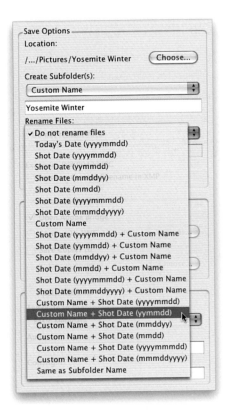

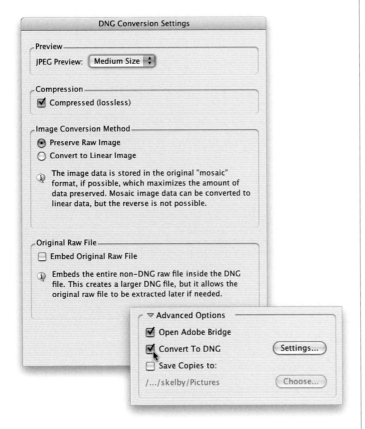

Step Seven:

Once you've chosen any of the naming conventions that have a custom name in it from the Rename Files pop-up menu, the name field is highlighted beneath it. Type in your custom name (in this case, I chose "Yosemite") and then in the field to the right of it, choose the number where you'd like the sequential numbering to start. An example of your renaming appears directly under the name field (as seen here). There's also a checkbox that lets you embed the original filename into your renamed file, just in case for some reason you need it one day. Now, I always turn this feature on, yet I've never needed to know a photo's original camera-given name thus far, but hey—ya never know.

Step Eight:

In the Advanced Options section, there's a checkbox that automatically opens Bridge (if it's not already open). I know what you're thinking: "That's an advanced option?" (Don't get me started.) Anyway, directly under that you have the ability to convert your RAW, JPEG, or TIFF files to Adobe's DNG format, which is a universal archival format (designed primarily for RAW files, whose formats today are mostly camera-specific), so that they can be opened and accessed in the future. DNG is a subchapter unto itself, so for more on Adobe's DNG initiative, visit www.adobe.com/products/dng/index.html. Here's my rule of thumb: If it's a RAW file, I convert it to DNG. If it's a JPEG or TIFF file, I don't (since a JPEG is a JPEG, so to speak). If you turn on the Convert To DNG checkbox and click the Settings button to the right, a dialog appears (shown here) where you can customize your DNG settings, including how large your preview is, how to save the RAW file, and whether to embed the original RAW file inside your DNG.

Continued

Step Nine:

There's one more option in the Advanced Options section and, to me, this is a critically important option. That's the option to automatically back up your imported photos to a different hard drive. Just turn on the Save Copies To checkbox and then click the Choose (PC: Browse) button to the right of it to choose an external hard drive, network, etc., where you want a copy of the photos you're importing backed up to. This is so incredibly important because at this point, if your computer's hard drive crashes, all your photos are gone. For good. But by turning this feature on, you'll have a second backup set on a totally separate hard drive (and yes, it has to be on a totally separate hard drive—backing up to a different folder on your same computer doesn't help, because if your computer's hard drive crashes, you lose the originals and the backup at the same time).

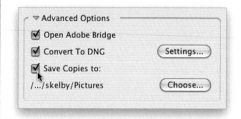

Step 10:

The next section down is the Apply Metadata section. This is where you're able to embed your name and copyright information into each file automatically, as it's imported. Simply click in the Author field and type in your name. Then click in the Copyright field, type in your copyright info (as shown here), and you're set. Now, you can have more information embedded upon import than this, but first you'd have to create a metadata template (which would appear in that pop-up menu at the top of this section). I show you how to create your own a little later, so for now, just use the Basic Metadata template and enter your name and copyright info (as shown here. Of course, enter your own name, not mine. I really didn't have to say that, did I?).

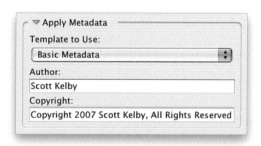

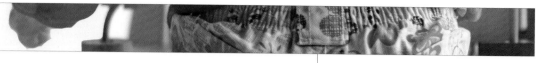

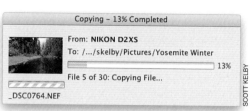

Step 11:

Well, that's the whole deal. So now all you have to do is click the Get Photos button (in the bottom right-hand corner of the Photo Downloader), and a download status dialog appears (shown here), showing you which files are being imported, how far along you are, etc.

Step 12:

Once your files are imported, they're displayed in Bridge as thumbnails (as shown here), and now you can begin sorting, ranking, and all the other cool stuff we're going to learn in the rest of this chapter. Back in Step One, I had you go to the File menu and choose Get Photos from Camera to bring up the Photo Downloader. If you'd like it to appear anytime you plug in your memory card reader (or even your camera), press Command-K (PC: Ctrl-K) to bring up Bridge's Preferences, and turn on the checkbox for When a Camera is Connected, Launch Adobe Photo Downloader (as shown here). On a PC, select Download Images Using Adobe Bridge CS3 in the Autoplay dialog and turn on the Always Do This for Pictures checkbox.

TIP: Besides the photos on your computer and the automatic backup saved to your separate hard drive, right now (before you start any editing) I would burn that imported folder of photos to a DVD+R disc and store it vertically (upright, like a book) in a safe, cool, dark, dry location. Also, don't apply any kind of adhesive label to the disc, and if you're going to write on it with a marker, make sure that it's non-solvent based. I know, this sounds like a lot of work, but these are your negatives, and perhaps the visual history of your life. It's worth protecting.

Creating a Contact Sheet for Your CD/DVD Jewel Case

If you took my advice from the last tutorial and burned an archival-quality CD or DVD backup of your original photos (before you started editing them), then you can save yourself a lot of time and frustration down the road if you create a CD/DVD-jewel-case-sized contact sheet now. That way, when you pick up the CD/DVD years later, you'll see exactly what's on the disc before you even insert it into your computer. Luckily, the process is pretty much automated—you make a few simple option choices, and Photoshop takes it from there.

Step One:

In Bridge, press Command-A (PC: Ctrl-A) to select all your photos (of course, make sure the photos you want to make a contact sheet for are the ones you see now onscreen). Then go under Bridge's Tools menu, under Photoshop, and choose Contact Sheet II (as shown here). *Note:* When you're not working in Bridge, you can find this contact sheet feature by going under Photoshop's File menu, under Automate, and choosing Contact Sheet II.

SCOTT KELBY

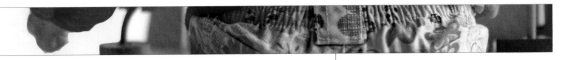

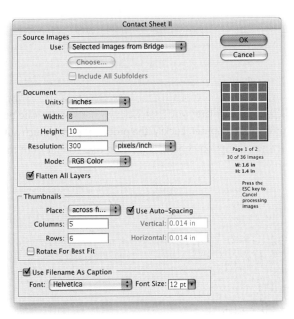

Step Two:

This launches Photoshop and opens the Contact Sheet II dialog (shown here). In the top section, where you would normally choose which photos you'd like in your contact sheet, the Use pop-up menu reads Selected Images from Bridge, since you already chose the photos you want for your contact sheet back in Step One. If you hadn't, then you'd choose a folder of images by selecting Folder from the Use pop-up menu and clicking on the Choose (PC: Browse) button.

Step Three:

The rest of the Contact Sheet II dialog is where you pick how you want your contact sheet to look. In the Document section, enter the width and height of your jewel case cover. (The standard size is 4.75x4.75", but I recommend using 4.5x4.5"; otherwise, the contact sheet places the thumbnails too close to the edge. By making it 1/4" smaller, as you'll see later, you can add 1/4" of white space around it, making it look much better.) For the Resolution field, I choose a low resolution of only 72 ppi for two reasons: (1) the thumbnails wind up being so small they don't need any higher resolution, and (2) Photoshop builds your contact sheet much faster using low-res images. I leave the Mode pop-up menu set to RGB Color (the default), and I choose to flatten all layers—that way I don't end up with a large, multilayered Photoshop document. I just want a document that I can print once and then delete.

The Thumbnails section is where you choose the layout. Luckily, Adobe put a preview on the far-right side of the dialog. Change the number of rows and columns (try setting them both at 6), and this live preview will give you an idea of how your layout will look.

Continued

Step Four:

At the bottom of the dialog, you'll see that Use Filename As Caption is turned on, and with good reason. One day when you go back to this CD/DVD looking for a particular photo, if there's no name below each thumbnail, you'll have to search through every photo on the disc to locate the one you saw on the case's contact sheet. However, if you include the filename below each thumbnail, then getting right to that shot takes just seconds.

Step Five:

There's also a Font pop-up menu for choosing from a handful of fonts for your thumbnail captions, and then you can choose a size from the Font Size pop-up menu. The font choices are somewhat lame, but believe me, they're better than what was offered in the original contact sheet feature, so count your blessings.

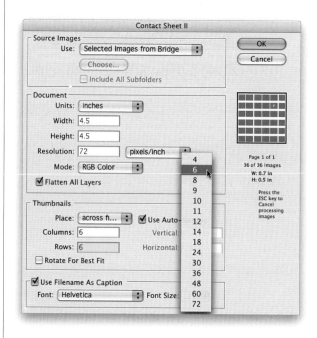

TIP: When you're choosing a font size for your contact sheet's thumbnail captions, if you have rows and rows of thumbnails (rather than just six) make sure you decrease the default Font Size setting of 12 points to something significantly lower, like 6 points. You'll need to do this because of the long file names assigned to the images from your digital camera (otherwise, you'll only see the first three letters of the filename, making the contact sheet worthless, like the one shown here). So how small should you make your type? That depends. The more thumbnails you're fitting on your contact sheet, the smaller you'll need to make the font size.

SCOTT KELBY

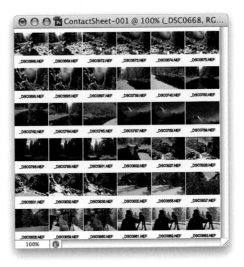

Step Six:

Now it's time to let 'er rip! With all your settings in place, just click OK. Within a minute or two, you'll have a contact sheet. But notice how tight the thumbnails are to the top and side edges? That's what I was talking about earlier when I said it's better to make your contact sheet's size slightly smaller than you need, so later (actually, in the next step), you can add some white space around it, which makes it less crowded, easier to use, and it just plain looks better.

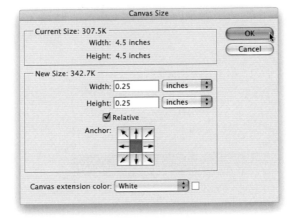

Step Seven:

Here's where we add that 1/4" of space back in, allowing some breathing room around the thumbnails in the contact sheet. Go under the Image menu and choose Canvas Size. When the dialog appears, ensure the Relative checkbox is on, enter 0.25 inches for the Width and Height fields, set the Canvas Extension Color pop-up menu to White, then click OK.

Continued

Step Eight:

Here's the contact sheet now, after adding 1/4" of white space around the top, bottom, and sides. Looks much better, doesn't it? (Contrast this with the previous contact sheet and you'll see the difference.)

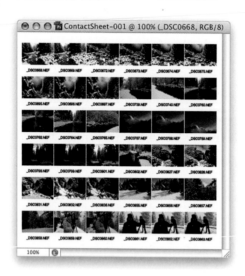

Step Nine:

This is more like a tip than a step, but a number of photographers add a second contact sheet to make it even easier to track down the exact image they're looking for. It's based on the premise that in every roll (digital or otherwise), there are usually one or two key shots—two really good "keepers"—that will normally be the ones you'll go searching for on this disc. So what they do is make an additional contact sheet with just the one or two key shots on that CD, which they'll use either as the cover or the inside cover of their CD jewel case. They include a description of the shots, which makes finding the right image even easier. *Note:* If you're only using one or two images, you don't need to use Contact Sheet II—you can just create this second cover yourself by dragging the images into a blank Photoshop document using the Move tool (V) and adding filenames, descriptions, etc., with the Horizontal Type tool (T).

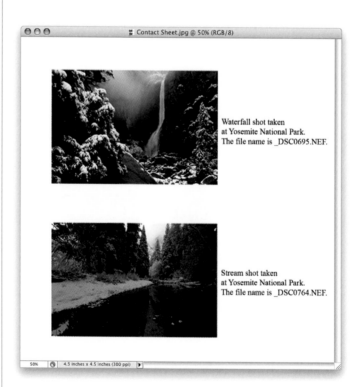

©ISTOCKPHOTO/STEFAN KLEIN

Step 10:
Here's the final result, after the contact sheet has been printed and fitted into your CD jewel case.

A Much Better View Is Just a Few Clicks Away

So, at this point, you've imported the photos onto your computer, you've backed them up, you've burned a CD/DVD, and made a contact sheet for the CD/DVD's case. Now, you've already got Bridge open, but if you didn't, there are three ways to access it: (1) When you're in Photoshop, click on the Go to Bridge icon on the far-right side of the Options Bar. (2) You can go under Photoshop's File menu and choose Browse. (3) You can bring it up with the keyboard shortcut Command-Option-O (PC: Ctrl-Alt-O).

Step One:
Now that your imported photos are in Bridge (well, they're not actually *in* Bridge—they're in a folder on your computer, and you're looking inside that folder using Bridge), these photos show up as thumbnails in the Content panel, which by default appears in the center of Bridge (as shown here). Bridge is generally pretty quick about displaying these thumbnails, but the more photos you have, the longer it will take to render the thumbnails. Also, it builds thumbnails from the top down, so even though you see thumbnails in the Content panel, if you scroll further down, other thumbnails could still be rendering. So you might have to be a little patient.

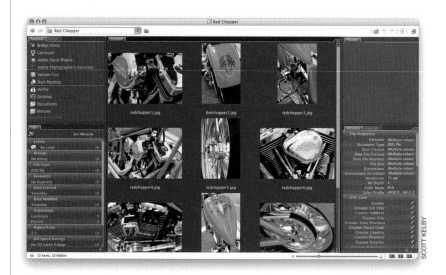

Step Two:
To change the size of the thumbnails, use the slider that appears at the bottom right of Bridge (as shown here). Dragging to the right makes the thumbnails larger, so you can pretty much imagine what happens when you drag to the left.

TIP: If you want to jump to the next larger (or smaller) size thumbnail, just click on the little rectangular icons on the far right (or left) of the thumbnail slider.

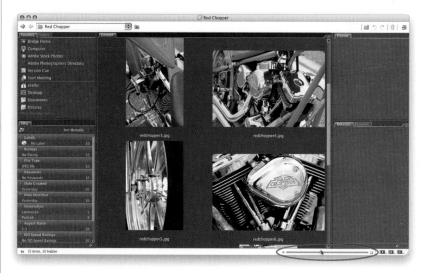

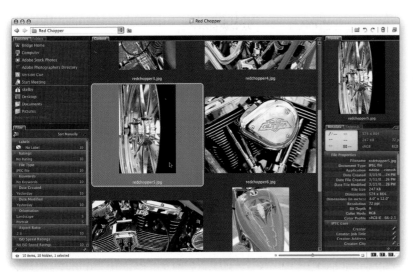

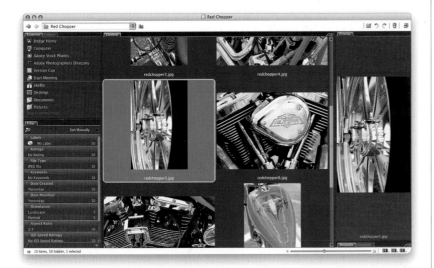

Step Three:

Click on any photo to select it, and once selected it also appears in the Preview panel on the top right of the Bridge window (this Preview panel is dramatically more useful than it looks, but we'll get to that in just a moment). At the instant you took this selected photo, your digital camera automatically embedded loads of background information (including the make and model of your camera, your ISO setting, exposure setting, the focal length of the lens you used, etc.), and that information appears in the Metadata panel directly below the Preview panel. This Metadata panel is very useful, but at this point it's kind of in the way, because it's keeping your Preview panel small—stuck up in that corner, so you can't really see a larger version of your photo.

Step Four:

One way to make your preview bigger is to make the Preview panel bigger, and to do that simply double-click directly on the Metadata panel's tab itself, and it quickly collapses (basically, it tucks itself out of the way) to the bottom of the right-side Panel area (as shown here). When it does this, the Preview panel expands to take up the extra available space and voilà—your preview is bigger. But it can get even bigger (which makes it even more valuable).

TIP: To collapse any panel, just double-click on its tab. To expand that panel, double-click on its tab again. However, if there's a panel you find you just don't use, then you can totally hide it from view—just go under the Window menu and choose the name of the panel you want to hide, and it's hidden. To make a hidden panel visible again—do the same thing.

Continued

Step Five:

To make the Preview panel really big (and really useful), move your cursor over the divider line that appears between the Preview panel and the center Content panel. Your cursor will turn into a two-headed arrow, and now you can click-and-drag over to the left—expanding the Preview panel, which makes the preview much larger (as shown here). This is still kind of a clunky layout, but we'll fix that in the next step.

TIP: By the way, if you ever want to quickly hide all the left side panels, just click on the double-sided arrow in the bottom-left corner of Bridge and that entire Panel area will tuck away. Or just press the Tab key to hide both side Panel areas.

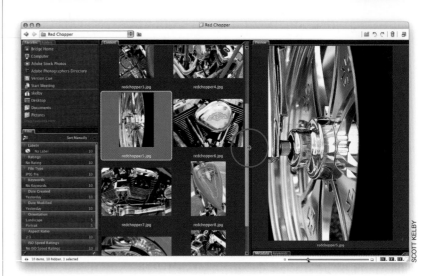

Step Six:

I think the "clunkiness" of the layout shown in Step Five comes from the fact that the thumbnails are still taking up too much space, and so are the panels along the left side. Plus, it seems like the Preview panel should be in the center, with your thumbnails more out of the way. So, here's what I do: go under the Window menu, under Workspace, and choose Vertical Filmstrip (as shown here) or just press Command-F6 (PC: Ctrl-F6) on your keyboard. This Vertical Filmstrip workspace is a built-in, pre-designed lay-out for Bridge (Adobe calls these "work-spaces"), which puts your thumbnails in a single column along the far-right side, and puts your Preview panel nice and big right in the center (where I've always thought it belonged). But we can even take this a step further, and create our own custom workspace (as you'll see in the next step).

SCOTT KELBY

Step Seven:

At this point, you're getting about as large a preview as you're going to get with a vertical (tall) photo (the full depth of your screen), but you could have a much larger preview with horizontal (wide) photos by hiding the panels along the left side. To do that, you could click-and-drag the divider line between the center Preview panel and the left side Panel area to the left a bit to give the Preview panel more space, but it's faster to just hide the entire left-side Panel area at once by double-clicking directly on that same divider line. This collapses the panels all the way to the left, leaving just that thin divider line still visible. Now, click on a horizontal (wide) photo and look how big your preview is (as seen here). Yeah, baby—that's what I'm talkin' about! To bring those left side panels back, double-click on that thin divider line again.

Step Eight:

This particular workspace layout is my favorite when I'm viewing the photos from a shoot because it always gives me the biggest possible horizontal and vertical previews, while still keeping the thumbnails in the Content panel visible. If you like this layout too, you can save this as your own custom workspace (so you can jump right to this layout anytime with just one click) by going under the Window menu, under Workspace, and choosing Save Workspace (as shown here). When the Save Workspace dialog appears, give your workspace a name (I named mine "Scott's Workspace." I know—how original), click Save, and now your workspace will appear in the Workspace submenu. Oh, but it gets better. Not now, in the next step.

Continued

Step Nine:

To put your new custom workspace just one click away, you're going to use those three little buttons marked 1, 2, and 3 in the bottom-right corner of Bridge (I know, you can't see them right here, so take a look at the graphic in the next step—down in the very bottom-right corner, you'll see the numbers 1, 2, and 3 right in a row). If you were to just click on the 1 button, it would return you to the Default workspace (as shown here). But it doesn't have to do that—you can change it by clicking-and-holding on that 1 button, and the pop-up menu of workspaces you see here will appear. Choose your custom workspace (in my case, it would be Scott's Workspace) from the pop-up menu. That's now the new default for this button.

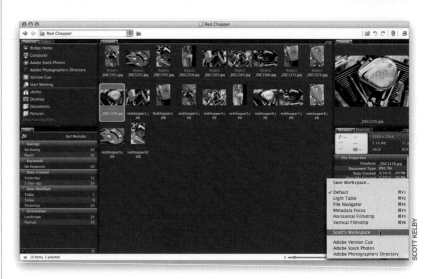

Step 10:

Now, anytime you click on the 1 button once, the layout switches to your custom workspace (as shown here). You can also program the 2 and 3 buttons with either more custom workspaces you create, or with a built-in workspace like the Horizontal Filmstrip. The only thing I don't like about that one is that it doesn't give as much room for either horizontal or vertical photos as the Vertical Filmstrip does.

TIP: Besides just hiding panels, you can also group panels you want together by clicking on a panel's tab, and dragging-and-dropping it onto another panel. This creates a "nested" panel, where you can now click on a tab to reveal that panel. That way, if you need all the panels visible, at least you could nest them together, all on the same side, to get a larger Preview panel.

SCOTT KELBY

Step 11:

Okay, ready for another thing you'll love about this Preview panel? It has a built-in Loupe feature for zooming in tight (perfect for checking your photo's sharpness without having to actually open it in Photoshop). Try this: Move your cursor out over your photo in the Preview panel, and you'll notice that your cursor changes into a Magnifying Glass cursor (shown circled here in red). Move your Magnifying Glass cursor over an area where you want to zoom in (a perfect place to check sharpness on portraits is to zoom in on an eye).

Step 12:

Now click once on the eye to bring up the Loupe, which shows you the enclosed area at its full 100% size view (as seen here). Once the Loupe is open, to reposition it, move your cursor inside the Loupe itself and your cursor changes to the Hand tool so you can click-and-drag the Loupe over the area you want to see magnified. To zoom in even closer, just press the + (plus sign) key on your keyboard and you jump to a 200% view (you can see the view magnification amount just below the photo). Click the + key again to zoom to 400%, and once again for the maximum view of 800%. To zoom back out, press the – (minus) key. To remove the Loupe, click once inside it. The Loupe has a neat feature: if you get so close to an edge that the Loupe would extend outside the Preview panel, it automatically flips to a different orientation. Pretty slick.

Continued

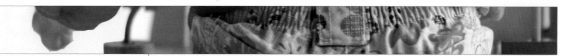

Step 13:

To compare two photos, click on one photo, press-and-hold the Command (PC: Ctrl) key and click on the photo you want to compare it with, and both photos will show up side by side, as shown here. This is incredibly handy when you're trying to compare similar photos (as we are here), or trying to find the "best of the bunch" between photos of the same subject.

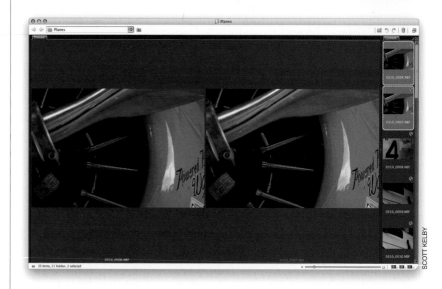

Step 14:

You're not limited to comparing two photos; just Command-click (PC: Ctrl-click) on any other photos you want to compare, and the Preview panel will automatically rearrange the size and position of all your selected photos to accommodate the newly-added photos (as shown here).

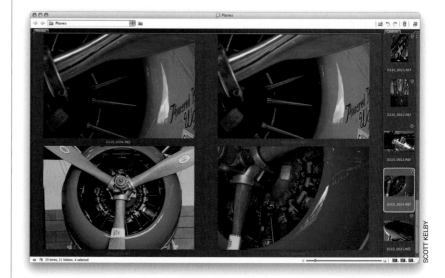

SCOTT KELBY

Step 15:
To remove a photo from the current group you're comparing, just Command-click (PC: Ctrl-click) on it in the Content panel to deselect it. (If you just did that and you're saying, "Hey, that didn't work!" you're probably Command-clicking within the Preview panel, and not over in the Content panel on the right side. It's a common mistake, so don't feel bad. Or foolish, or really embarrassed—it could happen to anyone. Well, not anyone, but I'll bet it's happened to plenty of people. Sure, they were goobers, but don't let that affect you. I think you're doing great despite that hugely embarrassing mistake you just made. In fact, at this point, it's probably best we keep this just between us.)

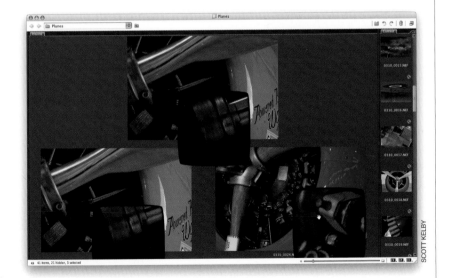

SCOTT KELBY

Step 16:
While your photos are in this compare view, you can still use the Loupe to zoom in tight, and in fact you can apply the Loupe to one photo, then just move over to another photo (while that first Loupe is still open) and click to add additional Loupes to the other photos you're comparing. You can reposition any Loupe by clicking inside it and dragging. Then, once you've got some Loupes in place, press-and-hold the Command (PC: Ctrl) key and click-and-drag within any one of the Loupes and they all now move together, which is very handy for inspecting areas on similar photos. Also, if you press Command–+ (plus sign; PC: Ctrl–+) to zoom in, all the Loupes zoom in together. This is a great trick to impress your friends with—it might help you regain some of that pride you lost in the previous step.

How to View Other Photos, Plus Moving and Deleting

So far we've been working with photos that we imported (okay, I changed photos a couple of times in the last tutorial because I was just getting tired of seeing the same photos over and over again, but I didn't tell you how I did it, so…here's how I did it. Plus, here's how to move photos, and delete them from just Bridge or from your computer altogether).

Step One:
There are two nested panels at the top of the left-side Panel area—Folders and Favorites. (If these left-side panels aren't visible, press Command-F1 [PC: Ctrl-F1] to return to Bridge's Default workspace, and then you'll see them.) The Folders panel gives you access to all the files and folders on your computer, so you can simply navigate to a folder of photos and click on the folder to see them. Of course, if you have an external hard drive connected, or DVD, or CD, etc., you'll see them listed too, and you can look inside them the same way. So, it's pretty much like the standard file structure of your computer.

Step Two:
The Favorites panel is kind of like your Bookmarks (or Favorites) in your Web browser, so if you find yourself constantly going to a particular folder of photos, you can save a shortcut to that folder in the Favorites panel. That way, you won't have to go digging through your hard drive to find it—it will be just one click away. To add a folder as a favorite, Control-click (PC: Right-click) on the folder and choose Add to Favorites from the contextual menu that appears, or you can just drag-and-drop that folder's thumbnail from the Content panel right into the bottom area of the Favorites panel.

Step Three:
Once you've saved that folder as one of your favorites, you'll see it added to the bottom of the list in the Favorites panel. Now, to jump directly to the photos in that folder, just click on it (as shown here).

Step Four:
If you look in the list of favorites in the Favorites panel, you can see Adobe has kind of already decided what it thinks might be some of your favorite destinations and added them to your list. If you'd like to remove any of them (so there's more room for the items you choose as your favorites), go to Bridge's General Preferences (press Command-K [PC: Ctrl-K]) and in the bottom section of the dialog, under Favorite Items, turn off the checkboxes for whichever Adobe-chosen items you don't want to appear in your Favorites panel (as shown here), then click OK. So, that's basically how to look at folders full of photos, and how to save your favorite folders (or discs, or drives, etc.) so they're more convenient. Now, on to moving photos from folder to folder.

Continued

Step Five:

Besides saving favorites and dragging-and-dropping photos between folders (which we'll cover next), there's another way to move or copy photos between folders that can help keep you from digging through the Folders panel (can you tell I don't like wasting a lot of time searching through different folders?). Give this method a try: Click on a photo you want to move to a different folder, then go under the File menu, under Move To, and you'll see a list of your recently viewed folders (as shown here). Now just choose which folder you want that photo to appear in, and you're set.

SCOTT KELBY

Step Six:

If, instead, you want to make a copy of your selected photo and move it into another folder, then you'd go under the File menu again, but this time you'd choose Copy To (as shown here). The same list of folders will appear, and you can choose one of these or you can choose which folder you want this copy saved into by selecting Choose Folder at the bottom of that same list. Now, of course you could always do this the manual way (which I would only recommend if you charge by the hour), which is to click on a photo, then go under the Edit menu and choose Duplicate. This makes a copy of your selected photo, then you can drag this copy right over to any folder you'd like, but that's a two-step process, where choosing Copy To does the whole thing for you at one time.

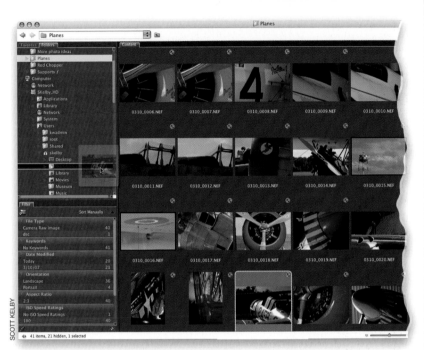

Step Seven:

Another nice feature of Bridge's Folders panel is that you can use it to move photos from one folder to another. You do this by clicking-and-dragging the thumbnail of the photo you want to move, then dropping that photo into any folder that appears in the Folders panel (when you move the dragged photo over a folder, the folder is highlighted letting you know that you've targeted that folder). That photo will now be removed from the currently selected folder and placed into the folder you dragged-and-dropped it into.

TIP: If you press-and-hold the Option (PC: Ctrl) key as you click-and-drag, instead of moving your original photo, Bridge will place a duplicate of your photo into that folder.

Step Eight:

Deleting photos is pretty simple—just click on the photo you want to delete, and hit the Delete key on your keyboard. When you do, a dialog appears asking you if you just want to mark this photo as a Reject (meaning, you're basically marking it for deletion later), or if you really want this file off your computer altogether. If you do want this file off your computer, then click the Delete button at the bottom of the dialog, and it moves that photo into your Trash (or on a PC, into your Recycle Bin). By the way, if you know that you really want a file deleted from your computer, you can skip this dialog altogether by just clicking on the file and pressing Command-Delete (PC: Ctrl-Backspace) instead.

Continued

Step Nine:

However, if instead you clicked the blue Reject button, all that happens is that now the word "Reject" will appear in red right above the filename (as shown in the close-up here). This rejected photo will still be visible in Bridge right along with all the rest of the photos in that folder, so if you'd like to hide the Rejects from view (I absolutely do—it doesn't make sense to keep rejected photos around just cluttering up things), go under the View menu and click on Show Reject Files to uncheck it. Now any photo tagged as a Reject (that sounds so cruel) will be hidden from view.

Step 10:

So, if labeling a photo as a Reject doesn't delete it from your computer, why do it at all? Well, once you turn off Show Reject Files it does become more useful because now, as soon as you label something as a Reject, it's hidden from view. But it has another purpose, and here's how I use it: When I bring in a shoot, I quickly go through and reject any photos that I can instantly see are totally messed up (in other words, they're terribly out-of-focus, or I see a shot I fired of my foot by accident, or shots taken with the lens cap on, etc.). I save time marking my Rejects by clicking on the file to be rejected, and then pressing Option-Delete (PC: Alt-Backspace). Once I've gone through the entire shoot, then I go to the Filter panel in the bottom-left Panel area of Bridge (this panel lets you narrow down, or "filter" down your field of photos using a wide variety of attributes, one of them being the type of label assigned to a photo). The first section at the top of the Filter panel is Ratings. Click on Reject in the Ratings section, and now only the photos you labeled as Rejects appear.

Step 11:

Now that you're seeing just the Rejects, I recommend taking a quick look at them to make sure some photo you didn't want labeled as a Reject didn't somehow accidentally wind up in this group (hey, it's not hard to accidentally mark the wrong photo as a Reject). After your quick look, if they are indeed all Rejects, press Command-A (PC: Ctrl-A) to select them all (as shown here), and then press Command-Delete (PC: Ctrl-Backspace) to delete them.

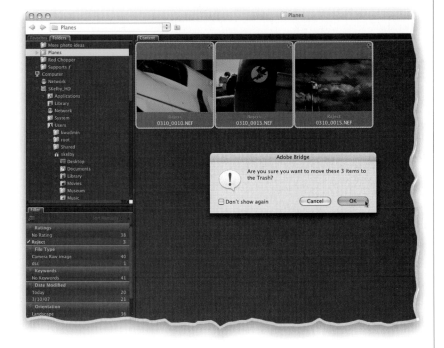

Step 12:

Once you press Command-Delete (PC: Ctrl-Backspace), a warning dialog appears (apparently they really want you to be darn sure before you delete anything for good) asking you if you are sure you want to move these selected photos to your computer's Trash (PC: Recycle Bin), as shown here. Of course, your answer is "Youbetcha!" but there is no Youbetcha button, so just click the OK button, and those files will then be removed from Bridge, removed from their folders, and placed in the Trash. So, there actually is an advantage to marking photos as Rejects instead of just deleting them as you go, and that is you get one last look at them (to check for mistakes) before they're gone for good.

Customizing the Look of Your Bridge

This latest version of Bridge gives you more control over the look, size, and layout of your Bridge than ever, so you can pretty much set this puppy up to look almost any way you'd like. Well, as long as you like the colors black, gray, and white anyway.

Step One:
Back in Bridge CS2, we only had one background color control, so everybody's Bridge was either solid black, solid gray, or solid white. In Bridge CS3, the default look is a dark gray (as seen here), but you now have control over three color areas: (1) the color behind your photos, (2) the color behind all the panels, and (3) the Accent color (which controls your highlight color). To customize these colors, press Command-K (PC: Ctrl-K) to bring up Bridge's Preferences dialog (shown in the next step).

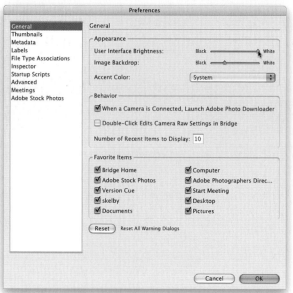

Step Two:
When the Preferences dialog appears, by default it brings up the General preferences, and at the top of the dialog is the Appearance section. The User Interface Brightness slider controls the color of all the panels except those that include photos (so, it doesn't control the background color of either the Content panel or the Preview panel). Go ahead and drag that slider all the way over to the right, and you'll notice that the text in each panel automatically changes from white to black to accommodate your new panel background color (as seen in the next step).

Step Three:

Although the text automatically changed to black (after all, you can't read white text on a white background), and the two panels that display your photos are still gray, the whole thing looks pretty horrid (but who am I to judge? Come on, it does look pretty horrid, right?). Want to really stretch the boundaries of good taste? Change the Accent color (the high-light color) to Emerald (from the Accent Color pop-up menu). You can try chang-ing the Image Backdrop color as well (this slider controls the background color behind the two panels that show you photos), but unless you change those panels to something else quick, it's still going to look pretty unsavory.

Step Four:

Personally, I like a color scheme similar to the one used by Adobe's new pho-tography application, Adobe Photoshop Lightroom. It has a light gray behind the photos, a darker gray behind the panels (though not as dark as the default gray used in Bridge CS3), and a medium gray as the text color. You don't have quite that level of control here in Bridge, but here's how it looks if you choose (1) a medium gray for the User Interface Brightness color, (2) a lighter gray for the Image Backdrop, and (3) the color Crystal as your Accent color, so when you select a photo, it highlights in a lighter gray (Crystal is one of the choices in the Accent Color pop-up menu). Of course, you can create any combination you'd like.

Continued

Step Five:

Besides just choosing background colors, you can also decide how much (or little) information the Content panel displays under each thumbnail. For example, by default the name of each file is displayed below the thumbnail, but you can add up to four additional lines of information (which are pulled from the metadata embedded in the file by your camera, or in Bridge itself). To turn on these extra lines of info, press Command-K (PC: Ctrl-K) to open the Preferences dialog, and in the list of preferences on the left side, click on Thumbnails to bring up the Thumbnails preferences. In the Details section, turn on the Show checkboxes beside each info line you want to add (as shown here), and then choose the specific types of info from the pop-up menus to their right.

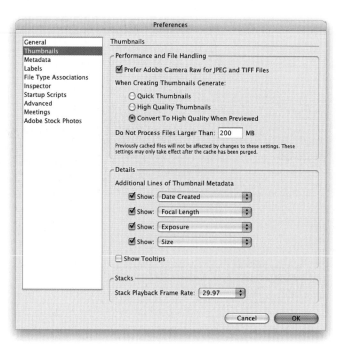

Step Six:

Click OK and you'll see those extra lines of info now appearing under your thumbnails (as shown here, in this close-up of one of the thumbnail cells).

TIP: If you ever want to see just the thumbnails and temporarily hide all those extra lines of metadata, just press Command-T (PC: Ctrl-T) and only the thumbnails will be displayed. This is a handy shortcut because all those extra lines of info take up space, and when you're displaying three or four extra lines, plus the file's name, and perhaps even a rating, fewer thumbnails fit in the same amount of space.

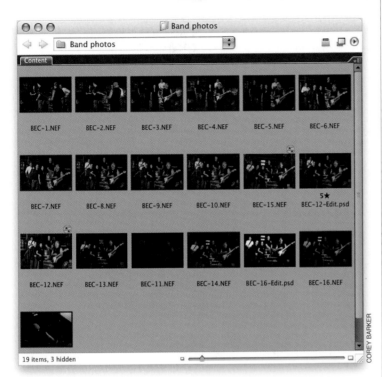

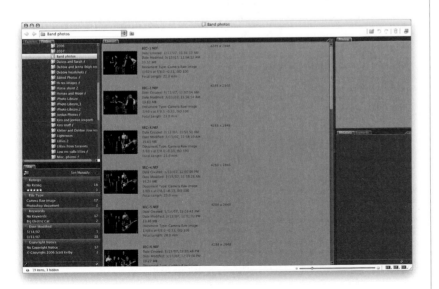

Step Seven:

Now we're onto the size of Bridge. Of course, you can just grab the bottom-right corner of Bridge and resize the window to whatever suits you, but if your goal is a smaller Bridge, then just click on the Switch to Compact Mode icon located in the top-right corner of Bridge. It will literally shrink in size leaving only small thumbnails visible (much like a small version of Bridge's Light Table workspace). The hidden advantage of Compact mode is that it floats in front of whichever applications are open (so if you're working in Photoshop CS3 or another Creative Suite application, Bridge will appear just like a floating panel). By the way, if you like the Compact mode but don't want this floating feature, turn off Compact Window Always On Top from Bridge's flyout menu (it's the right-facing arrow in the top-right corner).

Step Eight:

If you like Compact mode, you're gonna love Ultra-Compact mode (believe it or not, that's its real name—I love it!). First, switch to Compact mode and then click on the Switch to Ultra-Compact Mode icon (it's the first icon in the top-right corner). This hides the thumbnail area, leaving just the navigation pop-up menu, the viewing mode icons, and an arrow so you can reach Bridge's flyout menu.

TIP: There are two ways to view your content: as thumbnails (which you're already familiar with) or as details, which gives you a small photo thumbnail along with some of the EXIF metadata on each photo (as shown here). You access this Content panel view by going under Bridge's View menu and choosing As Details.

Getting Each Photo's Background Info (Called Metadata)

The Metadata panel is where you can go see all the background info on your photos, including all the EXIF metadata added by your digital camera at the moment you took the shot, along with any metadata added in Bridge itself (like your copyright info or custom filenames added when you imported the photos from your camera). Here's how to leverage that info:

Step One:

When you take a photo with today's digital cameras, at the moment you take the shot, the camera automatically embeds loads of information about what just took place—things like the make and model of the camera, the time the photo was taken, the exposure setting, the f-stop, shutter speed, etc. (this info is called EXIF camera data). Click on a photo in Bridge, and you'll see the basic camera data is displayed at the top of the Metadata panel in a layout similar to an LCD screen on a digital camera (as shown here). Once you bring the digital photo into Bridge, more information is embedded into the photo (stuff like the filename, when it was last edited, the file format it was saved in, its physical dimensions, color mode, etc.). All this embedded info comes under the heading of metadata, and that's why it appears in the Metadata panel. At the top of the panel, under the File Properties section is the info Photoshop embeds into your file. The next section down is IPTC Core metadata, which is where you can embed your own customized info (stuff like copyright, credits, etc.) into the photo (this is covered in detail in the next chapter). The Camera Data (EXIF) section displays data embedded by your camera.

Step Two:

Metadata is more than just interesting to look at—it can be incredibly useful in helping you find a particular photo (or group of photos), because this metadata is also automatically read by the Filter panel, which appears at the bottom of the left side Panel area. Here's how it works: click on any folder of photos, and their metadata is automatically added to this Filter panel. For example, click on a folder, and then look in the Filter panel. In the example shown here, it lists the dates the photos in that folder were created, and how many photos in that folder were created on each date. But here's where it gets cool: Go down a little further to the ISO Speed Ratings section. See where it says 800? To the right of that, it shows that five photos in this folder were taken at ISO 800. Click on the 800, and now only those five photos are displayed in Bridge (and a checkmark now appears before 800 to show you what's currently being displayed). I know, pretty cool (and very powerful)!

Step Three:

Okay, let's say you now want to see all the ISO 800 and ISO 1000 photos together. To do that, just click to the immediate left of 1000 to add a checkmark to that filter, and now both ISO 800 and ISO 1000 photos are displayed together (for a total of 11 photos). To remove a line of filtering, click on the checkmark again. To clear all the filters, click on the "No!" symbol in the bottom-right corner of the panel. So, to recap: if you have some idea of what you're looking for (for example, you remembered that these shots were taken indoors during a presentation), metadata filtering can help you quickly narrow the field.

Sorting and Arranging Your Photos

Ah, finally, we get to the fun part—sorting your photos—and there are a number of different ways to do this based on your own personal workflow. Some are ideal for managing just a few photos, some work better when you're managing hundreds (or thousands) of images, but at the end of the day the main job you're probably going to do here is to find the good photos, delete the bad photos, and narrow things down to just the "keepers" that you're actually going to show to the client. Here are some different strategies to get you there:

Step One:

If you have a small number of photos (in our case, we've got around 14 photos), then you can do simple drag-and-drop sorting, where you just click-and-drag the photos into the order you want them inside the Content panel. Generally, people want their best shots to appear at the top of Bridge's thumbnail window, followed by the "just okay" shots, and the lame shots (if you keep them at all) at the bottom. In the example shown here, I want to move the hats on the blue wall (Santa Fe47.jpg) photo up to the second position. So, to move that photo, click-and-drag it up to the second position (you'll see a small ghosted version of the photo as you drag it).

Step Two:

When you move that photo up there, you also see a solid yellow line letting you know exactly where that dragged photo is going to drop (you can see that yellow line back in Step One). Here you can see the photo has been moved from the second row, third position, up to the first row, second position. You can drag photos around just like you would on your own personal lightbox, putting photos into the exact order you want them. Again, this kind of drag-and-drop sorting is fine for managing a small number of photos, but outside of that it's just too slow and ineffective.

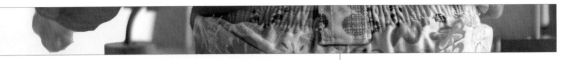

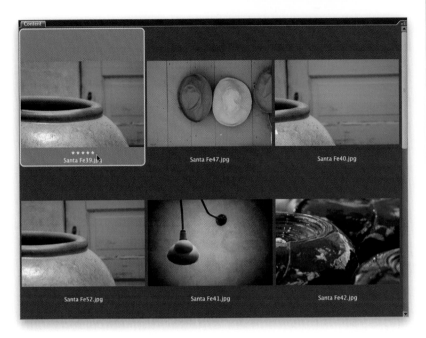

Step Three:

When you're sorting a large number of images, try rating them (rather than dragging them around). If you're an iPod user, you're probably familiar with how you rate songs on your iPod (or in iTunes), and this is very similar. You can rate your photos (from one to five stars) by first clicking on the photo you want to rate. Five tiny dots will be visible directly beneath your thumbnail. Click-and-hold on the first dot and a star will appear. Drag to the right to add up to five stars. That's it—you've rated the photo. (By the way, you can just click directly on the dot you want; you don't have to drag.) You can also rate by clicking on the photo and pressing Command-5 (PC: Ctrl-5), -4, -3, etc. To rate multiple photos at once (which is what you want to do), Command-click (PC: Ctrl-click) on your best images, give just one of them a 5-star rating, and all the other selected photos will receive the same rating.

Step Four:

Once you've rated your photos, you can sort them in order (5-star first, 4-star next, followed by the 3-star shots, and so on). To do that, go under the View menu, under Sort, and choose By Rating (as shown here). If you scroll to the top and don't see any rated photos, it means Ascending Order is selected (meaning your best photos are at the bottom—not the top), so go back under the View menu, under Sort, and turn off Ascending Order by choosing it from the menu. This method works fairly well, but there's a faster way to filter things down to see just the photos you want.

Continued

Step Five:

This is another area where the Filter panel (at the bottom of the left-side panels) really pays off. If you look in the Filter panel, you'll see a list of star ratings, and beside each rating it will show how many photos in your current folder have that rating (as seen here).

Step Six:

For example, in our case we've got two photos rated 1-star, two rated 2-star, three rated 3-star, only one rated 4-star, and six rated 5-star. If you wanted to see just that one 4-star rated photo, in the Filter panel you'd simply click on the four stars in the Ratings section and it filters your photos down so only your 4-star photos are visible (in this case, it's just this one photo). If you then click on the 3-star rating filter, it adds the 3-star photos (so now you're seeing just your 4-star and 3-star photos). As you click on other star-rating filters, they're added to your results. To remove a star rating set from view, Option-click (PC: Alt-click) on any star rating. If you Option-click on an unselected star rating, it then deselects all the other star ratings, and just shows that star-rating filter's results. (So, if you have the 3-star, 4-star, and 5-star rated photos all showing, then you Option-click on the 2-star rating filter, it hides the rest and only shows the 2-star rated photos.)

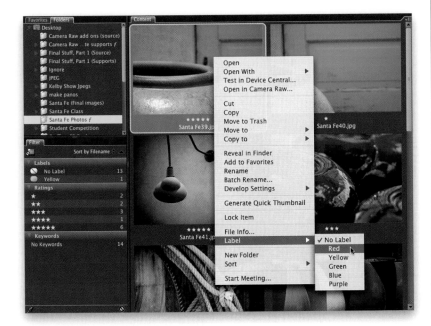

Step Seven:

Let's take things a step further: let's look at your 5-star rated photos (so go to the Filter panel and click on just the 5-star rating filter to see just those photos). Now, within that 5-star grouping, aren't there some that are better than others? I mean, isn't there a best 5-star photo? And a second best? So, how do you separate your best 5-star images from the pack? You'd add a color label, like the Red label added around the file's name shown here. (Seriously, imagine how good a photo would have to be to be a red 5-star photo. In fact, if you do rate one as a red 5-star, a pop-up menu appears where you can choose Submit to *National Geographic.* Kidding.)

Step Eight:

There are three ways to add a color label: (1) Select the photo (or photos), then Control-click (PC: Right-click) on it, and when the pop-up menu appears, you'll see a submenu called Label where you can choose the label color you want (as shown here). Or (2) you can assign labels using keyboard shortcuts (i.e., Command-6 assigns Red, Command-7 assigns Yellow, etc. Of course, for a PC it would be Ctrl-6, Ctrl-7, and so on), or (3) you can assign labels by going under the Label menu and choosing the label you want to assign.

TIP: If you've applied a rating to a photo and you want to remove the rating, just click on the thumbnail and press Command-0 (zero; PC: Ctrl-0). However, if this photo is labeled as well as rated, this will not remove the label color. To do that, you have to Control-click (PC: Right-click) on the selected thumbnail, go under the Label submenu, and choose No Label.

Continued

Step Nine:
Once you've assigned color labels to your best 5-star photos, they're just one click away. Go to the Filter panel, click on the 5-star rating (to filter down to just your 5-star photos), and you'll notice that color labels have been added above the star ratings. Click on the Red label, and now only your 5-star photos with a Red label (the best of the best) will be visible (as seen here). Now, personally I rarely use these labels because I'm normally just interested in finding the best, the worst, and I don't care about the rest. The one time I do use labels is when I'm looking for just one single photo. In that case, once I've filtered down, I use just the Red label to mark that one photo as "the one!"

TIP: Although you can't change the label colors, you can change their names by going to the Preferences dialog (under the Bridge menu on a Mac or the Edit menu on a PC) and choosing Labels from the categories on the left of the dialog. Now you can just type in your new custom label names beside each color (as shown here). By the way, there's a checkbox at the top of the Labels preferences that affects ratings as well, and by turning this checkbox off, it actually makes rating and labeling easier, because you rate with single keys (like 1 for one star, 2 for two stars, and so on), rather than Command-1, Command-2, etc. The same thing goes for labels—once that checkbox is off, you can just press 6 to label a selected photo Red, 7 for Yellow, and so on. In my book, easier is better and the fewer keys I have to hold down, the better.

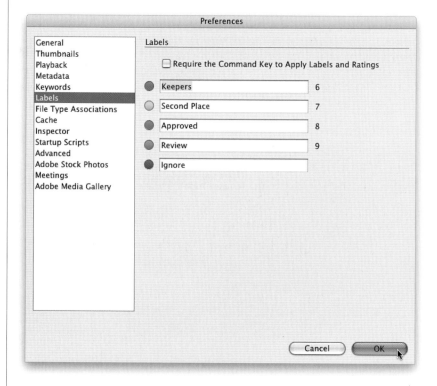

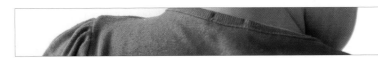

Ask yourself this question: "Is there really a reason to keep photos that you've rated 1-star on your computer?" (They're your "worst of the worst" photos.) They just take up drive space and otherwise impede the national economy, so you might as well delete them now and move on with your life. Here are a couple of ways to do just that:

Deleting Files (and Folders) in Bridge

Step One:

You can delete any photo from Bridge that you don't want by clicking on it (or select a number of photos by Command-clicking [PC: Ctrl-clicking] on them), then just pressing the Delete (PC: Backspace) key. This brings up the warning dialog shown here, which assumes you don't really want to delete this file—you just want to mark it as a Reject (you can then hide rejected photos from view under the View menu). Now, if you do indeed want to remove the selected photo from your computer, click the Delete button instead of Reject. However, clicking on a folder in Bridge and pressing the Delete key has no effect whatsoever.

Step Two:

Now, to delete a file or a folder of images in the Folders panel, click on the photo or folder and press Command-Delete (PC: Ctrl-Backspace), which brings up yet another warning asking, "Are you sure you want to move (file or folder name) to the Trash/Recycle Bin?" Before I clicked OK, I would turn on the Don't Show Again checkbox (as I did here), so in the future your selected file or folder just moves silently into the Trash without any warning dialogs or further input from you.

Exposure: 1/3s   Focal Length: 12.0mm   Aperture Value: ƒ/4.0

The Bridge
advanced bridge techniques

I know, "The Bridge" sounds a little too obvious a name for a chapter on advanced bridge techniques, but it beats the alternative of using the movie title *Bridge to Terabithia* (see, "The Bridge" doesn't sound all that bad now, does it?). It took me all of about four seconds in Apple's iTunes Store to come up with at least 30 song titles that not only included the term "the bridge," but actually were named exactly that. There were versions in the iTunes Store from everyone from Janis Ian to Eddie from Ohio whose song "The Bridge" appears on his album *I Rode Fido Home*. While listening to the free 30-second preview of Eddie's song, it was at that moment I knew I had to choose this version—the Eddie from Ohio version—as my chapter title. It was because no one (outside of close friends and relatives of Eddie himself) was ever going to

do an iTunes search for that song, and if by some cosmic solar accident someone like myself did come across his version of "The Bridge," the chances of a royalty coming Eddie's way were very slim indeed. That's sad in a way, because I think Eddie needs the money. I think Eddie may need the money for music lessons. (I'm kidding of course, Eddie doesn't need music lessons—he's got an album on iTunes, and now that his album *I Rode Fido Home* has gotten a write-up in print, it's only a matter of time before photographers around the world start going to iTunes and plunking down their 99¢ to download their own personal copy of what is soon to be a cult hit—"The Bridge" by Eddie from Ohio. This is precisely why they call me "The Star Maker." It's either that or "The Guy with the Tin Ear." I can't remember which.)

Creating Full-Screen Slide Shows

One of my favorite features of Adobe Bridge is the ability to play a full-screen slide show of your photos. But besides just showing off your work, seeing your photos at full-screen size really helps when you're choosing which photos from a shoot "make the cut" (so to speak). That's because while the slide show is running, you can delete any bad shots, apply ratings, rotate shots, etc. One of my pet peeves from the old Bridge (in CS2) was it didn't have a smooth dissolve transition between slides, but in CS3 we've got that and a whole lot more.

Step One:

If you'd like to see a full-screen slide show of the photos currently shown in Bridge, press Command-L (PC: Ctrl-L) and your slide show starts (as shown here). If you just want certain photos to appear in your slide show, select them by Command-clicking (PC: Ctrl-clicking) on them first, before you start your slide show. The slides advance automatically, but if you'd prefer to switch slides manually, press the Right Arrow key on your keyboard (to return to the previous slide, press the Left Arrow key. I know, that was pretty obvious. Sorry).

Step Two:

There are some options for how your slide show displays onscreen (most of these are new in CS3). To get to the new Slideshow Options dialog, start your slide show then press the letter L on your keyboard. This pauses your slide show and brings up the dialog you see here. *Note:* To pause your slide show without getting the dialog, press the Spacebar. To restart, press it again. To quit your slide show, press the Esc key on your keyboard.

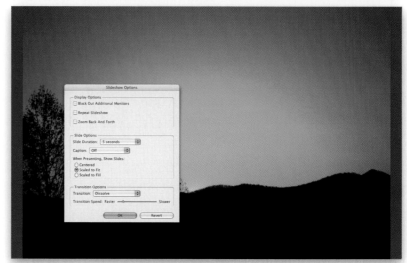

SCOTT KELBY

Step Three:

At the top of the dialog are the display options. The first option only applies to people working with two different monitors (turning this on blacks out the second monitor, so it doesn't distract from your slide show on the first monitor). The Repeat Slideshow checkbox does… come on, do I really have to describe this one? The last checkbox, Zoom Back And Forth, sounds like it would create something really annoying, but actually this is Adobe's name for the popular Ken Burns effect—where your photos slowly and smoothly move toward the screen (or away from it), giving your slide show some subtle motion. You should definitely at least give this a try to see if you like the effect (it's very popular).

Step Four:

The next set of options relates to the slides themselves, including how long each slide appears onscreen and whether any captions you've added to the photo's metadata will appear onscreen as well. The next option down is important, because it determines how big your photos appear onscreen. I don't like the default Scaled to Fit setting, because (depending on the size of your photos) it can leave gray bars on both sides of your image (look at the image in Step One to see what I mean). That's why I prefer either of the two other choices. The Scaled to Fill option scales your photo to fill the entire screen (which looks really good; see Step Three), and I recommend this option if you choose the Zoom Back and Forth effect. If you're not using Zoom Back and Forth, I like the Centered option, which displays your photos a little smaller but nicely centered on a gray background (as shown here).

Continued

Step Five:

The last set of options is the transition options, where you can choose from a pop-up menu of transitions. Thankfully, the default transition is a nice, smooth dissolve, but you can choose other transitions, as well as how fast (or slow) the transition effect takes before the next slide appears (you set this using the Transition Speed slider, just below the Transition pop-up menu, as shown here).

Step Six:

This is really more a tip rather than a step, but it's so cool (and such an improvement over how this worked in CS2) that I had to include it separately. If you're looking at your slide show and you see a RAW photo you'd like to edit, just press the letter R (easy to remember—R for RAW). It pauses your slide show and instantly opens that photo in Bridge's own Camera Raw, as shown here (remember—Bridge has Camera Raw built right in), so you can edit the photo. Once you're done editing, click the Done button and you return to the slide show. The changes you made are instantly applied and the slide show continues. This is cooler than it first sounds. Think about it—you're watching your slide show and you see a photo and think "I wonder what that would look like if it was a little warmer," so you press R to bring up Camera Raw, you move a white balance slider to the right, click Done, and bam, you're back in your slide show, and your photo looks warmer. Now come on—that is pretty slick.

TIP: If you click on a JPEG or TIFF photo and press Command-R (PC: Ctrl-R), it will open in Bridge's Camera Raw, so you can process it using Camera Raw's controls, even though they're not RAW images. Pretty cool.

SCOTT KELBY

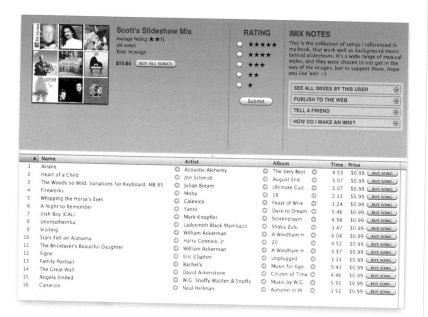

Step Seven:

There are other keyboard shortcuts for controlling your slide show (like ones for applying star ratings to your slide show photos, or to rotate them, etc.), but you don't have to remember all of them if you can remember just one—the letter H. If you press H on your keyboard while the slide show is running, a list of short-cuts appears onscreen (as shown here). To hide the shortcuts, press H again. Okay, now there is one cool shortcut that's not on this list—if you click your mouse button on a photo in the slide show, the slide show pauses and your photo zooms to 100%. To move around the photo while zoomed in, just click-and-drag. Click on the photo again and then press the Spacebar to restart the slide show.

Step Eight:

Sadly, Bridge CS3 still doesn't have a built-in background music feature, but that doesn't mean you can't have back-ground music. Here's what I do: I open Apple's iTunes (for a PC or Mac) and start my background music first. Then I jump over to Bridge and start my slide show. The effect is exactly the same—a full-screen slide show with background music. By the way, if you want some ideas for great slide show background music, in Apple's iTunes Store I created a 16-song iMix (basically, a playlist) of great slide show background music, called (surprisingly enough) "Scott's Slideshow Mix." You can listen to a 30-second pre-view of each track, and you can buy any of them for 99¢ each. To get to my iMix, launch your Web browser and type in this address: http://phobos.apple.com/WebObjects/MZStore.woa/wa/view PublishedPlaylist?id=222715 or just go to the iTunes Store and search for my iMix by its name, "Scott's Slideshow Mix."

Finding Your Photos Fast by Using Keywords

Imagine how great it would be if one day you needed a photo of a Gerbera daisy, and you were able to open Bridge, type "Gerbera Daisy" into the Find dialog, and within just seconds every Gerbera daisy photo you've taken (and only Gerbera daisy photos) would appear in Bridge? To get to this happy place, all you have to do is start adding keywords to your photos (which are basically just search terms you embed into your photos) while you're working in Bridge.

Step One:

First, make sure the Keywords panel is visible. If you choose the Default workspace, it's nested with the Metadata panel, so you could press Command-F4 (PC: Ctrl-F4) to switch to the Metadata Focus workspace, which puts the Keywords panel over on the left. Personally, I prefer to just choose the Default workspace, and then double-click on the tab for the Preview panel, which tucks that panel away up top, and expands the Keywords panel all the way down the right side (as shown here).

Step Two:

If you look in the Keywords panel, you'll see that Adobe has already included some keyword categories (Adobe calls them Keyword Sets), including Events, People, and Places, each with some of the most common keywords associated with these categories (for example, within the Events set the default keywords are Birthday, Graduation, and Wedding). These default sets and keywords are just there to basically give you an idea of how sets and keywords work, and to give you a starting place, but the real power comes from you creating and applying your own keywords (an Other Keywords set will automatically be created when you create a keyword).

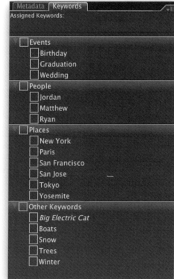

Step Three:

Any keywords that you've assigned to a photo will appear in the Keywords panel. For example, when you look in the Keywords panel, you'll see the generic keywords (Snow, Trees, Winter, Yosemite) I added after I imported photos I took out in Yosemite National Park. If I click on one of those photos, two things happen in the Keywords panel: (1) at the top of the panel, it displays all the keywords assigned to that photo, and (2) down in the list of keywords you'll see a checkmark beside each keyword assigned to your selected photo, as shown here (we actually use the term "tagged," as in, "That photo is tagged with Winter and Snow." It's important to use slang like this to build "street cred" with the kids—I mean, your colleagues).

Step Four:

The problem is, generic keywords will only get you so far. Here's why: Let's say that you're working on a client project and you need a photo of a little red chapel you remember shooting on one of your trips to Yosemite in winter. Well, you could look in your Yosemite folder, but there could easily be hundreds, or even thousands of photos in that folder. Instead, to narrow your search, you could go to the Filter panel and click on the keyword Winter, and now all the shots you took in winter would appear. That's nice, but what if there are 780 shots you took during the winter (as shown here)? You'll need to narrow your search further, but you really can't, because you only assigned these generic keywords.

Continued

Step Five:

If you want to save yourself from having to spend 30 minutes searching every time you need to find a particular photo, here's what to do: after you import your photos and get rid of the obviously bad, out-of-focus, totally trashed shots, go right then and tag your photos with specific keywords. At this point in the game, it takes just a few minutes, but it will turn your 30-minute searches into 30-second searches, so it's definitely worth doing. You start in the Keywords panel by clicking on the New Keyword icon at the bottom-right corner of the panel (as shown here). This adds a new high-lighted keyword field under whichever set was last selected in your keywords list, so type in the name you want to add as a keyword (I typed in "Red Chapel").

Step Six:

Now quickly scroll through your photos, and when you see a photo with that red chapel in it, Command-click (PC: Ctrl-click) on it to select it. Once you've got them all selected, just head over to the Keywords panel and turn on the check-box for Red Chapel (as shown here), and all the selected photos are now tagged with that keyword. So, that's basically the process—you create and assign key-words in the Keywords panel, but then to find photos, you can use the Filter panel (which I love), or the Find com-mand, which we're going to talk about in just a moment. But first, we need to add more keywords to this same photo because a year from now you might not remember that you used the keyword Red Chapel to describe this photo. So, I would add more keywords, like Church, Steeple, and any other descriptive terms that might help you find these photos six months or six years from now.

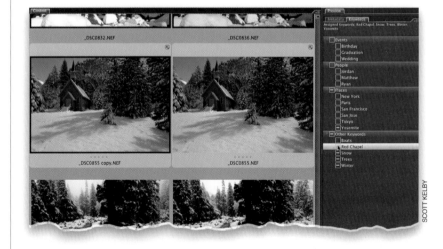

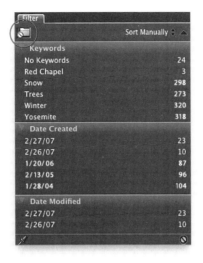

Step Seven:
So, now let's see just how adding these keywords has made your life easier by going back to our client project. Go to the Folders panel, find your Picture (or My Pictures) folder, and click on it to show its contents. Find your folder named Yosemite and click on it. Let's say that inside this folder are all the photos you've taken in Yosemite in the past five or six years (we'll assume you've been there a number of times). Go to the Filter panel, and before you start filtering things down, click on the little Folder icon in the upper-left corner of the panel, shown circled in red here (its icon is a folder with a tiny international symbol for "No!" on it. I have no idea why that "No!" symbol is there. Maybe the icon designer was angry that day). What this does is tells the Filter panel to search through not only the Yosemite folder, but any subfolders inside of it. So if you have folders for 2004, 2005, 2006, 2007, etc., it will search through all of them.

Step Eight:
Now, in the Filter panel, click on the keyword Winter, and all the photos anywhere inside that Yosemite folder that were taken in the winter will appear in your Content panel. This brought up 320 photos, so we need to filter things down a bit more. If you click on the keyword Red Chapel, it now displays all your photos with the keywords Winter or Red Chapel in them, but that's not what you want—you want to see *only* the photos with a Red Chapel in them. To do that, after you click on the keyword Winter, instead of just clicking on the keyword Red Chapel, press-and-hold the Option (PC: Alt) key and click in the space right before Red Chapel. This deselects all the Winter photos, and selects only the photos tagged with Red Chapel (as shown here).

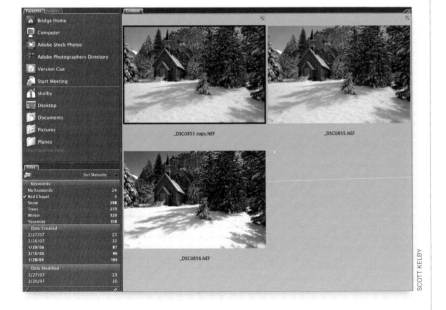

SCOTT KELBY

Continued

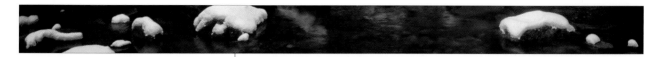

Step Nine:
You see how we got right to the photos we wanted in just four clicks? The first click was on the Pictures folder (which showed all your photos); the second click was on the Yosemite folder (which filtered us down to just the Yosemite photos); click three was in the Filter panel on the keyword Winter, so now we're seeing just the Yosemite shots taken in the winter; and the fourth click was on the keyword Red Chapel which brought us to our photos. Four clicks and you're there. That's the power of keywords. Now, the other way to quickly find photos is using the Find feature, so press Command-F (PC: Ctrl-F) to bring up the Find dialog (shown here).

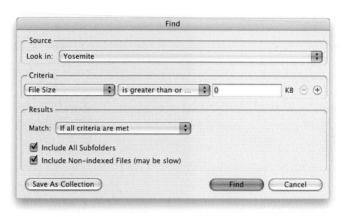

TIP: If you want to delete the default Keyword Sets that Adobe put in the Keywords panel, just go there and click on the category (like Events or People) and click on the Trash icon at the bottom of the Keywords panel. You delete individual keywords the same way.

Step 10:
When the Find dialog appears, go under the Criteria section and choose Keywords from the first pop-up menu (as shown here). From the second pop-up menu in the Criteria section, choose Contains, and then in the text field to the right, enter the keyword(s) you want to search for (in this case, "Red Chapel").

TIP: If you go to the Keywords panel and Control-click (PC: Right-click) on a keyword you want to search, and choose Find from the contextual menu that appears, it automatically chooses all the right criteria for you and inserts the keyword in the text field. A big timesaver!

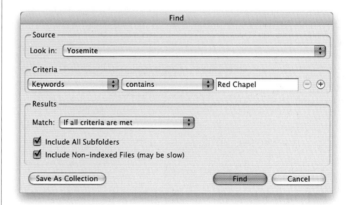

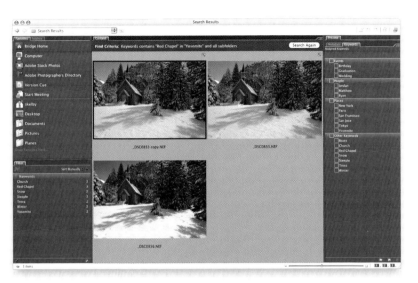

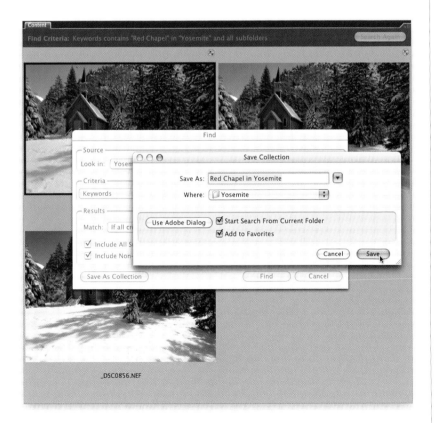

Step 11:

Click the Find button, and within a few seconds just the photos that have been tagged with the keyword Red Chapel will appear in the Content panel (as shown here). To search for more photos, click the Search Again button in the top right of the Content panel. To return to your regular Content panel, click the Go Back button in the top-left corner of Bridge (it's the left-facing arrow—just like the Back button in your Web browser).

Step 12:

Okay, so all your red chapel photos appear in the Content panel. Now what? Well, you can sort them, open them in Photoshop, etc., but if you think you'd like to have instant access to this exact same group of photos again (without having to do another Find), you can create a one-click collection. To do that, click on the Search Again button (or press Command-F [PC: Ctrl-F] if it's no longer there), and when the Find dialog appears, click on the Save As Collection button in the bottom-left corner. When the Save Collection dialog appears, name your collection, turn on the checkboxes for Start Search From Current Folder and Add to Favorites, then click Save (as shown here). Now you can get to these same photos in one click by going to the Favorites panel and clicking on Red Chapel in Yosemite. *Note:* Collections update live, meaning whenever you tag a new photo with the Red Chapel keyword, it will automatically be included in this collection (and collections are really just the results of a search, so it doesn't add any file size). Pretty handy, eh?

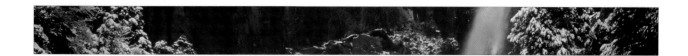

Seeing and Editing a Photo's Metadata

When you take a photo, your digital camera automatically embeds a host of background info right into your photo (called EXIF data), which includes the make and model of your camera, the lens you used, your exposure settings, etc. Bridge not only lets you see this information, but it also lets you embed your own custom info (like your copyright info, contact info, etc.). Bridge also shows the file properties (like the pixel dimensions, resolution, color mode, the file size, etc.). All this embedded info is known as your photo's metadata.

Step One:
Click on a photo in Bridge and then look at the Metadata panel on the bottom-right side of Bridge (I zoomed in on it here so you can see it more clearly) to see all the photo's embedded background info. On the top left of the panel, there's a little window that looks like a digital camera's LCD screen. This "fake LCD screen" displays some key EXIF data (shooting info) for that photo, like the f-stop, shutter speed, ISO setting, metering mode, etc. The section to the right of the screen shows some of the file info data, like the physical dimensions, file size (in this case, it's 69.91 MB), resolution, etc. Below these two boxes is the File Properties section, which shows the full file info data, instead of just the "quick glance" version. By the way, Bridge pulls this File Properties info from the photo itself, so this information is not editable by you (or me) in this panel. The only way to change this part of the metadata is to actually change the photo itself by opening it in Photoshop and changing the image size, or color mode, or resolution, etc. Then, when you save the file with the changes, the metadata is updated automatically to reflect them.

Tip: You can hide the fake LCD screen and the info box to the right of it by clicking on the tiny down-facing triangle in the top-right corner of the panel and choosing Show Metadata Placard from the flyout menu (as shown here). Choosing this hides those sections from view. If you change your mind, just choose Show Metadata Placard again.

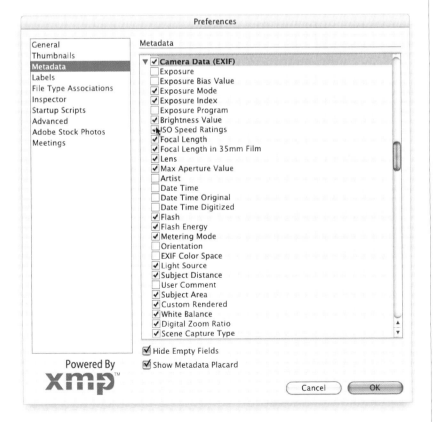

Step Two:

Now scroll down a little further until you come to the Camera Data (EXIF) section, as shown here (you'll scroll right by the IPTC Core info section, but don't worry, we'll look at that next). This section shows the information embedded by your digital camera at the moment you pressed the shutter button. Info in this Camera Data (EXIF) section can't be edited at all—it was put there by your camera and it stays there, so all you can do is look at it (you'll use this info later, and then you'll understand why it's so useful). So, for now, just take a look at it and comment out loud something along the lines of, "That's really cool the way it knows everything about my photo."

Step Three:

Now, there is a long list of Camera Data (EXIF) fields you can't add info into (many more than the average photographer will ever need). That's why most folks set up this list to display only the fields they really want to see. To do this, click on the tiny down-facing triangle in the top-right corner of the Metadata panel and choose Preferences from the flyout menu that appears. This brings up Bridge's Preferences dialog with the Metadata category selected. Scroll down to Camera Data (EXIF) and you'll see the full list of available camera data fields (scary, ain't it?). Only the fields with checkmarks by them will be visible, so to hide a field in the list, just click on the checkmark beside that field. Also, ensure the Hide Empty Fields checkbox is turned on at the bottom, so when you click OK, only the checked fields with information will be visible.

Continued

Step Four:

Okay, so although the camera data isn't editable, there is one section where you can add your own info—it's the IPTC Core section (named for the International Press and Telecommunications Council). This is where you can add info directly into the file, like your copyright info, your contact info, the rights usage for the photo, your website, etc. So, let's add some. In the Metadata panel, scroll down to IPTC Core and click on the right-facing triangle to the left of the words IPTC Core to reveal that section (shown here). If you see a little pencil icon on the far-right side of any field, you can write your own custom info into that field. If you added some metadata during the import process (like your copyright info), you'll see that info has been added to those fields.

Step Five:

To enter your own info, click once in the blank field to the right of the item you want to edit and all the text fields will appear. To see how this works, click to the right of Creator: Address (it's near the top). When the field appears, just type your street address. To move on to the next field down (in this case, it's the Creator: City field), just press the Tab key on your keyboard. If you want to jump directly to any field, just click on it. When you're done adding your own custom data, either press the Return (PC: Enter) key on your keyboard or click on the checkmark icon at the very bottom of the Metadata panel.

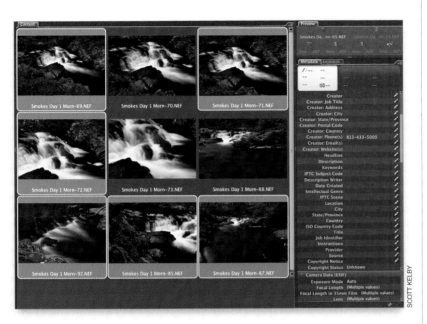

SCOTT KELBY

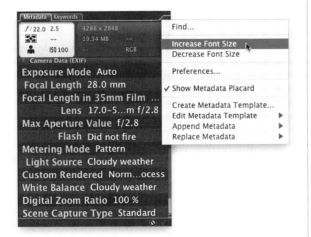

Step Six:

Applying your own custom info on a photo-by-photo basis can really be slow and tedious, but luckily you can apply your info to as many photos as you'd like, all at once. If you want to apply this info to all the photos in the folder you're currently working with, press Command-A (PC: Ctrl-A) to select them all, then click to the right of the info field you want to add to activate it. Now just type in your info, and when you're done press the Return (PC: Enter) key on your keyboard, and all those photos will now have that custom metadata applied. But what if you just want to add (or edit) metadata on certain photos? (Maybe you want to add your contact phone number to some photos you're going to post on the Web.) Then do this instead: Click on the first photo you want to edit, then press-and-hold the Command (PC: Ctrl) key and click on all the other photos you want to affect. Once they're selected, click to the right of the phone number field, type your phone number in the active field, press the Return key, and it's done. Much faster and easier.

TIP: Because there's so much metadata included in each photo, Adobe had to make the panel's font size really small. Luckily, you can increase it by clicking on the Metadata panel's flyout menu (in the top-right corner of the panel) and choosing Increase Font Size. If it's still not big enough, choose it again. Still not big enough? Choose it again and again, until it's so large your next-door neighbors can read it through your front window. Take a look at the example shown here where I just chose Increase Font Size two times.

Maximize Your View by Using Two Monitors

Bridge CS3 is the first version of Bridge to enable you to effectively use two monitors for your work. The setup we've all been clamoring for is to have our thumbnails and other panels visible on one screen, and then just see a really large preview of our selected photo on the second monitor. Here's how to set up your CS3 just like that:

Step One:

Go under Bridge's Window menu and choose New Synchronized Window (as shown here).

Step Two:

This will create an identical second floating window, but before you just drag it over to that second monitor, there are some things you'll need to do to set this new synchronized window up so it displays just a large-sized preview of the currently selected thumbnail. Start by going under the Window menu and you'll see that just about all the panels have a checkmark by them (indicating that they're visible). Well, you want them all hidden except Preview, so go and choose each one, as shown here (except for Preview, of course), and now all those other panels will be hidden from view.

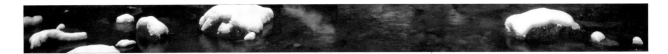

Step Three:

Once you hide these panels, you'll notice that the Content panel is still visible because it's the one panel you can't hide. So, what you need to do is click on the divider bar between the Content panel and the Preview panel, and drag it all the way over to the far-left side. This hides the Content panel from view leaving just the Preview panel visible (as shown in the image in Step Four).

Step Four:

Now you can click-and-drag this window over to your second monitor, and as you click on a thumbnail in the first window, the large preview will appear in the second monitor (as shown below). One last thing: go ahead and save this setup as a custom workspace by going under the Window menu, under Workspace, and choosing Save Workspace. Now you're just one click away from this two-monitor setup. *Note:* You can also save a custom workspace you've created by clicking-and-holding on the 1, 2, or 3 button in the bottom-right corner of Bridge, and then choosing Save Workspace from the pop-up menu.

Batch Renaming Your Files

If you didn't rename your photos when you first imported them from your memory card (or if the photos were already on your computer), then you can use Bridge to automatically rename an entire folder full of images. This is really helpful because you can give your photos descriptive names, rather than the cryptic secret code names assigned by your digital camera (which tends to give your photos fun names like DSC_0486.JPG or DSC_0784.NEF). So, here's how to batch rename a folder full of (or just selected) photos fast!

Step One:

First, you have to tell Bridge which photos you want to rename. If it's just a certain number of images within your main window, you can press-and-hold the Command (PC: Ctrl) key and click on only the photos you want to rename. But a more likely scenario is that you'll want to rename all the photos open in your Content panel, so go under Bridge's Edit menu and choose Select All, or press Command-A (PC: Ctrl-A). All the photos in your Content panel will be highlighted. Now, go under Bridge's Tools menu and choose Batch Rename.

Step Two:

When the Batch Rename dialog appears, you need to select a destination for these renamed photos by choosing an option. Will they just be renamed in the folder they're in now? Do you want them renamed and moved to a different folder, or do you want to copy them into a different folder? If you want to either move or copy them, you'll need to click on the Browse button. In the resulting dialog, navigate to the folder you want your photos moved (or copied) into after they're renamed. In our example, we'll just rename them right where they are (which is probably what you'll do most of the time).

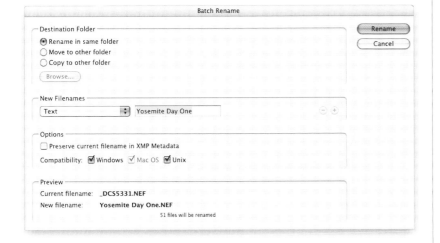

Step Three:

Under the New Filenames section of the dialog, the first pop-up menu shows Current Filename by default. You want to click on this pop-up menu and instead choose Text. A text field will appear to the right, so just click within that field and type in your own custom filename (I entered "Yosemite Day One"). At the bottom of the dialog, there's a live before-and-after preview of your custom filename so you can see how it will look. So far, so good, but there's a problem: In your folder, you can only have one photo (or any file for that matter) exactly named Yosemite Day One, so you'll need to add something to the end of the filename (like a number) so each photo is named something different (like Yosemite Day One001, Yosemite Day One002, and so on).

Continued

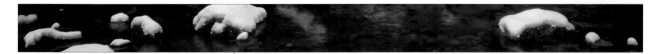

Step Four:

To use the built-in auto-numbering, click once on the small + (plus sign) to the right of the text field to add another customized set just below your original naming options. From the pop-up menu, choose Sequence Number (to have Bridge automatically add a sequential number after the name); in the center text field, enter the number you want to start with (I typed the number 1); then, from the pop-up menu on the far right, choose how many digits you want for your sequence (I chose Three Digits, as shown here). Look at the preview at the bottom of the dialog to see how the name looks now—Yosemite Day One001.NEF. (By the way, if you want a space between the last word and the number, just press the spacebar once after you type in your name in the text field.)

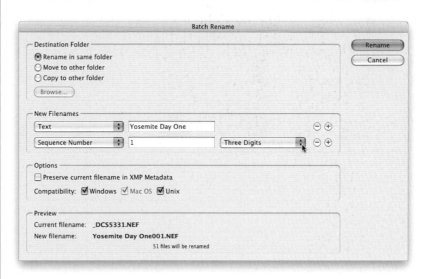

Step Five:

When you click the Rename button, Batch Rename does its thing. If you chose to rename your files in the same folder, you can just take a peek at Bridge, and you'll see that your selected thumbnails are now updated with their new names (as seen here). If you chose to move all your files to a different folder and then clicked the Rename button, the Content panel will be empty (that makes sense because you moved the images to a new folder and the Content panel is displaying the current folder, which is now empty). So, you'll need to go to the Folders panel in Bridge and navigate your way to the folder to which you moved (or copied) all your photos (and best of all, they'll be sporting their new, more descriptive names).

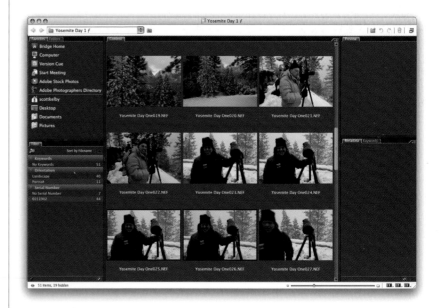

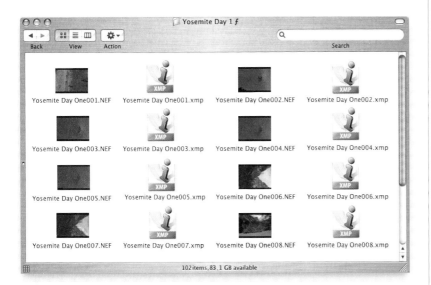

Step Six:

Batch Renaming doesn't just change the thumbnails' names, it applies this name change to the actual image file. To check it out, leave Bridge and go to the folder on your hard disk where these photos are stored. Open that folder and you'll see the new filenames have been assigned there as well.

TIP: If you want to take this renaming thing a step further, you can click on that little + (plus sign) again to add another set of naming options. In the first field, choose Current Filename, which adds the original filename at the end of your new filename. Hey, some people dig that. Instead, what I do is go under the Options section, and turn on the checkbox for Preserve Current Filename in XMP Metadata. That way the original filename is embedded into the file, just in case you have to go searching for the original file one day.

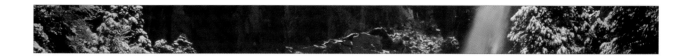

Creating Metadata Templates

I'm pretty sure the last thing you want to do in Bridge is spend a lot of time typing, but you'll probably at least want to embed your copyright info, your contact info, your website, and on and on. That's why you'll want to know how to create a metadata template, which allows you to enter all that info only once, then you can embed it all automatically with just one click of your mouse.

Step One:
You'll need to start with a photo on which to base your template. So navigate to a folder of images within Bridge that you'd like to assign some copyright and contact info to and click on one of the thumbnail images in that folder. Then go under the Tools menu and choose Create Metadata Template (as shown here).

Step Two:
This brings up the Create Metadata Template dialog (shown here). You'll see a checklist of IPTC Core metadata categories on the left-hand side, but only the ones with checkmarks by them will be visible. So turn on the checkboxes for those you want visible, then in the fields to the right, type in the information that you'd like to turn into a template (in the example shown here, I just added my basic contact info). Don't forget, if you scroll down, there are many more fields you can add info to (including the all-important copyright fields).

Step Three:

Once you've entered all the information you'd like in your template, type in a name for it in the Template Name field at the top of the dialog (this is the name you'll see listed when you go to apply this template later or during the import process, so be descriptive). Now click the Save button at the bottom of the dialog (as shown here).

Step Four:

Now that your template has been created, applying it is simple. Just select the photos you want to have that info embedded into (as shown here, where I Command-clicked on our photos—on a PC you would Ctrl-click on them). Then go under the Tools menu, under Append Metadata, and choose your saved template (as shown here, where I'm choosing the template I just created named "My Basic Contact Info"). From now on, this template will appear in this list, so you can apply it anytime. Also, you can create and save as many of these templates as you'd like, with each one having a different set of info (so you could have one with detailed copyright info, or one that just has copyright info and nothing else, or one that you'd use when selling a digital image file to a client, etc.).

Stripping Out Metadata from Your Photos

Well, technically I'm not sure if this belongs in a chapter about Bridge, except that so much of what we're talking about is metadata, so I hope you don't mind if I stick it here. Okay, so why would you want to strip out the very metadata that we clearly hold so dear? Well, it contains personal information about you, your whereabouts on a certain day, your equipment, your lenses, your settings, etc. Stuff your clients don't need to know (whether you're giving them the file or selling your work to a stock photo agency). Here's how to quickly strip it out:

Step One:
Go under the Window menu, under Workspace, and choose the preset workspace Metadata Focus. This displays your thumbnails with the main metadata for each photo displayed to the right of it. That's the info we're going to strip out, along with a bunch more that's not displayed here. To see the rest, double-click on the Keywords and Favorites panels' tabs to collapse them and have the Metadata panel expand into that empty space. If you distribute these photos "as is," all that metadata will be included along with the photo, and it will be viewable to anyone with a photo editing program. So, double-click on any photo thumbnail to open it in Photoshop CS3.

Step Two:
Once the photo is open in Photoshop, go under the File menu and choose New. When the New dialog appears, click on the Preset pop-up menu at the top and near the bottom of the pop-up menu you'll see the name of your open photo. Select the photo's name, and the exact Width, Height, Resolution, and Color Mode settings from your open photo will be copied into the New dialog's fields. All you have to do is click OK and a new document with the same specs as your open photo will appear onscreen.

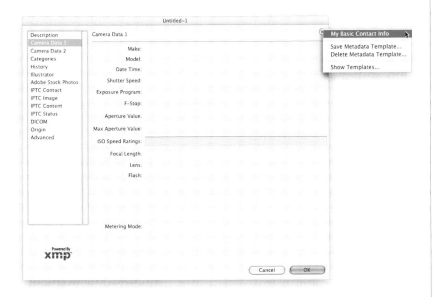

Step Three:
Once your new blank document is open in Photoshop, click back on the photo you opened. Now press V to get the Move tool, press-and-hold the Shift key, and then click-and-drag your photo onto the new blank document. Because you're pressing-and-holding the Shift key while you're dragging, the photo will appear in the exact position it did in the original. However, this dragged copy is on its own separate layer, so press Command-E (PC: Ctrl-E) to merge this layer with the Background layer (this flattens the document). Since the document you dragged your photo onto was a new blank document, it has no metadata whatsoever, and your photo, which comes over as a layer, doesn't carry any of its own metadata with it.

Step Four:
Lastly, go under the File menu and choose File Info. When the dialog appears, on the left side, click on Camera Data 1 and you'll see that all the fields are blank. However, if you click on IPTC Contact, you'll see that all your copyright and contact info has been stripped out, too. Luckily, when you create a metadata template in Bridge, it is also available in Photoshop. So if you'd like to add your IPTC Contact and copyright info back in, just click on the right-facing triangle in the top-right corner of the dialog and from the flyout menu, choose the metadata template with the info you'd like to embed (as shown here). By the way, if you find yourself doing this a lot, this is an ideal thing to record as an action, so the whole process is totally automated (more on actions later).

Stay Organized Using Stacks

Another cool thing Adobe added in Bridge CS3 is the ability to stack similar photos together, which is a big help in limiting clutter and making things more organized. It's kind of the same metaphor we use with folders on our computer—we put similar things together in folders to keep them organized, and it's the same with stacks. Of course, we have the advantage that the photo on top of the stack gives us an idea of what's in the stack, so we can tell at a glance what's inside. Here's how to start using stacks to bring more order to your shoots:

Step One:

To stack photos together, first click on the photo that you want to represent the stack (in other words, click first on the photo you want visible on top). Then, press-and-hold the Command (PC: Ctrl) key, and click on the other similar photos you want in your stack. In our example here, there are basically two kinds of photos: architectural elements, and animal and plant shots. So I clicked on the first shot in the upper-left corner first, then I Command-clicked on the other visible architectural element shots next (there are seven photos selected here in all).

Step Two:

Now, in the Menu bar, go under the Stacks menu and choose Group as Stack, or just press the keyboard shortcut Command-G (PC: Ctrl-G).

SCOTT KELBY

Step Three:

Once you do either of those, when you look in the Content panel, you'll see that the photo you clicked on first now has a number in the top-left corner (which is there to tell you how many photos are in that particular stack. Here there is a 7), plus you'll see a thin stroke (that looks like the outline of a traditional slide mount) around your thumbnail (as shown here). Those are your two indicators that this is a stack. By stacking these similar photos together, you can now see other photos that you would have had to scroll down to see.

SCOTT KELBY

Step Four:

To reveal the contents of your stack, just click directly on the number up in the top-left corner, and the stack expands (as shown here). If you actually want to cancel your stack (and have your photos return to just being individual photos), press Command-Shift-G (PC: Ctrl-Shift-G).

TIP: If you click on a stack and press the Return (PC: Enter) key, only the top photo (the visible photo) in that stack will open in Photoshop. However, if you look closely, you'll see that there are two slide mount outlines around each stack. If you click directly on the second slide mount (the one in back), when you press the Return key it opens all the photos in that stack in Photoshop. By the way, if those photos are in RAW format, they will open in Camera Raw instead.

Continued

Step Five:

Adding more stacks is easy (and the more stacks you make, the more organized you'll be, because you'll have to deal with fewer thumbnails). Just Command-click (PC: Ctrl-click) on the photos you want in your stack, and then press Command-G (PC: Ctrl-G). It's as easy as that. Here I've created another stack, but this time it's a stack for animals. By adding this second stack, I can now see the rest of the photos in my shoot all within the same window (as seen here).

Step Six:

To add photos to an existing stack, first click on the stack you want to add them to, then Command-click (PC: Ctrl-click) on the other photos you want to add (in this case, I clicked on the architectural elements stack, then I clicked on the other seven photos). Now press Command-G (PC: Ctrl-G; the same keyboard shortcut we've been using), and those photos are added to the stack. We're now down to just these two stacks. Now, we could have broken this down into more stacks if we wanted to—maybe one for flowers, one for monkeys, etc.—but the idea is to reduce clutter by grouping similar photos together, with the top photo representing the contents. How many (or few) stacks you create is up to you.

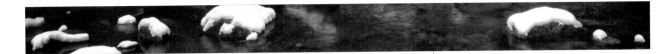

Step Seven:

If you have more than 10 photos in your stack and you place your cursor over its thumbnail, a little horizontal slider will appear across the top of your stack (as seen here). If you click-and-drag this slider to the right, it will scroll through and show you the thumbnails of the photos in that stack. That's pretty sweet because you don't have to expand the stack. Also, to the immediate left of this slider is a tiny Play button. If you click it, it will play a quick mini-slide-show of the photos in that stack, right within that small thumbnail window. Here's the thing: if you have a fast computer, this is just about useless, because it goes so fast you can't tell what's what. However, if you're working on some really sluggish mush-puppy, it's perfect!

Step Eight:

One last thing: remember when I mentioned that the first photo you click on becomes the top photo in the stack (and the one visible when the stack is collapsed)? Well, after you've created your stack, you can choose any photo as the top photo by first expanding the stack (click on the number in the thumbnail's top-left corner), and then Control-clicking (PC: Right-clicking) on the photo you'd like as the top photo. When the contextual menu appears, under Stack, choose Promote to Top of Stack (as shown here) and that photo will now represent the stack. Of course, when the stack is expanded, you can drag-and-drop photos into the order you want.

Exposure: 1/30s   Focal Length: 70mm   Aperture Value: f/11.0

Raw Deal
processing your images using camera raw

Okay, this title is actually taken from a movie starring California Governor Arnold Schwarzenegger called *Raw Deal*. I found the movie poster for it online, and I must admit it was the movie's tag line that sold me on using it as my chapter title. The tag line was: "The system gave him a Raw Deal. Nobody gives him a Raw Deal." The word "Nobody" was underlined. Like this: Nobody. So here's the weird thing: shouldn't it have been, "Nobody gives him a Raw Deal!" with the "him" either italicized or underlined? But the "Nobody" was underlined instead. Makes you stop and think, doesn't it? Anyway, on the movie poster itself, Arnold is holding a really large automatic weapon (I know—how unusual) while wearing a small white under-shirt, so his arms and chest look really huge. Ya know, if I had arms and a chest the size of Arnold's, I'm not sure I'd even own a shirt.

I'd go shirtless everywhere, and I don't think anyone would give me even an ounce of heat about it. I think restaurants and grocery stores would quickly ease their "no shirt—no service" policy and welcome me right in. Especially if I was carrying that large automatic weapon like he is. Why, I'll bet people get right out of his way. Now, this movie was released in 1986 (I think I was about 6 months old then), and at that time there was no shooting in RAW, so this was years before the RAW wars broke out. (Everybody thought one day we'd have a huge war over oil reserves in the Middle East. But no one had anticipated that long before that, the entire world would be embroiled in a bitter RAW vs. JPEG war that would threaten to take neighboring TIFF and PSD right into the conflict with it. I can't believe you're still reading this. You're my kind of people— ya know, for just one person.)

Getting RAW, JPEG, and TIFF Photos Into Camera Raw

Although Adobe Camera Raw was created to process photos taken in your camera's RAW format, Adobe Photoshop CS3 has the first version of Camera Raw that's not just for RAW photos, because now you can process your JPEG and TIFF photos in Camera Raw as well (so even though your JPEG and TIFF photos won't have all of the advantages of RAW photos, at least you'll have all of the intuitive controls Camera Raw brings to the table). So, here's how to get your photos into Camera Raw and which Camera Raw to use when (the one in Adobe Bridge or the one in Photoshop CS3 itself).

Step One:
We'll start with the simplest thing first—opening a RAW photo from Bridge CS3. If you double-click on a RAW photo in Bridge, it takes the photo over to Photoshop and opens it in the Camera Raw interface (as shown here). I know, you were probably expecting something sexier than that, but that's all there is to it—double-click and it recognizes that it's a RAW file, takes it over to Photoshop, and opens it in Camera Raw. So far, so good.

Step Two:
If you want to open more than one RAW photo at a time, in Bridge Command-click (PC: Ctrl-click) on all the photos you want to open (as shown here), then double-click on any one of them. It follows the same scheme—it takes them over to Photoshop and opens them in Camera Raw.

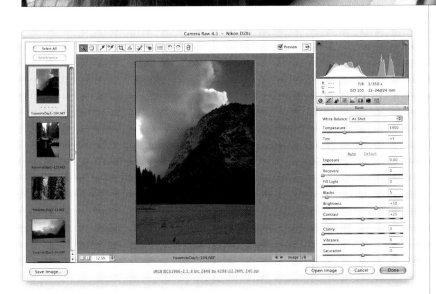

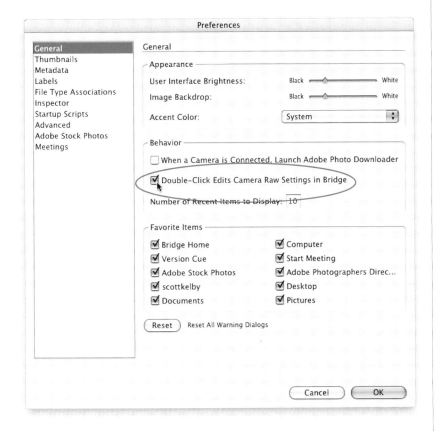

Step Three:
On the left side of the Camera Raw dialog, you can see a filmstrip with all the RAW photos you had previously selected in Bridge. At this point, only the top photo is selected, so changes you make will only affect that one photo (even though you have a number of others open). To have the changes you make to the top photo affect all the photos in the filmstrip, click the Select All button (at the top of the filmstrip), and then make your changes (for example, click the Select All button, drag the Temperature slider all the way to the right, and watch the filmstrip thumbnails update with the very warm white balance. Now click the Cancel button on the bottom right).

Step Four:
So far, we've been processing our RAW photos in Photoshop's Camera Raw, but Bridge has its own separate Camera Raw built right in. That's so you can have Bridge processing multiple RAW images in the background, leaving Photoshop free for you to work on something else (so, basically it's a productivity thing). If you want to open one or more RAW photos in Bridge's Camera Raw, click on the photo (or Command-click [PC: Ctrl-click] on multiple photos) and press Command-R (PC: Ctrl-R), and those photos will open in Bridge's Camera Raw (which is identical to Photoshop's Camera Raw). If you find yourself doing this quite often, then you'll probably want to press Command-K (PC: Ctrl-K) to bring up Bridge's Preferences, and then turn on the checkbox for Double-Click Edits Camera Raw Settings in Bridge (as shown here). Now, double-clicking on a photo opens RAW photos in Bridge's Camera Raw, rather than Photoshop's.

Continued

Step Five:

Now, if you're not using Bridge, and you want to open a RAW photo in Camera Raw, just double-click on it from right within the Mac's Finder window (or within Windows Explorer on a PC) and it will open in Photoshop's Camera Raw. But what if you want to open a JPEG or TIFF photo in Camera Raw? On a Mac, just go under Photoshop's File menu and choose Open. In the Open dialog, navigate to the JPEG or TIFF photo you want to import and click on it. If you click on a JPEG photo, the Format pop-up menu will show JPEG (and it will open in Photoshop, like any other JPEG). So to open this JPEG photo in Camera Raw, you have to choose Camera Raw from the Format menu (as shown here). On a PC, under the File menu, you'll choose Open As, then navigate to a JPEG or TIFF, click on it, and choose Camera Raw from the Open As pop-up menu.

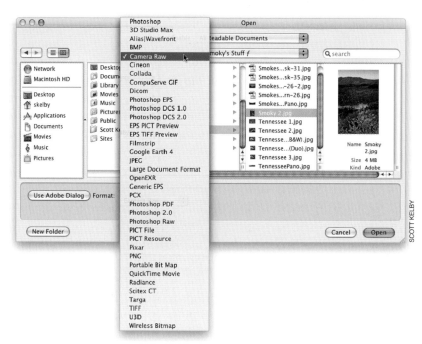

Step Six:

When you click the Open button, that JPEG photo is opened in the Camera Raw interface, as shown here (notice how JPEG appears up in the title bar, just to the right of Camera Raw 4.1?). *Note:* When you make adjustments to a JPEG or TIFF photo in Camera Raw and you click either the Open Image button (to open the adjusted photo in Photoshop) or the Done button (to save the edits you made in Camera Raw), unlike when editing RAW photos, you are now actually affecting the pixels of the original photo. Of course, there is a Cancel button in Camera Raw and even if you open the JPEG photo in Photoshop, if you don't save your changes, the original JPEG or TIFF photo remains untouched.

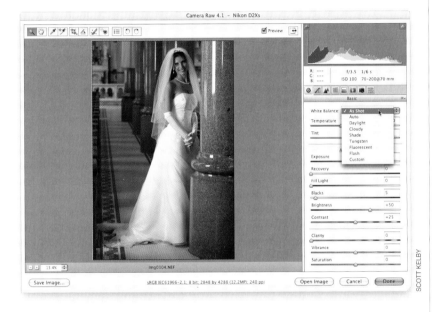

If you've ever taken a photo indoors, chances are the photo came out with kind of a yellowish tint. Unless, of course, you took the shot in an office, and then it probably had a green tint. Even if you just took a shot of somebody in a shadow, the whole photo probably looked like it had a blue tint. Those are white balance problems. If you've properly set your white balance in the camera, you won't see these distracting tints (the photos will just look normal), but most people shoot with their cameras set to Auto White Balance, and well…don't worry, we can fix it really easily in Camera Raw.

The Essential Adjustments: White Balance

Step One:
On the right side of the Camera Raw dialog, there's a section for adjusting the white balance. Think of this area as "the place we go to get rid of those yellow, blue, or green tints that appear on our photos taken indoors." There are three ways to correct this, and we'll start with the easiest—choosing a new white balance from the White Balance pop-up menu. By default, Camera Raw displays your photo using your camera's white balance setting, called the As Shot white balance. Here, my camera's White Balance setting (it was set to Flash) made the photo look too warm with a yellowish tint.

Continued

Step Two:

To change the white balance, click on the White Balance pop-up menu and choose a preset. As I mentioned in Step One, the white balance setting in my camera was set to Flash, but I wasn't shooting with a flash—I was shooting with a single Westcott Spiderlite TD5 (which is a daylight-fluorescent continuous light with a softbox attached). So, you could choose Fluorescent (as shown here), which removes most of the yellowing seen in Step One, but to me it now looks a little too blue (look at her veil). (By the way, you will only get these white balance presets when working on a RAW image. They are not available for JPEGs or TIFFs.)

Step Three:

This is going to sound pretty simplistic, but it works—just take a quick look at the seven different white balance presets and see if any of them look more natural to you (look for one without the yellow tint, but less blue). This process takes around 14 seconds (I just timed it). Some will be way off base immediately (like Shade, which looks way too yellow, or Tungsten, which looks way too blue). What surprised me about this particular photo was the preset that looked best (to me anyway). It was the Auto white balance preset (as shown here), which seldom does the best job, unless you're shooting in mid-afternoon on a bright sunny day (which I avoid like the plague). Anyway, this is why it pays to take a quick look at all seven presets. Notice her veil looks less blue, and the warm yellow look is gone? Ahhhhh, that's better.

Step Four:

Although the Auto setting is the best of the built-in presets here, when it comes to portraits, most people tend to look better when they're a little bit on the warm side (with even a little bluish cold tint, they look…well…cold. Or pale. Or worse yet, deceased). So, although I would use the Auto white balance preset, I would only use it as a starting point. Then I would drag the Temperature slider to the right (toward the yellow side of the slider) to warm the photo back up just a little bit. After all, the lighting was nice and warm in the church, and Debbie has a dark tan, so go ahead and drag the Temperature slider a little to the right (away from blue, and toward yellow) to bring back some of the warmth, without making the whole photo look too yellow (so, don't drag too far to the right).

Step Five:

The second method of setting your white balance is to simply use just the Temperature and Tint sliders (although most of the time you'll only use the Temperature slider, as most of your problems will be too much [or too little] yellow or blue). The sliders themselves give you a clue on which way to drag (blue is on the left and it slowly transitions over to yellow). This makes getting the color you want so much easier—just drag in the direction of the color you want. By the way, when you adjust either of these sliders, your white balance preset changes to Custom (as shown).

Continued

Step Six:

The third method, using the White Balance tool, is perhaps the most accurate because it takes a white balance reading from the photo itself. You just click on the White Balance tool in the toolbar at the top left (it's circled in red here), and then click it on something in your photo that's supposed to be a light gray (that's right—you properly set the white balance by clicking on something that's light gray). So, take the tool and click it once on the glove on her forearm (as shown here) and it sets the white balance for you. If you don't like how it looks (there's a good chance it's too blue), then just click on a different light gray area.

Step Seven:

Now, here's the thing: although this can give you a perfectly accurate white balance, it doesn't mean that it will look good. White balance is a creative decision, and the most important thing is that your photo looks good to you. So don't get caught up in that "I don't like the way the white balance looks, but I know it's accurate" thing that sucks some people in—set your white balance so it looks right to you. You are the bottom line. You're the photographer. It's your photo, so make it look its best. Accurate is not another word for good. Okay, I'm off the soapbox, and it's time for a tip: Want to quickly reset your white balance to the As Shot setting? Just double-click on the White Balance tool up in the toolbar (as shown here).

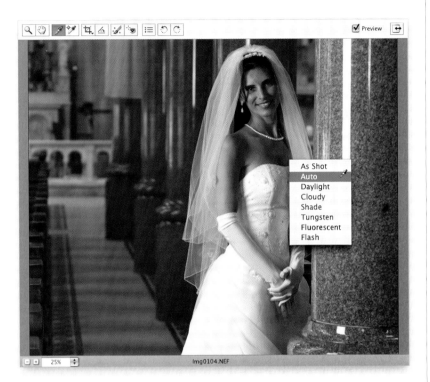

As Shot
Auto
Daylight
Cloudy
Shade
Tungsten
Fluorescent
Flash

Img0104.NEF

Step Eight:
One last thing: once you have the White Balance tool, if you Control-click (PC: Right-click) within your photo, a White Balance preset contextual menu appears under your cursor (as shown here), so you can quickly choose a preset.

TIP: To help you find the neutral light gray color in your images, I've included a swatch card for you in the back of this book (it's perforated so you can tear it out), and it has a special Camera Raw white balance light gray swatch area. Just put this card into your scene (or have your subject hold it), take the shot, and when you open a file in Camera Raw, click the White Balance tool on the neutral gray area on the swatch card to instantly set your white balance.

Step Five:

So, now you know how to spot a clipping problem, but what do you do to fix it? Well, in previous versions of Camera Raw, there was really only one thing you could do—drag the Exposure slider back to the left until the clipping warnings went away (which stinks, because lowering the exposure usually made the whole photo underexposed). But thankfully, in CS3 we have the Recovery slider (for recovering clipped highlights). Start by setting the Exposure slider first until the exposure looks right to you—if you see some small areas are clipping, don't worry about it. Now, drag the Recovery slider to the right and as you do just the very brightest highlights are pulled back (recovered) from clipping. Here I still have that white clipping warning turned on, and from just dragging the Recovery slider a tiny bit to the right, you can see that the red clipped areas have been greatly reduced.

Step Six:

Like the Exposure slider, you can use that same press-and-hold-the-Option (PC: Alt)-key trick while you're dragging the Recovery slider, and the screen will turn black, revealing just the clipped areas. As you drag to the right, you'll actually see the clipped areas go away (as shown here). These two warnings (the highlight triangle, and the black preview window showing which colors have clipped and where) do exactly the same thing. It's really just up to you which of the two you like using best.

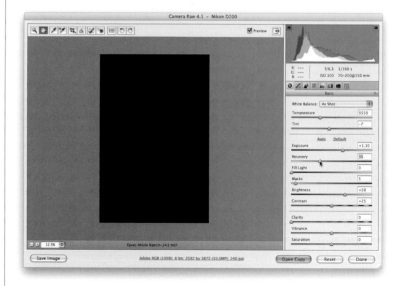

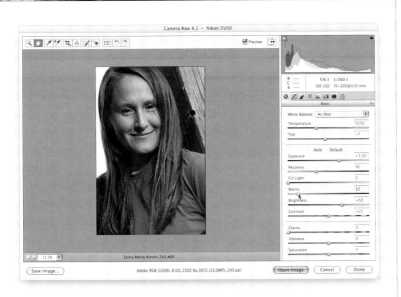

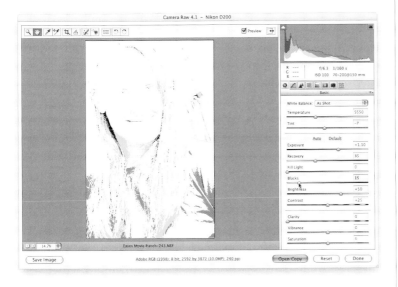

Step Seven:

Next, I adjust the shadow areas using the Blacks slider. Dragging to the right (as shown here) increases the amount of black in the darkest shadow areas of your photo. Dragging to the left opens up (lightens) the shadow areas. See how the slider bar goes from white on the left to black on the right? That lets you know that if you drag to the right, the blacks will be darker. Increasing the blacks will usually saturate the colors in your photo as well, so if you have a really washed out photo, you may want to start with this slider first instead of the Exposure slider.

Step Eight:

You can also use the press-and-hold-the-Option (PC: Alt)-key trick with the Blacks slider. As you might expect, this works in the opposite way the highlight warning works; instead the preview area turns solid white, and any areas that are solid black have lost detail and actually have turned to solid black. If you see other colors (like red, green, or blue), they're getting clipped too, but not as significantly as the overall shadows. So, I'm not nearly as concerned about a little bit of clipping in color. If there's significant shadow clipping, the only fix is to drag to the left to reduce the amount of blacks in the shadows. Here you can see some areas in the Yellow channel are turning to solid black—probably not a big deal (look at the photo without the warning on to see if those are areas of important detail. More on this in a moment). Also, some shadow areas in her hair are clipping to solid black. Do I really care? Are these important detail areas? Not to me, so I would ignore warnings in those areas.

Continued

Step Nine:

Here's the other shadow clipping warning (the one you get from clicking on the triangle in the top-left corner of the histogram). Now, any clipped deep shadow areas will appear in solid blue (as shown here). Again, I don't care about these areas turning solid black—they don't hold important detail.

TIP: Personally, I'm not nearly as concerned about shadows (blacks) clipping as I am highlights clipping. But, in many cases, some highlight clipping is perfectly acceptable. For example, clipping specular highlights, like a bright reflection on a car's bumper or the center of the sun, isn't a problem—there wouldn't be important detail (or any detail for that matter) anyway. So, as long as we make sure important areas aren't clipped off, we can keep dragging either the Exposure slider or the Blacks slider to the right until some important areas begin to clip.

Step 10:

The next slider down is Brightness. Since you've already adjusted the highlights (Exposure slider) and the shadows (Blacks slider), the Brightness slider adjusts everything else (I relate this slider to the midtones slider in Photoshop's Levels dialog, so that might help in understanding how this slider differs from the Exposure or Blacks sliders). Of the three main adjustments (Exposure, Blacks, and Brightness), this one I personally use the least—if I do use it, I usually just drag it a very short amount to the right to open up some of the midtone detail. There are no warnings for midtones, but if you push it far enough to the right, you could see some highlight clipping.

Step 11:

If you don't want to manually adjust these sliders (in other words, you're a total wuss), you can always click the Auto button (known in RAW circles as "the wuss button" or "the total wuss button"). It's a button that doesn't look like a button. It's just the underlined word Auto, and it appears just below the Tint slider. If you click on it (as shown here), Camera Raw automatically tries to adjust the photo for what it feels is the proper exposure. Sometimes this works okay, sometimes it does very little (other than adjusting the Exposure and Recovery sliders to eliminate highlight clipping, as in our example here), and sometimes it seems to way overexpose the photo (okay, more than sometimes. I'd say fairly often). It seems like it pushes the Exposure slider as far to the right as it can without clipping the highlights, which I guess in theory gives you a full range of exposure, but in reality it gives you what looks like (to me anyway) an overexposed photo.

Step 12:

If you don't like the Auto results, you can click on the Default button (to its immediate right) to reset the photo to the Camera Raw default settings (which is what the photo looked like the first time you opened it in Camera Raw, as seen on the left here). In the After photo, the only other change I made was to add a subtle vignette effect (shown on page 118). Okay, so that's the deal on setting your highlights, shadows, and midtones, and how to keep from clipping important details. Now, when you turn the page, let's do a quick four-step adjustment using these tools in the order that I would use them if I were processing a photo in Camera Raw.

Before

After

Continued

Step 13:

Here I've opened a different photo, also shot in RAW, so we can practice the process in the same order I would normally edit a photo in Camera Raw. I always start with setting the white balance, and in the image shown here, the whole photo seems to have a bit of a yellow color cast. That's there because I didn't set the white balance in my camera to reflect the tungsten (standard indoor) lighting in the room.

Step 14:

To set the white balance (or "reset" to the proper white balance, I should say), get the White Balance tool (I) and click on something that you think should be a light gray (in the example shown here, I clicked on the edge of a plate on the right side of the photo—shown circled here in red). Now, although I used the White Balance tool here, if I know the lighting situation the photo was shot in, I usually go straight to the White Balance pop-up menu and just choose a white balance preset (so for example, if this had been shot in an office, I would have chosen the Fluorescent preset).

Step 15:

After setting the white balance, I then adjust the exposure using the Exposure slider. In the example shown here, I dragged the Exposure slider to the right until the image looked bright enough, but when it looked right to me, the highlights were beginning to clip a little bit (I could see the clipping warning up in the top-right corner of the histogram). So I immediately went to the Recovery slider and dragged it over to the right (as shown here) until the clipping warning went away.

Step 16:

This isn't a backlit photo, or one that required fill flash, so I would skip right over the Fill Light slider and go to the Blacks slider. Drag it to the right (as shown here) to increase the darkness of the shadows and to add contrast to the photo and saturation to the colors. If I felt the photo needed more detail in the midtones (in other words, it looked kind of dark and muddy in the midtones), I would drag the Brightness slider to the right, but I didn't think it was necessary in this photo. That's it—four easy steps in the exact order that I do them for my own work. Those steps again are: (1) setting the white balance, (2) setting the exposure, (3) compensating for highlight clipping using the Recovery slider, and (4) increasing the Blacks amount.

Adding "Snap" to Your Images Using the Clarity Slider

This is one of my favorite new features in Camera Raw 4.1, and whenever I show it in a live class, it never fails to get "Ooohhs" and "Ahhhhs." I think it's because it's just one simple slider, yet it does so much to add "snap" to your image. The Clarity slider (which is well-named) basically increases the midtone contrast in a way that gives your photo more punch and impact, without actually sharpening the image (much like certain Curves adjustments in Photoshop can add snap and punch to your photos).

Step One:
The Clarity slider (new in Camera Raw 4.1) is found near the bottom of the Basic panel in Camera Raw, right above the Vibrance and Saturation sliders. Like the Sharpening controls, if you want to see the effects of applying "clarity," first zoom in to a 100% view (you can choose 100% from the pop-up view menu as shown here). Then, click-and-drag the Clarity slider to the right to increase the amount of snap in your image (I heard that at one point in the development the Adobe engineers toyed with the name "Punch" to describe it, as they thought it added punch to the image).

Step Two:
To get the most possible clarity out of your image, keep dragging the slider to the right until you see those little halos start to appear around edge areas in your image (you know, those halos we're always trying to avoid). Well, once you see them, just back off a little (dragging back to the left) until they're gone and your clarity is set. Now, of course, that's for adding maximum clarity. You can always just click-and-drag the slider to the right until the photo has the amount of midtone punch you want it to have. Here's a before/after with the Clarity on the After photo set to 90.

Before   *After*

Since you're processing your own images, it only makes sense that you get to choose what resolution, what size, which color space, and how many bits per channel your photo will be, right? These are workflow decisions, which is why you make them in the Workflow Options dialog. Here are my recommendations on what to choose, and why:

Setting Your Resolution, Image Size, Color Space, and Bit Depth

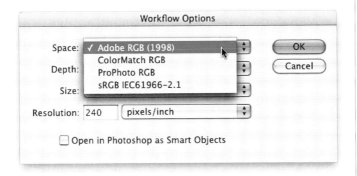

Step One:
Once you've made all your edits, and the photo is generally looking the way you want it to, it's time to choose your resolution, size, etc. Directly below the Camera Raw preview area (where you see your photo), you'll see your current workflow settings—they are underlined in blue like a website link. Click on that link to bring up the Workflow Options dialog (which is seen in the next step).

Step Two:
We'll start at the top by choosing your photo's color space. By default, it shows the color space specified in your digital camera, but if you're editing a RAW photo, you can ignore that and choose the color space you want the photo processed with. I recommend choosing the same color space that you have chosen as Photoshop's color space. For photographers, at this point in time, I still recommend that you choose Adobe RGB (1998) for Photoshop's color space, and if you've done that, then you would choose Adobe RGB (1998) here, from the Space pop-up menu. See my color management and printing chapter (Chapter 5) for more on why you should use Adobe RGB (1998).

Continued

Step Three:

When it comes to choosing your photo's bit depth, I have a simple rule I go by: I always work in 8 Bits/Channel (Photoshop's default), unless I have a photo that is so messed up that after Camera Raw, I know I'm still going to have to do some major Curves adjustments in Photoshop just to make it look right. The advantage of 16-bit is those major Curves adjustments wouldn't damage the photo as much (you'd get less banding or posterization) because of the greater depth of 16-bit. The reasons I don't use 16-bit more often are: (1) many of Photoshop's tools and features aren't available in 16-bit, (2) your file size is approximately double, which makes Photoshop run a lot slower, and (3) 16-bit photos take up twice as much room on your computer. Some photographers insist on only working in 16-bit and that doesn't bother me one bit. (Get it? One bit? Aw, come on, that wasn't that bad.)

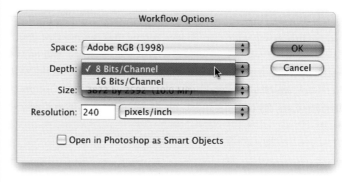

Step Four:

The next option down is size. By default, the size displayed in the Size pop-up menu is the original size dictated by your digital camera's megapixel capacity (in this case, it's 3872 by 2592 pixels, the size generated by a 10-megapixel camera). If you click-and-hold on the Size pop-up menu, you'll see a list of image sizes Camera Raw can generate from your RAW original (the number in parentheses shows the equivalent megapixels that size represents). The sizes with a + (plus sign) by them indicate that you're scaling the image up in size from the original. The − (minus sign) means you're shrinking the size from the original, which quality-wise isn't a problem. Usually, it's fairly safe to increase the size to the next largest choice, but anything above that and you risk having the photo look soft and/or pixelated.

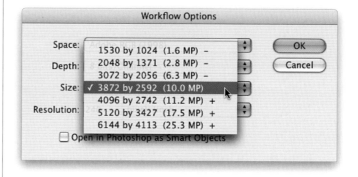

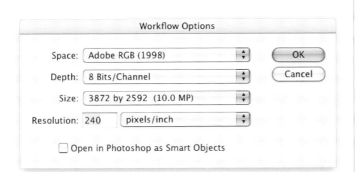

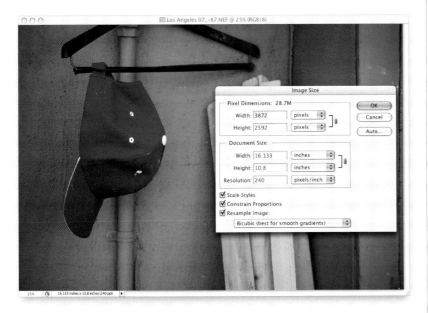

Step Five:
The last Workflow Options choice is what you want the resolution of your processed file to be. The topic of resolution is something entire training DVDs are dedicated to, so we won't go in-depth about it here, but I'll give you some quick guidelines. If your photo will wind up on a printing press, use 300 ppi (you don't really need that much, but many print shops still think you do, so just play it safe at 300 ppi). When printing to an inkjet printer at larger than 8x10" size, I use 240 ppi (although some argue that the sweet spot for Epson printers is 360 ppi, so you might try printing the same image at both resolutions and compare). For prints smaller than 8x10" (which are viewed at a very close distance), try 300 ppi. If your photos are only going to be viewed on the Web, you can use 72 ppi. (By the way, the proper resolution is debated daily in Photoshop discussion forums around the world, and everybody has their own reason why their number is right. So, if ever you're bored one night….)

Step Six:
When you click OK and then click Open Image in the Camera Raw dialog, your photo is processed using those settings and opened in Photoshop (here's the processed photo in Photoshop with the Image Size dialog open, so you can see the settings). These workflow settings now become your defaults, so you don't have to mess with them again, unless: (a) you want to choose a different size, (b) you need to work in 16-bit, or (c) you need to change the resolution. Personally, I work at the original size taken by my camera, in 8-bit mode, and at a resolution of 240 ppi, so I don't have to change these workflow options very often.

Cropping and Straightening

There are some distinct advantages to cropping your photo in Camera Raw, rather than in Photoshop CS3 itself, and perhaps the #1 benefit is that you can return to Camera Raw later and return to the uncropped image (here's a difference in how Camera Raw handles RAW photos vs. JPEG and TIFF photos: this "return to Camera Raw later and return to the uncropped image" holds true even for JPEG and TIFF photos, as long as you haven't overwritten the original JPEG or TIFF file. To avoid overwriting, when you save the JPEG or TIFF in Photoshop, change the filename).

Step One:
The fifth tool in Camera Raw's toolbar is the Crop tool. By default, it pretty much works like the Crop tool in Photoshop (you click-and-drag it out around the area you want to keep), but it does offer some features that Photoshop doesn't—like access to a list of preset cropping ratios. To get them, click-and-hold on the Crop tool and a pop-up menu will appear (as shown here). The Normal setting gives you the standard drag-it-where-you-want-it cropping. However, if you choose one of the cropping presets, then your cropping is constrained to a specific ratio. For example, choose the 2 to 3 ratio, click-and-drag it out, and you'll see that it keeps the same aspect ratio as your original uncropped photo.

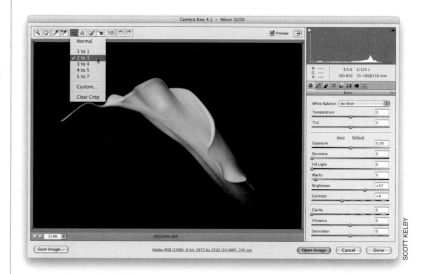

Step Two:
Here's the 2-to-3-ratio cropping border dragged out over my image. The area that will be cropped away appears dimmed, and the clear area inside the cropping border is how your final cropped photo will appear. If you reopen this RAW photo later, the cropping border will still be visible onscreen, so you can move its position, resize it, or remove it altogether by simply pressing the Esc key, or the Delete (PC: Backspace) key on your keyboard (or by choosing Clear Crop from the Crop tool's pop-up menu).

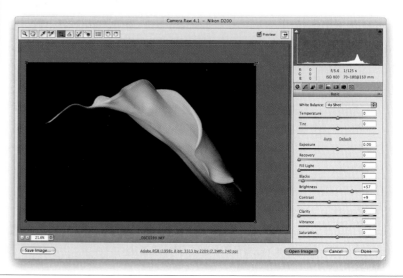

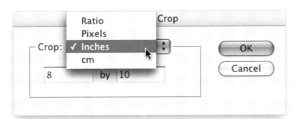

Step Three:

If you want your photo cropped to an exact size (like 8x10", 13x19", etc.), choose Custom from the Crop tool's pop-up menu. You can choose to crop by inches, pixels, centimeters, or a custom ratio. In our example, we're going to create a custom crop so our cropped photo winds up being exactly 8x10", so choose Inches from the pop-up menu (as shown here), then type in your custom size. Click OK, click-and-drag out the Crop tool, and the area inside your cropping border will be exactly 8x10".

Step Four:

Once you click on the Open Image button in Camera Raw, the image is cropped to your specs and opened in Photoshop (as shown here). If instead, you click on the Done button, Camera Raw closes and your photo is untouched, but it keeps your cropping border in position for the future.

TIP: As I mentioned earlier in this chapter, the size of your photo (and other information about your photo) is displayed directly under the preview area of Camera Raw (in that blue underlined text that looks like a Web link). When you drag out a cropping border, the size info for the photo automatically updates to display the dimensions of the currently selected crop area.

Continued

Step Five:

If you save a cropped JPEG or TIFF photo out of Camera Raw (by clicking on the Save Image button on the bottom left of the Camera Raw window), the only way to bring back those cropped areas is to reopen the photo in Camera Raw. However, if before saving, you choose Photoshop from the Format pop-up menu (as shown), a new option will appear called Preserve Cropped Pixels. If you turn on that option before you click Save, when you open this cropped photo in Photoshop, it will appear to be cropped, but the photo will be on a separate layer (not flattened on the Background layer). So the cropped area is still there—it just extends off the visible image area. You can bring that cropped area back by clicking-and-dragging your photo within the image area (try it—click-and-drag your photo to the right or left and you'll see what I mean).

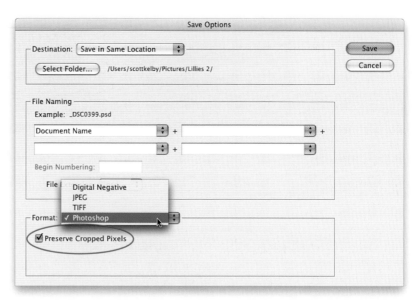

Step Six:

If you have a number of similar photos you need to crop the same way, you're going to love this: First, select all the photos you want to crop in Camera Raw (either in Bridge, or on your computer), then open them all in Camera Raw. When you open multiple photos, they appear in a vertical filmstrip along the left side of Camera Raw (as shown here). Click on the Select All button (it's above the filmstrip) and then crop the currently selected photo as you'd like. As you apply your cropping, look at the filmstrip and you'll see all the thumbnails update with their new cropping instructions. A tiny Crop icon will also appear in the bottom-left corner of each thumbnail, letting you know that these photos have been cropped in Camera Raw.

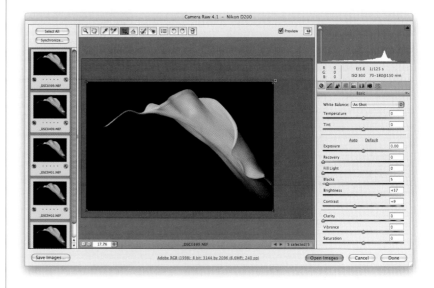

Step Seven:

Another form of cropping is actually straightening your photos using the Straighten tool. It's a close cousin of the Crop tool because what it does is essentially rotates your cropping border, so when you open the photo it's straight. In the Camera Raw toolbar, choose the Straighten tool (it's immediately to the right of the Crop tool, and shown circled here in red). Now, click-and-drag it along the horizon line in your photo (as shown here). When you release the mouse button, a cropping border appears and that border is automatically rotated to the exact amount needed to straighten the photo (as shown in Step Eight).

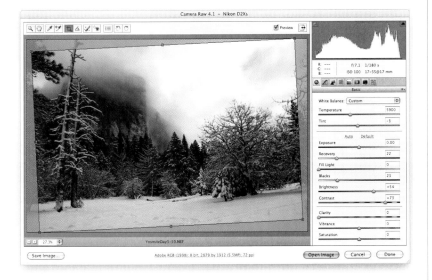

Step Eight:

You won't actually see the rotated photo until you open it in Photoshop (which means, if you click Save Image or Done, Camera Raw closes, and the straightening information is saved along with the file. So if you open this file again in Camera Raw, that straightening crop border will still be in place). If you click Open Image instead, the photo opens in Photoshop, but only the area inside the cropping border is visible, and the rest is cropped off. Again, if this is a RAW photo (or you haven't overwritten your JPEG or TIFF file), you can always return to Camera Raw and remove this cropping border to get the original uncropped photo back.

TIP: If you want to cancel your straightening, just press the Esc key on your keyboard, and the straightening border will go away.

Editing Multiple Photos at Once

One of the coolest things about Camera Raw is the ability to apply changes to one RAW photo, and then quickly and easily apply those same changes to as few, or as many, other images as you'd like. It's a form of built-in automation, and it can save an incredible amount of time in editing your shoots (plus, if you use Bridge's Camera Raw, rather than Photoshop's, you can have your photos processing in the background, while you're working on something else in Photoshop. Now that is some serious productivity!).

Step One:

There are two different ways to do this, and the first starts in Bridge. The key to making this type of automation work is that the photos you want to edit all are shot in similar lighting (that's why this is so popular with studio photographers), or they have some other similar problem. This is because the idea is to make changes to one photo, and apply those exact changes to a bunch of other similar photos.

Step Two:

So, with that in mind, go to Bridge, click on a photo to edit, and press Command-R (PC: Ctrl-R) to open the photo in Bridge's Camera Raw (as shown here). Go ahead and adjust the photo the way you'd like (in our example, I started by taking the White Balance tool [I] and clicking on her dress to remove most of the overly warm yellowish color. Next, I increased the Exposure a bit, and raised the Recovery amount to 100% to tame the sunlight coming through the top windows. The bride's face is in the shadows a bit, so I increased the Fill Light amount to bring some light into her face. Lastly, I moved the Contrast slider to the right just slightly). When you're done, don't open the image, just click the Done button.

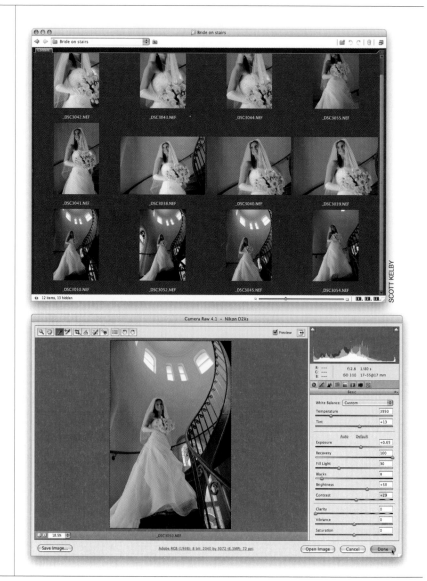

SCOTT KELBY

Step Three:

When you click that Done button, you're returned to Bridge, and the thumbnail for the photo you just edited now reflects the changes you made. Press-and-hold the Command (PC: Ctrl) key and select all the other photos in Bridge that you want to have those exact same edits (the white balance, exposure, recovery, fill light—all of it). Now, Control-click (PC: Right-click) on any one of those selected photos, and a contextual menu will appear. Go under Develop Settings and choose Previous Conversion (as shown here).

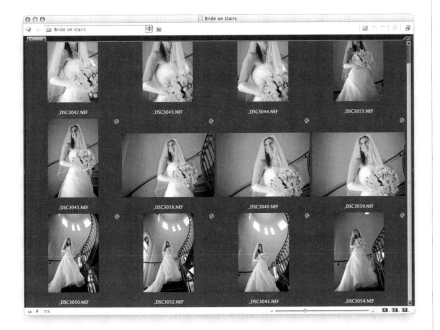

Step Four:

All the changes you made to the previous photo are now applied to all your selected photos in Bridge (as shown here, where you can see the white balance is now better [it's less yellow], the exposure has been tweaked, etc.). Now, what if you only wanted to apply certain edits you made—like just the white balance settings, and not all the other stuff? Then you'd use the other method (on the next page).

TIP: If after applying those edits to your photos, you decide one or more of them doesn't look good with those edits, then Control-click (PC: Right-click) to bring up that contextual menu again, but this time go under Develop Settings and choose Clear Settings. This removes any changes made in Camera Raw.

Continued

Step Five:

With this method, in Bridge, start by Command-clicking (PC: Ctrl-clicking) on all the photos you want to edit first (so they're all selected), then press Command-R (PC: Ctrl-R) to open them all in Camera Raw. Thumbnails of all the open photos appear in a vertical filmstrip along the left side of the window (as seen here). Click on any one of the photos and make your edits (in this case, we made the white balance a bit cooler, so her dress is white, rather than tinted yellow, as well as a few other adjustments). Now click the Select All button at the top left (to select all the open photos), and then click on the Synchronize button (right beneath it). This brings up the Synchronize dialog (shown in the inset), where you choose which of the edits you made to the first photo will be applied to the rest of your selected photos. In our case, we only want the white balance setting applied, so choose White Balance from the Synchronize pop-up menu at the top (as shown) and it automatically deselects all the other checkboxes.

Step Six:

When you click OK, the white balance setting—and only the white balance setting—from your edited photo will be applied to all your selected photos in Camera Raw, as shown here where you can see in the filmstrip how the other thumbnails are now updated and her dress no longer has that yellowish tint.

TIP: If you only want certain photos to be affected, and not all the ones open in Camera Raw, then in the filmstrip just Command-click (PC: Ctrl-click) on only the photos you want affected, then click the Synchronize button.

We finally have pro-level sharpening in Camera Raw 4.1 (along with the bonus that the sharpening is applied to your image's luminosity [like the Lightness channel in Lab color] and not the color, so you avoid problems that come with sharpening the full-color image). So, when do you sharpen here, and when in Photoshop? If you're going to be making lots of edits in Photoshop, do it there as the last thing before you save or print. If you're doing most of your editing in Camera Raw, and very little in Photoshop, apply your sharpening in Camera Raw.

Sharpening in Camera Raw

Step One:
When you open a RAW image in Camera Raw, by default it applies a small amount of sharpening to your photo (not the JPEGs or TIFFs—only RAW images). You can adjust this amount (or turn if off altogether, if you like) by clicking on the Detail icon, as shown here, or using the keyboard shortcut Command-Option-3 (PC: Ctrl-Alt-3). At the top of this panel is the new Sharpening section, where by a quick glance you can see that sharpening has already been applied to your photo. If you don't want any sharpening applied at this stage (it's a personal preference), then simply click-and-drag the Amount slider all the way to the left, to lower the amount of sharpening to 0 (zero), and the sharpening is removed.

Step Two:
If you want to turn off this "automatic-by-default" sharpening (so image sharpening is only applied if you go and manually add it yourself), first set the Sharpening Amount slider to 0 (zero), then go to the Camera Raw flyout menu and choose Save New Camera Raw Defaults (as shown here). Now, RAW images taken with that camera will not be automatically sharpened.

Continued

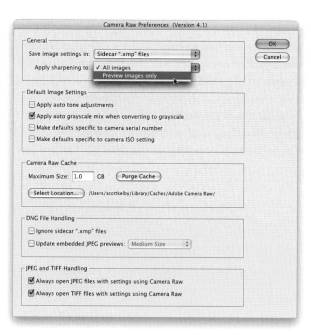

Step Three:

Before we charge into sharpening, there's one more thing you'll want to know. If you don't actually want sharpening applied, but you'd still like to see what the sharpened image would look like, you can sharpen just the preview, and not the actual file. Just press Command-K (PC: Ctrl-K) while Camera Raw is open, and in the Camera Raw Preferences dialog, choose Preview Images Only in the Apply Sharpening To pop-up menu (as shown here), and then click OK to save this as your default. Now the sharpening only affects the preview you see here in Camera Raw, but when you choose to open the file in Photoshop, the sharpening is not applied.

Step Four:

When this new Sharpening section was first introduced, I'd watch friends and students use it, and you'd see them drag the Amount slider all the way over to the right (to 150) and back to 0 (zero) again and back to 150 again, and they'd say, "It's not doing anything!" That's because, even though it says right within the Detail panel itself "Zoom preview to 100% or larger to see the effects of the controls in this panel," virtually no one sees that. I guess we're so excited to actually have more than just one Sharpening slider that we can't wait, so we start dragging it back and forth wildly, cussing at the screen, but all the while we're looking at a Fit in View preview, rather than at 100%, so we don't see the sharpening we're applying. So, forgive me if you did read that message in the panel, and this seems totally obvious to you, but (here goes) before you do any actual sharpening, set your view to 100% (as shown here), or you really won't be able to see the sharpening as you apply it (sorry...it had to be said).

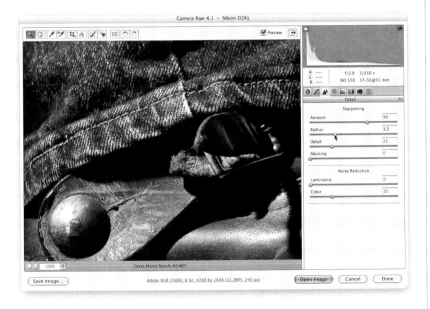

Step Five:

Now that you're at a 100% view, drag the Amount slider all the way to the right so you can see, in fact, that when you're at 100%, the sharpening does indeed work. Again, dipping into the realm of the painfully obvious, dragging the Amount slider to the right increases the amount of sharpening. Compare the image shown here, with the one in Step Four (where the Sharpening Amount was set to the default of 25), and you can see how much sharper the image now appears, even though I only dragged it to around 133.

TIP: To have Camera Raw expand to fill your entire screen, click the Full Screen icon to the right of the Preview checkbox, at the top of the dialog.

Step Six:

The next slider down is the Radius slider, which determines how far out the sharpening is applied from the edges being sharpened in your photo. This pretty much works like the Radius slider in the Unsharp Mask filter, which is probably why the default is 1 (because that's probably where we'll leave it most of the time). I use less than a Radius of 1 if the photo I'm processing is only going to be used on a website, in video editing, or something where it's going to be at a very small size or resolution. I only use a Radius of more than 1 when the image is visibly blurry and needs some "emergency" sharpening. If you decide to increase the Radius amount above 1 (unlike the Unsharp Mask filter, you can only go as high as 3 here), just be careful, because if you go much above 1, your photo can start to look fake and oversharpened. You want your photo to look sharp, not sharpened, so be careful out there.

Continued

Step Seven:

The next slider down is the Detail slider, which determines how much of the edge areas are affected by sharpening. You would apply lower amounts of Detail if your photo is slightly blurred, and higher amounts if you really want to bring out texture and detail, (which is why this slider is aptly named). So, how much Detail you apply depends on the subject you're sharpening. With an image like the one we've been working on here, with lots of texture in the leather, it's an ideal candidate for a high amount of Detail, so I dragged the slider to the right (all the way to 89), until the detail really came out in the leather (as seen here).

Step Eight:

The last Sharpening slider—Masking— is easier to understand, and for many people I think it will become invaluable. Here's why: when you apply sharpening, sharpening gets applied to everything fairly evenly. But what if you have an image where there are areas you'd like sharpened, but other areas of softer detail you'd like left alone. Of course, if you were applying the Unsharp Mask filter in Photoshop, you could duplicate the layer first, then sharpen it, then add a layer mask and mask (paint) away those softer areas you don't want sharpened, right? Well, that's kind of what the Masking slider here in Camera Raw does—as you drag it to the right, it reduces the amount of sharpening on non-edge areas. The default Masking setting is 0 (zero), so sharpening is applied evenly to everything with an edge to be sharpened. As you drag to the right (as shown here), the non-edge areas are masked from sharpening.

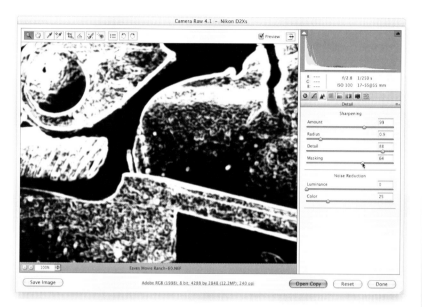

Step Nine:

All four sliders in the Sharpening section of the Detail panel let you have a live preview of what the sharpening is affecting. Just press-and-hold the Option (PC: Alt) key as you drag—your screen will turn grayscale, and the areas that the slider you're dragging will affect appear as edge areas in the preview window. This is particularly helpful in understanding the Masking slider, so press-and-hold the Option key and drag the Masking slider to the left. When Masking is set to 0, the screen turns solid white (because sharpening is being evenly applied to everything). As you drag to the right, the preview (shown here) now shows the only parts of the photo receiving sharpening. If you drag all the way to 100, you'll see that only the most obvious edges are now receiving full sharpening.

Step 10:

Here's a before and after of our boot shot, with no sharpening applied (Before), and then a nice crisp amount applied (After) using these settings—Amount: 120, Radius: 1, Detail: 70, Masking: 10. To see your own before/after press the letter P to toggle the Preview on/off.

Before

After

Double-Processing to Create the Uncapturable

As good as digital cameras have gotten these days, when it comes to exposure, the human eye totally kicks their butt. That's why we shoot so many photos where our subject is backlit, and with our naked eye we can see the subject just fine (our eye adjusts). But when we open the photo, the subject is basically in silhouette. Or how about sunsets where we have to choose which part of the scene to expose for—the ground or the sky—because our camera can't expose for both? Well, here's how to use Camera Raw to overcome this exposure limitation.

Step One:

Open the photo you want to double-process (by the way, although you can do this with JPEG and TIFF photos in Camera Raw, you'll get better results using photos shot in RAW, because you're going to be pushing the tones in some of these photos to their max, and having that extra headroom will keep you from having as much banding or posterization). In this example, the photo is exposed for the background, so the foreground is totally in the shadows. That's okay, just click the Open Image button to open this version of the photo exposed for the sky in Photoshop.

Step Two:

Now go back to Bridge (or wherever the original image is), and reopen the same RAW file in Camera Raw. This time, you're going to expose for the foreground, without any regard for how the sky looks (it will totally blow out, but who cares— you've already got a version with a great sky open in Photoshop). So, push the Exposure slider way over to the right, and maybe the Fill Light slider and the Brightness slider, if necessary, until the foreground looks like the one you see here.

Step Three:
Click the Open Image button in Camera Raw to open this much brighter version of the photo. Now you should have both versions open in Photoshop: the brighter one exposed for the foreground and the original darker one, which was exposed for the sky when shot in the camera. Arrange the windows so you can see both onscreen at the same time (as shown here).

Step Four:
Press V to get the Move tool, press-and-hold the Shift key, and drag-and-drop the darker version on top of the lighter version. The key to this part is holding down the Shift key while you drag, which perfectly aligns the dark version (that now appears on its own layer in the Layers panel, as seen here) with the lighter version on the Background layer. (This exact alignment of one identical photo over another is referred to as being "pin registered.") You can now close the shadow document without saving, as both versions of the image are contained within the lighter version's document.

Continued

Step Five:

Go to the Layers panel, press-and-hold the Option (PC: Alt) key, and click on the Add Layer Mask icon at the bottom of the Layers panel (as shown here). This puts a black mask over the layer with the photo exposed for the sky, covering it so you only see the lighter image on the Background layer. Next, you get to reveal the sky and the mountain by painting over them.

Step Six:

Press the letter B to get the Brush tool, then click on the down-facing arrow next to the word Brush in the Options Bar and choose a medium-sized, soft-edged brush from the Brush Picker. Now, press the letter D to set your Foreground color to white, and start painting over the areas of the photo that you want to be darker (in this case, the mountain in the background and the sky). As you paint with white directly on that black mask, the white reveals the darker version beneath the mask. This particular photo is tricky because of the trees, so you might consider lowering the opacity of your brush to 40% up in the Options Bar (as shown here), that way if you accidentally paint over some of the edges of the trees, it won't look so obvious.

Step Seven:

When you get to the mountain part, you might have to paint over it several times to get it dark enough (only if you lowered the opacity, like I mentioned in the previous step). If the dark areas seem too dark, slightly lower the opacity of the dark layer in the Layers panel. So what you wind up with is an image like the one shown here—one where the foreground and background are blended and both are properly exposed.

Step Eight:

A "smarter" way to do this double processing is to make your image a Smart Object (so there's no dragging-and-dropping, pin registering, and extra open files to slow things down). Here's how: when you're done editing the original image, instead of clicking Open Image, press-and-hold the Shift key and the Open Image button changes into Open Object (shown here).

Step Nine:

Click Open Object, and your RAW image opens as a Smart Object (notice the Smart Object icon in the bottom-right corner of its thumbnail in the Layers panel [for more on Smart Objects, see Chapters 4 and 12]). Now, if you simply duplicated this layer, the new layer would be tied to the original layer, and any tonal changes you made to this duplicate would automatically be applied to the original (bottom) layer. So, Control-click (PC: Right-click) just to the right of your layer's name, and choose New Smart Object via Copy (as shown here), which breaks the link between the two, so they can be edited separately.

Step 10:

In the Layers panel, double-click directly on this duplicate layer's thumbnail and it opens in Camera Raw. Lower the exposure until the sky looks good, and click OK. Your Smart Object duplicate layer is updated, leaving the original brighter bottom layer untouched. Now you can pick up with Step Five (adding a layer mask, as shown here) and continue on as usual painting in the darker sky. By the way, if you always want your RAW-processed images to open as Smart Objects, click the Workflow Options link at the bottom of the Camera Raw dialog, and when the dialog appears, turn on Open in Photoshop as Smart Objects.

Fixing Chromatic Aberrations (That Colored-Edge Fringe)

Chromatic aberration is a fancy name for that thin line of colored fringe that sometimes appears around the edges of objects in photos. Sometimes the fringe is red, sometimes green, sometimes purple, blue, etc., but all the time it's bad, so we might as well get rid of it. Luckily, Camera Raw has a built-in fix that does a pretty good job.

Step One:

Open the photo that has signs of chromatic aberrations (colored-edge fringe). If chromatic aberrations are going to appear, they're usually right along an edge in the image that has lots of contrast (like between the white edges of this building, and the green grass and trees behind it). If the aberrations are bad enough, you'll be able to see them right off the bat, but if you just suspect they might be there, you'll have to zoom in for a closer look (by the way, if you're using a quality camera with quality lenses, you might have to look far and wide before coming across a photo suffering from this problem. As it was, I had to go back and dig up this photo from my wife's old point-and-shoot camera).

Step Two:

Press Z to get the Zoom tool in the Camera Raw dialog and zoom in on an area where you think (or see) the fringe might be fairly obvious. In the example shown here, I zoomed directly in on the right side of the roof and sure enough, it has a red fringe running along the edge. To remove this fringe, click on the Lens Corrections icon (it's the sixth icon from the left at the top of the panel area) to bring up the Chromatic Aberration sliders.

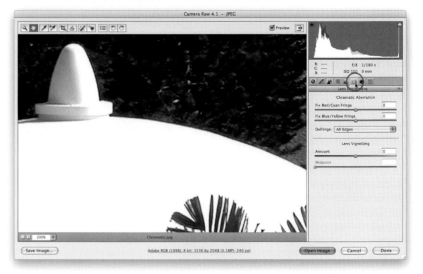

KALEBRA KELBY

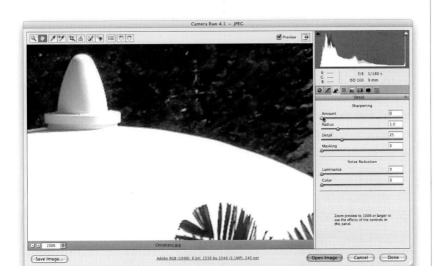

Step Three:

There are only two sliders and you just drag toward the color you want to fix (they're labeled—the top one fixes red or cyan fringe; the bottom fixes blue or yellow fringe). But before you begin dragging sliders, you may want to click on the Detail icon (the third icon from the left at the top of the panel area) and lower the Sharpening Amount to 0%, because sharpening can also cause color fringes to appear (and you want to make sure you're curing the right problem).

Step Four:

Since the fringe in this particular case is red, move the top Chromatic Aberration slider to the left (toward red), which reduces the red fringe (just make sure you don't drag so far toward red that you create a cyan fringe. Hey, I'm just sayin').

TIP: Although you can edit TIFFs and JPEGs in Camera Raw, there is one "gotcha!" Once you edit one of those in Camera Raw, if you click the Done button (rather than opening the image in Photoshop), you'll need to always open that photo in Camera Raw to see the edits you made. That's because those edits live only inside of Camera Raw; if you bypass Camera Raw and open an edited TIFF or JPEG directly into Photoshop, the Camera Raw edits you made earlier won't be visible.

Adjusting Contrast Using Curves

When it comes to adding contrast to a photo, I pretty much avoid the Contrast slider in the Basic panel as much as possible, because it's too broad, and too lame (much like the Contrast slider in Photoshop's Brightness/Contrast dialog was [before it was improved in CS3], which was too broad, and too lame. I just had a dejá vu). Anyway, when it comes to creating contrast, try the Tone Curve instead, and you'll never go back to that one broad and lame slider that is too broad and too lame. (I know. I did it again. I'm mean, "Oops, I did it again.")

Step One:
After you've done all your exposure and tone adjustments in the Basic panel, and you want to add contrast, skip the Contrast slider and click on the Tone Curve icon (it's the second icon from the left). There are two different types of curves available in Camera Raw 4.1: the Point curve (available in previous versions of Camera Raw), and the new Parametric curve. We'll start with the Point curve, so click on the Point tab within the Tone Curve panel. Here's what the photo shown here looks like with no added contrast in the Point curve (notice that the pop-up menu above the curve is set to Linear, which is a flat, unadjusted curve).

Step Two:
The normal, default setting for this curve is a Medium Contrast curve. If you want to create much more dramatic contrast, choose Strong Contrast from the Curve pop-up menu (as shown here), and you can see how much more contrast this photo now has, compared with how it looked in Step One. The difference is the Strong Contrast settings create a much steeper curve, and the steeper the curve, the more contrast it creates.

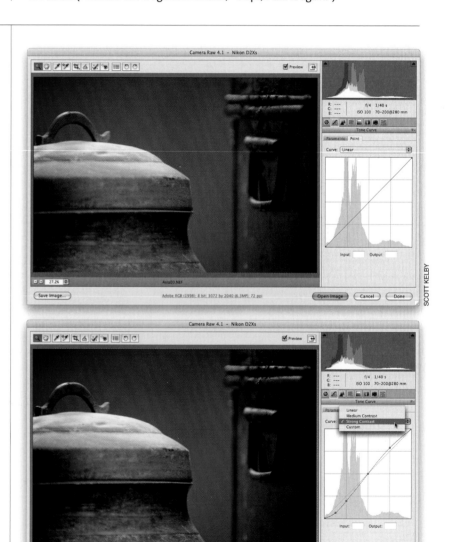

SCOTT KELBY

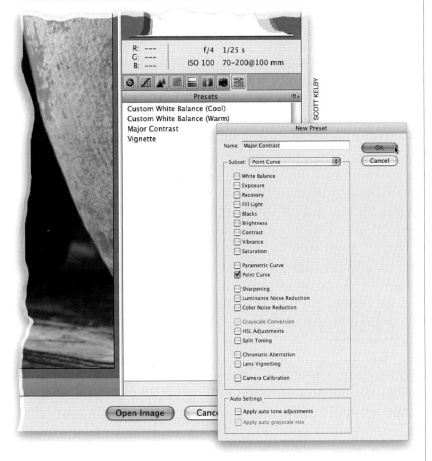

SCOTT KELBY

Step Three:

If you're familiar with Photoshop's Curves and want to create your own custom curve, start by choosing any one of the preset curves, then either click-and-drag the adjustment points on the curve or use the Arrow keys to move them (although I think it's easier to click on a point, then use the Up and Down Arrow keys on your keyboard to move that part of the curve up or down). If you'd prefer to start from scratch, choose Linear from the Curve pop-up menu, which gives you a flat curve. To add adjustment points, just click along the curve. To remove a point, just click-and-drag it right off the curve (drag it off quickly, like you're pulling off a Band-Aid).

Step Four:

If you create a curve that you'd like to be able to apply again to other photos, you can save this curve as a preset. To do that, click on the last icon in the row of icons to bring up the Presets panel. Next, click on the New Preset icon (which looks just like Photoshop's Create a New Layer icon) at the bottom of the Presets panel. This brings up the New Preset dialog (shown here). If you just want to save this curve setting, from the Subset pop-up menu near the top, choose Point Curve, and it unchecks all the other settings available as presets, and leaves only the Point Curve checkbox turned on (as shown here). Give your preset a name (I named mine "Major Contrast") and click OK.

Continued

Step Five:

If you're not comfortable with adjusting the Point curve, try the new Parametric curve, which lets you craft your curve using sliders rather than adjusting points. This is very popular with photographers because it's so easy to use and unlike Photoshop's curves, it keeps you from creating a curve that would pretty much trash the photo. When you click on the Tone Curve icon, it's the Parametric panel that appears first (maybe even Adobe knows you're going to like it better). There are four sliders, which control the four different areas of the curve, but before you start "sliding," I thought I'd mention that the adjustments you make here are added on top of the default Point curve setting of Medium Contrast. If you'd like to start from scratch with this tool, then click on the Point curve tab, choose Linear from the Curve pop-up menu, and then click back on the Parametric curve tab.

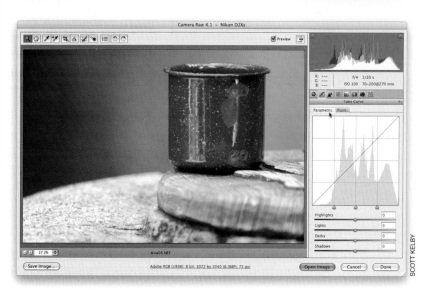

Step Six:

The Highlights slider controls the highlights area of the curve (the top of the curve), and dragging it to the right arcs the curve upward, making the highlights brighter. Right below that is the Lights slider, which covers the next lower range of tones (the area between the midtones and the highlights). Dragging this slider to the right makes this part of the curve steeper, and increases the upper midtones. The Darks and Shadows sliders do pretty much the same thing for the lower midtones and deep shadow areas. But remember, dragging to the right opens up those areas, so to create contrast, you'd drag both of those to the left instead. Here, to create some real punchy contrast, I dragged both the Highlights and Lights sliders to the right, and the Darks and Shadows sliders to the left.

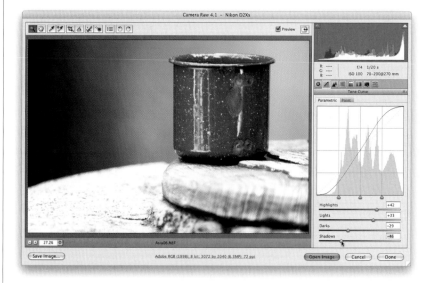

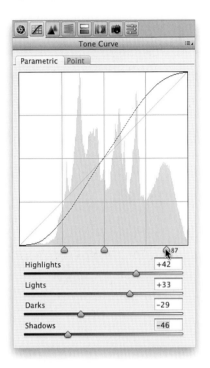

Step Seven:

One of the advantages of the Parametric curve is that you can use the region divider controls directly under the curve itself to choose how wide a range each of the four sliders covers. For example, if you move the far-right controller to the right (as shown here), it expands the area controlled by the Lights slider. Now the Highlights slider has less impact, and this also flattens out the upper part of the curve, so the contrast is decreased. If I drag that same region divider controller way back to the left instead, it expands the area controlled by the Highlights slider, which steepens the curve, making the brightest areas even brighter, and increasing contrast.

Step Eight:

If your goal is extraordinary contrast (maybe you're creating black-and-white photos where you want that super-contrasty look), then you want the steepest curve you can get away with (without damaging the photo, of course). Besides dragging the Highlights and Lights sliders to the right, and the Darks and Shadows sliders to the left, you can compress the tones so the Shadows and Highlights sliders affect much larger areas. You do this by dragging the two outside region divider controls in toward the center (as shown here), which adds even more steepness to the curve.

Fixing (or Creating) Edge Vignetting

If you're looking at a photo and the corners of the photo appear darker, that's lens vignetting. This is either a problem or a cool effect, depending on how you view it. Generally, I look at it this way: If it's just the corners, and they're just a little bit dark, that's a problem and I fix it. However, sometimes I want to focus the viewer's attention on a particular area, so I create a vignette, but I expand it significantly beyond the corners so it looks like an intentional effect (like a soft spotlight effect), not a lens problem. Here's how to fix (or create) vignettes:

Step One:
In the photo shown here, you can see the dark areas in the corners (that's the bad vignetting I was talking about). This vignetting is normally caused by the camera's lens, so don't blame yourself (unless you bought a really cheap lens—then feel free to give yourself as much grief as you can bear).

Step Two:
To remove this vignetting from the corners, click on the Lens Corrections icon (it's the sixth icon from the left) to bring up the Lens Vignetting controls. Click on the Amount slider and drag it to the right until the vignetting in the corners disappears (dragging to the right essentially brightens the corners, which hides the vignetting). Once you begin moving the Amount slider, the Midpoint slider beneath it becomes available. That slider determines how wide the vignetting repair extends into your photo (in other words, how far out from the corners your repair extends), so drag it to the right to expand the lightening farther toward the center of your photo.

Step Three:

Now for the opposite: adding vignetting to focus attention (by the way, in the Special Effects for Photographers chapter, I also show you how to get the same effect outside of Camera Raw). This time, in the Lens Vignetting section you're going to drag the Amount slider to the left, and as you drag left you'll start to see vignetting appear in the corners of your photo (as seen in Step Four). But since it's just in the corners, it looks like the bad kind of vignetting, not the good kind, so you'll need to go on to the next step.

Step Four:

To make the vignetting look more like a soft spotlight falling on your subject, drag the Midpoint slider quite a bit to the left, which increases the size of the vignetting and creates a soft, pleasing effect that is very popular in portraiture. That's it—how to get rid of 'em and how to add 'em. Two for the price of one!

TIP: If you want to see a before/after of just the changes you've made in a current panel, press the letter P to toggle that panel's Preview checkbox on/off. However, if you want to see a before/after of all the edits you've made in Camera Raw, then you'll need to choose Image Settings (from the Camera Raw flyout menu) to see the before version, and then from that same menu choose Custom Settings to see the after version. I agree—it's clunky.

Saving RAW Files in Adobe's Digital Negative (DNG) Format

At this point in time, there's a concern with the RAW file format because there's not a single, universal format for RAW images—every digital camera manufacturer has its own proprietary, closely-guarded RAW file format. That may not seem like a problem, but what happens if one of these camera companies stops supporting a format or switches to something else? What if in just five or 10 years from now there was no easy way to open your saved RAW photos? Adobe recognized this problem and created the Digital Negative (DNG) format as an open-source (open to everyone) format for the long-term archiving of RAW images.

Step One:

Saving your RAW file as an Adobe DNG file is easy—you just click the Save Image button in the Camera Raw dialog (as shown here) to bring up the Save Options dialog (seen in the next step). *Note: There's really no need to save TIFF or JPEG files as DNGs—this is really just about preserving your proprietary RAW photos for future generations.*

Step Two:

To save your file as a DNG, choose Digital Negative from the Format pop-up menu near the bottom of the dialog (as shown here). When you choose Digital Negative, the Compressed (Lossless) checkbox is turned on (which is fine, as lossless means no loss of quality), as it creates smaller file sizes without throwing away image data (like when you compress as a JPEG). You can choose to embed the original RAW file into your DNG. This makes the file size significantly larger, so I don't generally choose this option (but if you're the paranoid type and have loads of free hard drive space, go for it!). You can also choose to convert your RAW file to a linear image, which I only recommend if you're planning on opening this DNG in a RAW processing application other than Camera Raw, because it makes the file size much larger. That's it—click Save and you've got a DNG.

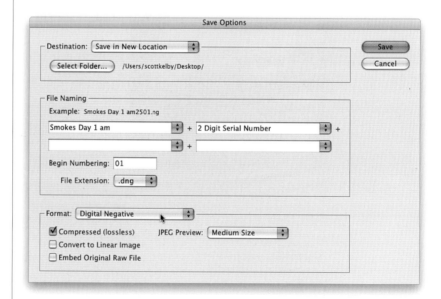

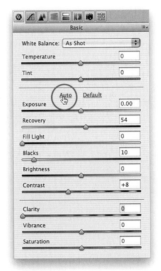

If you're not quite comfortable with manually adjusting each image, Camera Raw does come with a one-click Auto function, which takes a stab at correcting the overall exposure of your image (including shadows, fill light, contrast, and recovery). If you like the results, you can set up Camera Raw's preferences so every photo, upon opening in Camera Raw, will be auto adjusted using that same feature. Ahhh, if only that Auto function worked really well.

Letting Camera Raw Auto Correct Your Photos

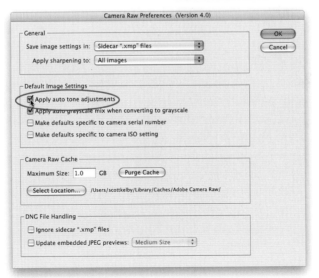

Step One:

Once you have an image open in Camera Raw, you can have Camera Raw take a stab at setting the overall exposure (using the controls in the Basic panel) for you by clicking on the Auto button (shown circled in red here). Although I used the four individual Auto checkboxes in previous versions of Camera Raw, I dunno maybe it's my camera, maybe it's me, but so far this Auto button in CS3 hasn't met a photo it didn't want to overexpose. But if you've tried it and you like the results (hey, it could happen), then you might want to make it auto process every image you open in Camera Raw.

Step Two:

To do that, click on the Preferences icon up in Camera Raw's toolbar (it's the third from the right), and when the Camera Raw Preferences dialog appears, turn on the checkbox for Apply Auto Tone Adjustments (shown circled in red here), then click OK. Now, Camera Raw will evaluate each image and try to correct it. If you don't like its tonal corrections, then you can just click on the Default button, which appears to the right of the Auto button (the Auto button will be grayed out because it's already been applied).

Split Toning Effects Made Easy

Split toning is another new feature in CS3's Camera Raw 4.1, and it debuted in Adobe's pro-photography workflow application Photoshop Lightroom, where it's gained lots of fans. What this does is lets you apply one tint to your photo's highlights, and one tint to your photo's shadow areas, and you even can control the saturation of each tint, and the balance between the two.

Step One:

Creating split toning effects (which used to be a traditional darkroom technique) is now incredibly easy and although split toning effects can be applied to both color and B&W photos, the look you probably see most often is the effect applied to a B&W image. So start in the HSL/Grayscale panel (the fourth icon from the left) by turning on the Convert to Grayscale checkbox at the top (as seen here).

Step Two:

Once your photo has been converted to black and white (as shown here), click on the Split Toning icon (it's the fifth icon from the left at the top of the panel area, as seen here), which makes the Split Toning sliders visible. At this point, dragging either the Highlights or Shadows Hue slider does absolutely nothing, because for some reason the Saturation sliders are set to 0. So you can drag them, but not a dang thing happens. Try it and you'll see. Seriously, I don't mind waiting, go ahead. See, I told you (I knew you had to try it yourself). Luckily, there is a hidden tip that will let you temporarily see the hues at their full saturation as you drag—just press-and-hold the Option (PC: Alt) key, then click-and-drag.

SCOTT KELBY

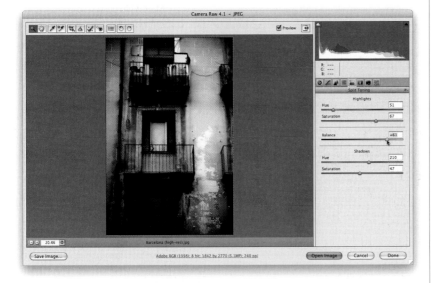

Step Three:

Once you find a highlight hue you like, release the Option (PC: Alt) key, and drag the Highlights Saturation slider to the right. The further you drag, the more saturated your highlight tint becomes. Once that's in place, do the same thing with the Shadows Hue slider (press-and-hold the Option key, drag the Hue slider to pick your hue, then release the Option key and slowly drag the Shadows Saturation slider to the right). In the example shown here, we have a yellow tint in the highlights and a blue tint in the shadows. I know what you're thinking, "Scott, I'm not sure I like split toning." I hear ya—it's not for everybody, and it's definitely an acquired taste (and I'm not quite sure I've acquired it yet), but some people love 'em. There's a name for these people. Freaks! (Kidding.)

Step Four:

There is one more control—a Balance slider which lets you control whether your split tone favors your highlight or shadow color. Just drag left, then back right (as shown here), and you'll instantly see what this slider does. At this point, it's perfectly fine to have feelings of confusion, and be asking yourself questions like, "Did people actually try to do this on purpose in traditional darkrooms?" Yes, Timmy. Yes they did, but that doesn't mean you have to get your hands dirty, because now you can just slide some sliders and best of all, you can keep the lights on.

TIP: You can use split toning to create a nice duotone effect—just put the same tint (like a sepia tone or dark brown) in both the highlights and shadows.

Adjusting Individual Colors

Since you can't make selections in Camera Raw, being able to tweak individual areas of color within your photo is very important, and there's a new tool (well, actually a whole new panel) in CS3's Camera Raw that gives you wide control over the hue, saturation, and luminance (lightness) of each color without having to make selections.

Step One:

Here's the original image and we want to make tweaks to some of the colors in it (I don't really want to do that—I actually like it the way it is, but if you can just pretend for the sake of this project that I actually do want to mess with the colors, then later I promise to mess some other photo's colors up really good). You tweak your individual colors in the HSL/Grayscale panel, so click on its icon in the top right of the dialog (it's the fourth one from the left).

Step Two:

So, let's say you want the yellow in the center area of the photo to be a brighter, more vibrant yellow. You'd click on the Luminance tab, and you'd see eight sliders, each controlling the vibrance for one particular range of color. If you look at the colors inside the sliders themselves, you can see that they're lighter on the right, and richer on the left, so to make the yellows more rich and vibrant, you'd drag the Yellows slider to the left (as shown here). If you had dragged to the right, the yellows would have become lighter, and closer to white, not deeper and more vibrant like we have here.

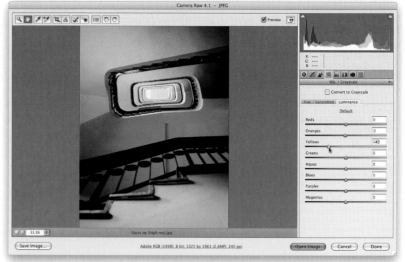

SCOTT KELBY

Step Three:

Next, the reds in the photo are pretty overpowering, so to reduce the amount of red in the photo, you'd click on the Saturation tab, then drag the Reds slider way over to the left (towards gray) to desaturate the reds quite a bit (as seen here). This really backed off the red and made the yellow stand out even more. If you look closely, you can see a little bit of a blue tint in the side of the stair closest to you, so in the next step we'll try to bring that out, and to tweak some other colors to really change the color makeup of the photo.

Step Four:

To actually change colors (not just adjust an existing color's saturation or vibrance), you click on the Hue tab. The controls are the same, but take a look at the color inside the sliders themselves now—you can see exactly which way to drag to get which color. Start up top by dragging the Reds and Oranges sliders to the right over toward orange, which changes the color of the reds pretty dramatically, don'tcha think? Now drag the Yellows slider a little bit toward orange as well, and you can also match up the color in the center with what was the red walls of the second floor. Lastly, if you drag the Aquas slider to the right and the Blues slider all the way to the left, you can really start to see the blue come out in the side of the bottom stairs (to add even more blue now, go to the Saturation tab and increase the saturation, and maybe even the luminance of the blues, which gives you the final color-tweaked image you see here, which I don't like better than the original, but since you were willing to go along with it, I went ahead and trashed it. Okay, kid—I owe you one).

Converting to Black and White Using a Channel Mixer (of Sorts)

Okay, technically it's not a channel mixer, but it's the next best thing—it's the HSL controls you used in the previous tutorial, but now you're using them to create custom color-to-B&W conversions. Here how it works:

Step One:
Here's the original color photo, taken late in the day in Taos, New Mexico. The photo is just like it came in from the camera, so it looks pretty flat (but we'll fix that shortly).

Step Two:
Converting from color to black and white is simple—just click on the HSL/Grayscale icon (it's the fourth icon from the left) and then turn on the Convert to Grayscale checkbox at the top of the panel (as seen here). This brings up the Grayscale Mix tab (which is like an expanded version of Photoshop's Channel Mixer). When you turn on that checkbox, Camera Raw performs an Auto adjustment as your starting point. It's not terrible, but it usually looks a little flat to me.

Step Three:
There's also a Default button (it looks like a link, but it's a button), just to the right of the Auto button (which looks like a link, too) and if you click on it, it sets all the Grayscale Mix sliders back to zero, which generally looks even worse than the Auto adjustment (as seen here), so I don't recommend it.

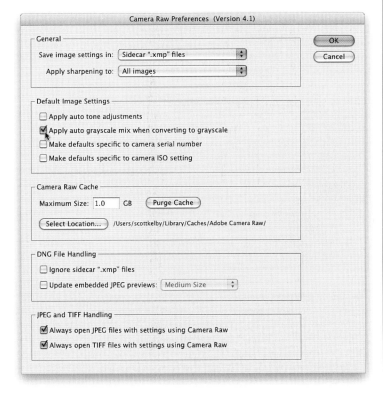

Step Four:
If for some reason you like this "zero'd out" look more than the Auto adjusted look (hey, it's possible), press Command-K (PC: Ctrl-K) to bring up Camera Raw's Preferences dialog and turn off the checkbox for Apply Auto Grayscale Mix when Converting to Grayscale (the checkbox is shown turned on here, so you'd turn that checkbox off).

Continued

Step Five:

The color sliders in the Grayscale Mix are pretty much like the HSL sliders for adjusting color. The catch is you can't see which colors you're adjusting because the photo is already converted to black and white. So, what I do is press the letter P to toggle the Grayscale Mix preview on/off. That way I can take a peek back at the original colors, and try to figure out which slider would adjust which parts of my image. When I did that here, I saw that the color of the church was orangish, so I dragged the Oranges and Yellows sliders to the right to make the front of the church a little brighter. I also dragged the Blues slider way over to the left (as shown here) to darken up the sky a bit. If you're not sure which slider does what, just drag any slider back and forth and you'll know pretty quickly what it affects (if anything).

Step Six:

By now you've probably come to the same realization that I have, and that is the Grayscale Mix sliders alone aren't enough to make a decent B&W photo. You need to add some serious contrast, including pushing the highlight exposure and shadows to create a B&W photo with any decent depth. So, go do that. You start back in the Basic panel and adjust the photo like you would any other—drag the Exposure slider to the right to increase the exposure in the highlights. If it starts to clip the highlights, drag the Recovery slider to the right to bring those clipped highlights back. Increase the Blacks (as shown here) to make the shadow areas nice and rich, and if the front of the church gets too dark, drag the Fill Light slider to the right to open up those areas.

Step Seven:

Of course, when it comes to adding contrast, nothing beats the Tone Curve. So click on the Tone Curve icon (second from left), then click on the Point Curve tab, and choose Strong Contrast from the Curve pop-up menu (as shown here). In our example, I went with just the default Strong Contrast curve, but if you wanted to "juice" that curve and make it a little steeper (for more kick in your contrast), then click on the top-right point and nudge it upward using the Up Arrow key on your keyboard. Then click on the second point from the bottom left and nudge it downward using the Down Arrow key (again, I didn't do that here, but…well…ya could).

Step Eight:

The before and after is shown below, with the Auto conversion on the left and our tweaked version on the right, which makes our case that we can't rely on the Grayscale Mix alone to give us that rich B&W photo we're hoping for.

Before (the Auto grayscale conversion)

After (tweakin' it a bit)

Simple Retouching in Camera Raw

And by simple, I mean it better be really simple, like removing a blemish, or a mole, or some dust in your photo that was originally some dust on your lens. If it's any more complicated than that, you'd better head over to Photoshop and use the Healing Brush, or the Patch tool, or the Clone tool, or just about anything other than the somewhat limited, but sometimes useful, Retouch tool in Camera Raw (it's actually fairly useful if you have sensor dust, because the spot would be in the same place on every photo. More on this in a moment).

Step One:
This photo has some simple problems that can be fixed using the Retouch tool. You start by clicking on the Retouch tool (the fifth tool from the right in the toolbar), and a set of options pops down from the toolbar (seen here). Using the tool is pretty simple—just move your cursor over the center of a spot that needs to be removed (in this case, it's that group of spots on the wall to the left of the green door), then click, hold, and drag outward and a red and white circle will appear, growing larger as you drag outward. Keep dragging until that circle is a little larger than the spot you're trying to remove (as shown here).

Step Two:
When you release the mouse button, a second circle (this one is green and white) appears to show you the area where Camera Raw chose to sample your repair texture from (it's usually very close by), and your spot or blemish is gone (as seen here).

TIP: So, what determines if you can fix a blemish here in Camera Raw? Basically, it's how close the blemish, spot, or other object you need to remove is to the edge of anything. This tool doesn't like edges (the edge of the pot, the edge of a door, a wall, a person's face, etc.), so as long as the blemish (spot, etc.) is all by itself, you're usually okay.

Step Three:
To remove a different spot (like the one on the far left of the yellowish pot), you use the same method: move over that spot; click, hold, and drag out a circle that's slightly larger than the spot; then release the mouse button. In this case, Camera Raw did sample a nearby area, but unfortunately it also sampled two little spots and it copied those to the area where we were retouching, making the retouch look very obvious with two identical sets of spots right next to each other.

Continued

Step Four:

If this happens, here's what to do: move your cursor inside the green and white circle and drag that circle to a different nearby area (here, I dragged downward and to the left to a clean nearby area), and when you release the mouse button, it resamples texture from that area. Another thing you can try, if the area is at all near an edge, is to go up to the options section and choose Clone rather than Heal from the Type pop-up menu (although I use Heal about 99% of the time, because it generally works much better).

Step Five:

When you're done retouching, just change tools and your retouches are applied (and the circles go away). Here's the final retouch after removing the price sticker from the bottom-right side of the pot. Use this tool the next time you have a spot on your lens or on your sensor (so the same spot is in the same place in all the photos from your shoot). Then fix the spot on one photo, open multiple photos, and paste the repair onto the other selected RAW photos using Synchronize (see "Fixing Spots or Sensor Dust on Multiple Photos at Once" in Chapter 8).

Removing Red Eye in Camera Raw

Camera Raw now has its own built-in Red Eye Removal tool, and there's a 50/50 chance it might actually work. Of course, my own experience has been a little less than that (more like 40/60), but hey—that's just me. Anyway, if it were me, I'd probably be more inclined to use the regular Red Eye tool in Photoshop CS3 itself, which actually works fairly well, but if you're charging by the hour, this might be a fun place to start. Here's how to use this tool, which periodically works for some people, somewhere. On occasion. Perhaps.

Step One:
Open a photo in Camera Raw that has the dreaded red eye (like the one shown here, taken by my assistant Kathy at one of her many drinking parties. I'm kidding of course, she doesn't have that many. At least, not since the accident). Anyway... to get the Red Eye Removal tool, you can press the letter E or just click on its icon up in Camera Raw's toolbar (as shown here).

Step Two:
You'll want to zoom in close enough so you can see the red-eye area pretty easily (as I have here, where I just simply zoomed to 100%, using the zoom level pop-up menu in the bottom-left corner of the Camera Raw dialog). The way this tool works is pretty simple—you click-and-drag the tool over the one eye (as shown here) and as you drag it makes a red and white box over the eye (seen here). That tells Camera Raw where the red eye is located.

Continued

Step Three:

When you release the mouse button, theoretically it should snap down right around the pupil, making a perfect selection around the area affected by red eye. You'll notice that the key word here is "theoretically." In our real example, it made a tiny rectangle on the bottom of her left pupil, which is all of about useless. If that happens to you (and if you download and use this same photo from my website, it will), then press Command-Z (PC: Ctrl-Z) to Undo that attempt, and let's try again, but before we do that, let's try to help the tool along by increasing the Pupil Size setting (in the options section) to around 100 (as seen in the next image).

Step Four:

Now, with the Pupil Size setting at 100, it did what we hoped it would, and that is it snapped right down around the pupil, and it removed the red from that area. Once that eye looks good, go over to the other eye, drag out that selection again (as shown here), and it does the same thing (the before and after are shown on the next page). One last thing: if the pupil looks too gray after being fixed, then drag the Darken amount to the right. Give it a try on a photo of your own. It's possible it might work.

Before

After

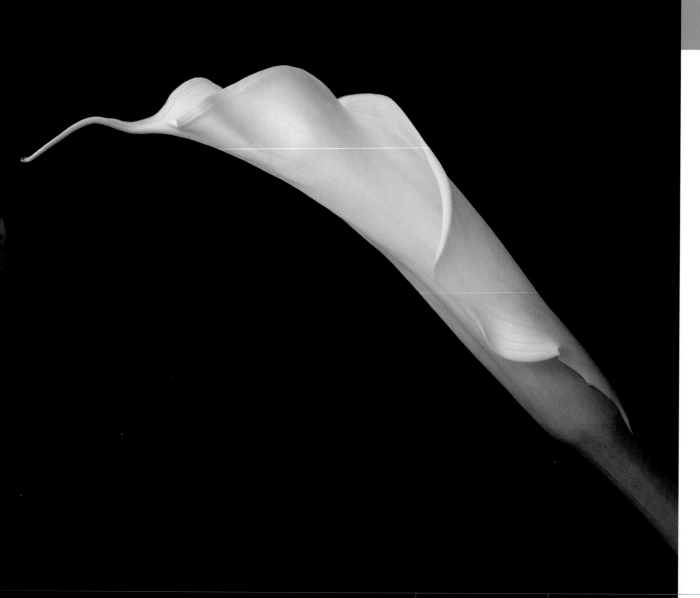

Exposure: 1/160s   Focal Length: 70mm   Aperture Value: ƒ/5.6

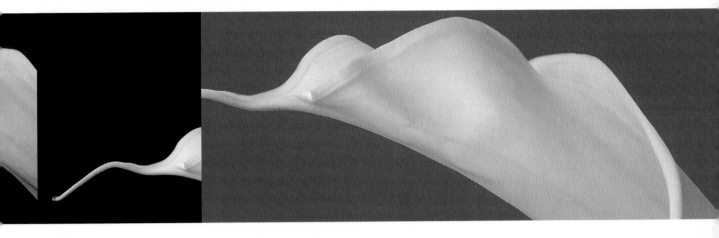

Resized
resizing and cropping your images

I could only find one song with the title "Resized," and I think it's a perfect fit for a chapter on resizing and cropping your photos. The song is by a band called Bungle and this particular song features Laura Pacheco. It's from their album *Down to Earth.* I'm telling you this like you're going to go and buy the CD, but trust me—you're not. That's because I'm going to try and talk you out of doing just that. Here's why: the full-length song is five minutes and 55 seconds. After hearing just the free 30-second preview of it on Apple's iTunes Store, I imagine there are some people (not you, mind you, but some people) who might become somehow adversely affected by its super-fast-paced hypnotic beat and might do things that they might not normally do while listening to selections from the Eagles or James Taylor. In fact, I would advise against even listening to the 30-second free preview if any of these conditions are present: (1) it's late at night and you have all the lights out, (2) the lights are out and you have a strobe light flashing, (3) the lights are out, a strobe is flashing, and you're holding a large butcher knife, or (4) the lights are out, a strobe is flashing, you're holding a large butcher knife, and you've just been fired from your job. "Resized" would make a great background track for *House of the Dead VII,* because it's not one of those gloomy Metallica songs— it actually has a fast pop-like beat, but at the same time, it makes you want to grab a butcher knife (not me, of course, and certainly not you, but you know…people like that one really quiet guy who works in accounting. I'd keep him away from that song. Especially if he ever gets fired).

Just a Quickie About the CS3 Interface

When you first look at Adobe Photoshop CS3, the interface looks a lot different than previous versions, but it's really not as different as you'd think. I don't want to spend a lot of time on the interface (I know you want to get your hands dirty, so I'll keep this to a minimum—just these two pages then we're off and running), but I do want to show you two things: (1) how to quickly return to the CS2 look if you're more comfortable with that, and (2) I thought I'd show you my own workspace which is a pretty efficient setup for photographers.

Step One:

Here's the default CS3 interface, with a single-column Toolbox on the far left and two columns of panels on the right (in *most* places, they're no longer called "palettes," they're officially called "panels." I have no idea why—they probably did it just to mess with us). The advantage of multiple columns is it lets you keep your panels out of the way until you need them (so they're not cluttering your screen). You can collapse each column of panels down to just their icons (or just their icons and names), so you pop 'em out when you need them, then tuck 'em out of the way when you don't. There's even an Auto-Collapse Icon Palettes preference (found in Photoshop's Preferences, under Interface) that tucks individual panels away automatically once you click on anything else.

Step Two:

To see an individual panel, click on its icon, and it pops out (like the Character panel shown here). To tuck it back out of the way, either click on its icon again, or on the tiny right-facing triangles on the top right of the panel itself. To expand an entire column of panels (like the panels on the far right here), click once on the tiny left-facing triangles on the top right of a column. To manually drag out a column, click-and-drag the double lines at the top left of the column.

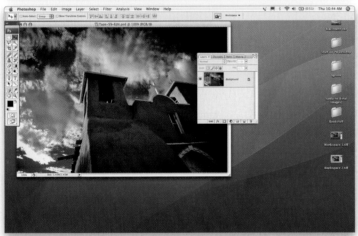

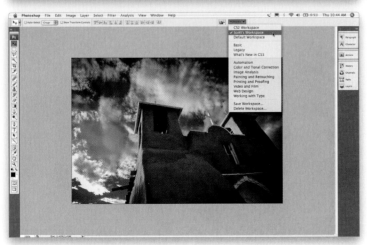

Step Three:

If you press the letter F, your floating image window is replaced by a medium gray background, and your photo is centered onscreen (as seen here). The Palette Well (that used to be up in the Options Bar in CS2), has been replaced with those darker gray areas on either side of your screen where you now stack as many columns and rows of panels as you have space for. Press F again, and it expands the gray background full screen, and hides those panel wells. Press F once again for full-screen mode (a solid black background with no visible menus).

Step Four:

If you want to return to the CS2 look (shown here), start by clicking on the right-facing triangles at the top left of the Toolbox to expand it back into the two-column Toolbox from CS2. Then, to make your panels float like palettes, just click on the panel's name tab, and drag it out over your desktop. To nest other panels with it, just click-and-drag a panel's name tab and move it over your floating panel. When you see the panel highlight, release your mouse button and it nests.

Step Five:

Here's my workspace: The single column Toolbox is on the left (once you get used to it, it's great because it takes up less space). On the right, I chose only the panels I use most often, and I manually dragged the two lines at the top left of the column to the left until the names of the icons appeared, because after all this time I still don't recognize them just by the icons. Up in the Options Bar, you now have one-click access to your workspaces (as seen here), so choose Save Workspace, give yours a name, and you're set. Now, let's get to work!

Cropping Photos

After you've sorted your images in Adobe Bridge, one of the first editing tasks you'll probably undertake is cropping a photo. There are a number of different ways to crop a photo in Photoshop. We'll start with the basic garden-variety options, and then we'll look at some ways to make the task faster and easier. At the end of this project, I've added a new way to see your cropping that won fame when it was added to Adobe Photoshop Lightroom, but I figured out an easy way to get the exact same cropping trick here in Photoshop CS3.

Step One:
Press the letter C to get the Crop tool (you could always select it directly from the Toolbox, but I only recommend doing so if you're charging by the hour).

Step Two:
Click within your photo and drag out a cropping border. The area to be cropped away will appear dimmed (shaded). You don't have to worry about getting your crop border right when you first drag it out, because you can edit the border by clicking-and-dragging the points that appear in each corner and at the center of each side.

Step Three:

If you don't like seeing your photo with the cropped-away area appearing shaded (as in the previous step), you can toggle this shading feature off/on by pressing the Forward Slash (/) key on your keyboard. When you press the Forward Slash key, the border remains in place, but the shading is turned off (as seen here).

Step Four:

While you have the cropping border in place, if you need to rotate your photo, you can do that as well (so basically, you're doing two things at the same time: cropping and rotating). You rotate the cropping border by just moving your cursor anywhere outside the border. When you do this, the cursor will change into a double-headed arrow. Just click, hold, and drag up (or down) and the cropping border will rotate in the direction you choose (as shown here).

Continued

Step Five:

Once you have the cropping border right where you want it, press the Return (PC: Enter) key to crop your image. The final cropped image is shown here, where we cropped off the windows on the left (the daylight coming through them was drawing your attention over there, which we don't want), and we also cropped away a distracting pillow on the right side of the couch. You can see the uncropped image on the previous page.

TIP: If you drag out a cropping border and then decide you don't want to crop the image, you can either press the Esc key on your keyboard, click on the "No" symbol in the Options Bar, or just click on a different tool in the Toolbox, which will bring up a dialog asking if you want to crop the image. Click on the Don't Crop button to cancel your crop.

Step Six:

Another popular way to crop is to skip the Crop tool altogether and just use the Rectangular Marquee tool (M) to put a selection around the area of your photo you want to keep. You can reposition the selection by clicking inside the selected area and dragging. When your selection is positioned where you want it, go under the Image menu and choose Crop. The area outside your selection will be cropped away instantly. Press Command-D (PC: Ctrl-D) to Deselect.

Step Seven:

Okay, are you ready for the ultimate cropping experience? (There's a sentence that's probably never been written before.) It's inspired by Lightroom's popular Lights Out full-screen cropping method. In Lights Out mode, as you crop, it surrounds your photo with solid black, so you see a live preview of what the final cropped photo will look like as you crop. It's pretty sweet, and once you try it, you won't want to crop any other way. Luckily, you can do the same thing here in Photoshop CS3. Start by taking the Crop tool and dragging it over part of your photo (it doesn't matter where or what size). In the Options Bar, there's an Opacity field, which lets you choose how light the area you're cropping away is going to display onscreen. Click on the right-facing triangle and increase the Opacity to 100%, so it's solid black (as shown here).

Step Eight:

Now press the Esc key to remove your cropping border. Press Tab, then the letter F three times to hide all of Photoshop's panels and menus, plus this centers your photo onscreen surrounded by solid black (as seen here). That's it—you're in "Lights Out cropping mode" because you made any cropped-away area solid black, which matches the black full-screen area surrounding your photo. So, try it yourself—get the Crop tool again, drag out a cropping border, then drag any one of the cropping handles inward and you'll see what I mean. Pretty sweet, eh? When you're done cropping, press Return (PC: Enter), then press the letter F once more to leave full-screen mode, then press the Tab key to bring your panels, menus, and Toolbox back.

Cropping Using the "Rule of Thirds"

The "rule of thirds" is a trick that photographers sometimes use to create more interesting compositions. Basically, you visually divide the image you see in your camera's viewfinder into thirds, and then you position your horizon so it goes along either the top imaginary horizontal line or the bottom one. Then, you position the subject (or focal point) at the center intersections of those lines. But if you didn't use the rule in the viewfinder, no sweat! You can use Photoshop to crop your image using the rule of thirds to create more appealing compositions.

Step One:
Open the photo you want to apply the rule-of-thirds cropping technique to (the shot here is poorly composed, with the subject right in the center, and too much headroom above—it just screams "snapshot!"). So, start by creating a new blank layer by clicking on the Create a New Layer icon at the bottom of the Layers panel.

Step Two:
Now, go to the Toolbox and get the Custom Shape tool (as shown here), or press Shift-U until you have it.

SCOTT KELBY

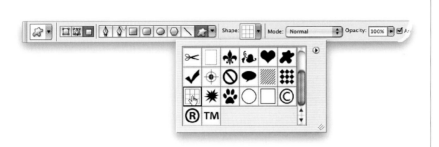

Step Three:
The Custom Shape tool's options will appear up in the Options Bar. First, click on the third icon from the left (so your shape will draw pixels, instead of a Shape layer or a path). Next, click on the downward-facing triangle to the immediate right of the current shape, and the Shape Picker will pop down (as shown here). In the default set of shapes there is a Grid shape, and that shape is already divided into equal thirds, so click on that shape to choose it.

Step Four:
You're going to need to see the exact size you want to crop down to, so go under the Window menu and choose Show Info. This brings up the Info panel (shown here), which displays the Width and Height for any shape you draw. So now take the Custom Shape tool and drag out a grid, and as you drag, keep an eye on the Info panel's Width and Height fields (our goal is to print a 13x19" print, so we're going to want our final grid size to be 13" wide by 19" tall). Now, start dragging (don't worry about positioning the grid right yet—just keep your eye on that Info panel, and your wrist steady, so you can drag out exactly a 13x19" grid. Also, don't worry about damaging your photo—that's why we created that new blank layer in Step One, so your grid will appear on this new layer).

Continued

Step Five:

Press the letter V to switch to the Move tool, and click-and-drag your rule-of-thirds grid into the position you'd like it (ideally, your subject, or point of interest, would appear at one of the four places within the grid where the lines intersect. I've marked all four here as a visual reminder).

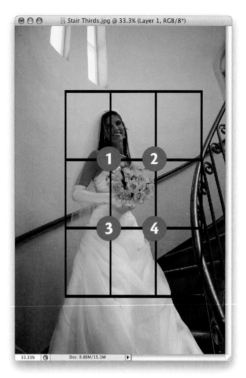

Step Six:

Once the grid is positioned right where you want it, get the Rectangular Marquee tool (M) and click-and-drag out a selection that is the exact same size as the grid (as shown here).

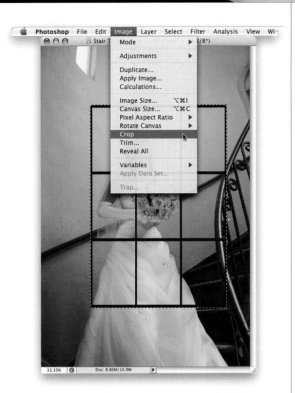

Step Seven:

Now go under the Image menu and choose Crop (as shown here).

TIP: You can also use the Crop tool to make your canvas area bigger. First, open a photo, then press the letter F (to make the gray area outside your photo visible). Take the Crop tool (C), and drag out over a small area inside your photo. Now, you can drag any corner or side point of your cropping border right outside your image area, off into that gray area surrounding your photo (so you can visually position where you want more canvas area). Then, when it's right where you want it, press the Return (PC: Enter) key and the area outside your image area now becomes white canvas area. Not bad, eh?

Step Eight:

When you choose Crop from that menu, it crops the photo based on your current selection, so basically it crops the photo down to the edges of your grid. Now, go to the Layers panel and drag Layer 1 (your grid layer) into the Trash (at the bottom of the Layers panel) to delete it. You can now see your final cropped photo—cropping using the rule of thirds. In the example shown here, I added my Three-Step Portrait Finishing Technique to sharpen the photo, soften the photo, and burn in the edges. You can find this technique in Chapter 10—the Special Effects for Photographers chapter.

Cropping to a Specific Size

If you're outputting photos for clients, chances are they're going to want them in standard sizes so they can easily find frames to fit their photos. If that's the case, you'll find this technique handy, because it lets you crop any image to a predetermined size (like 5x7", 8x10", and so on).

Step One:

Let's say our image measures 15x10", and we want to crop it to be a perfect horizontal 10x8". First, press the C key to get the Crop tool, and up in the Options Bar on the left, you'll see Width and Height fields. Enter the size you want for the width, followed by the unit of measurement you want to use (e.g., "in" for inches, "px" for pixels, "cm" for centimeters, "mm" for millimeters, etc.). Next, press the Tab key to jump over to the Height field and enter your desired height, again followed by the unit of measurement.

Step Two:

Click within your photo with the Crop tool and drag out a cropping border. You'll notice that as you drag, the border is constrained to a horizontal shape, and once you release the mouse button, no side points are visible—only corner points. Whatever size you make your border, the area within that border will become a 10x8" photo. In this example, I dragged the border so it almost touched the top and bottom to get as much of the subject as possible.

Step Three:
After your cropping border is onscreen, you can reposition it by moving your cursor inside the border (your cursor will change to an arrow). You can now drag the border into place, or use the Arrow keys on your keyboard for more precise control. When it looks right to you, press Return (PC: Enter) to finalize your crop, and the area inside your cropping border will be 10x8". (I made the rulers visible by pressing Command-R [PC: Ctrl-R], so you could see that the image measures exactly 10x8".)

TIP: Once you've entered a Width and Height in the Options Bar, those dimensions will remain in place until you clear them. To clear the fields (so you can use the Crop tool for freeform cropping to any size), just go up in the Options Bar and click on the Clear button (while you have the Crop tool active, of course).

COOLER TIP: If you already have a photo that is the exact size and resolution that you'd like to apply to other images, you can use its settings as the crop dimensions. First, open the photo you'd like to resize, and then open your ideal-size-and-resolution photo. Get the Crop tool, and then in the Options Bar, click on the Front Image button. Photoshop will automatically input that photo's dimensions into the Crop tool's Width, Height, and Resolution fields. All you have to do is crop the other image, and it will share the exact same specs as your ideal-size photo.

The Trick for Keeping the Same Aspect Ratio When You Crop

Okay, let's say you want to crop a photo down in size, but you want to keep the aspect ratio the same as the original photo from your camera (so when you crop, the photo will be smaller in size, but it will have the exact same width-to-height ratio as the original photo). You could pull out a calculator and do the math to figure out what the new smaller size should be, but there's a faster, easier, and more visual way. (By the way, although the Crop tool within Camera Raw gives you a menu of preset ratios, you can only use those presets on a RAW image, but this technique works on any photo.)

Step One:
Open the photo you want to crop. Press Command-A (PC: Ctrl-A) to put a selection around the entire photo.

Step Two:
Go under the Select menu and choose Transform Selection. This lets you resize the selection itself, without resizing the photo within the selection (which is what usually happens).

Step Three:
Press-and-hold the Shift key, grab a corner point, and drag inward to resize the selection area. Because you're holding the Shift key as you scale, the aspect ratio (the same ratio as your original photo) remains exactly the same. Once you get the selection near the size you're looking for, move your cursor inside the bounding box, and then click-and-drag to position your selection where you want to crop. Then, press Return (PC: Enter) to complete your transformation.

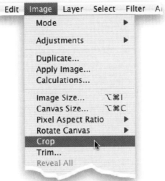

Step Four:
Now that you've used your selection to determine the crop area, it's time to actually crop, so go under the Image menu and choose (no big surprise here) Crop.

Step Five:
Once you choose Crop, the image is then cropped to fit within your selection, so just press Command-D (PC: Ctrl-D) to Deselect. Because you followed the steps shown here, your cropped image maintains the same aspect ratio as your original photo.

Creating Your Own Custom Crop Tools

Although it's more of an advanced technique, creating your own custom tools isn't complicated. In fact, once you set it up, it will save you time and money. We're going to create what are called "tool presets." These tool presets are a series of tools (in this case, Crop tools) with all our option settings already in place. So we'll create a 5x7", 6x4", or whatever size Crop tool we want. Then, when we want to crop to 5x7", all we have to do is grab the 5x7" Crop tool preset. Here's how:

Step One:

Press the letter C to switch to the Crop tool, and then go under the Window menu and choose Tool Presets to bring up the Tool Presets panel (or click on it in the panel dock on the right side of your screen, where it's nested by default). You'll find that five Crop tool presets are already there, all set to 300 ppi. That's great if you need these sizes at 300 ppi; but if you don't, you might as well drag these tool presets onto the Trash icon at the bottom of the panel. (Also, make sure that the Current Tool Only option is turned on at the bottom of the panel so you'll see only the Crop tool's presets, and not the presets for every tool.)

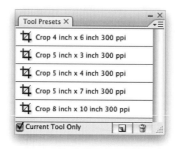

Step Two:

Go up to the Options Bar and enter the dimensions for the first tool you want to create (in this example, we'll create a Crop tool that crops to a wallet-size image). In the Width field, enter 2. Then press the Tab key to jump to the Height field and enter 2.5. *Note:* If you have the Rulers set to Inches under the Units section in Photoshop's Units & Rulers Preferences (Command-K [PC: Ctrl-K]), then when you press the Tab key, Photoshop will automatically insert "in" after your numbers, indicating inches.

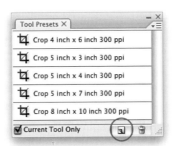

Step Three:

In the Tool Presets panel, click on the Create New Tool Preset icon at the bottom of the panel (to the left of the Trash icon). This brings up the New Tool Preset dialog, in which you can name your new preset. Name it "Crop to Wallet Size," click OK, and the new tool is added to the Tool Presets panel.

Step Four:

Continue this process of typing in new dimensions in the Crop tool's Options Bar and clicking on the Create New Tool Preset icon until you've created custom Crop tools for the sizes you use most. Make the names descriptive (for example, add "Portrait" or "Landscape").

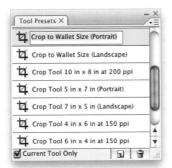

TIP: If you need to change the name of a preset, just double-click directly on its name in the panel, and then type in a new name.

Continued

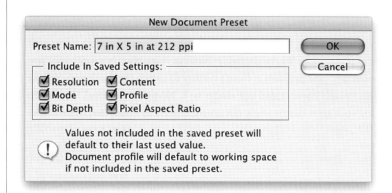

Step Three:

This brings up the New Document Preset dialog. In the Preset Name field, enter your new resolution at the end of the size. You can turn on/off the checkboxes for which parameters you want saved, but I use the default setting to include everything (better safe than sorry, I guess).

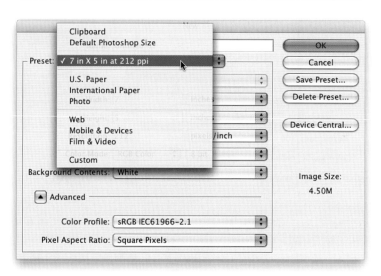

Step Four:

Click OK and your new custom preset will appear in the New dialog's Preset pop-up menu. You only have to go through this once. Photoshop CS3 will remember your custom settings, and they will appear in this Preset pop-up menu from now on.

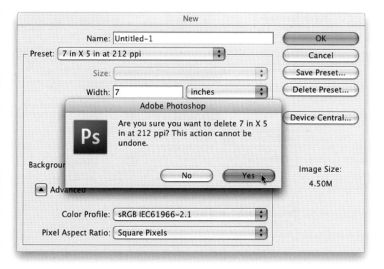

Step Five:

If you decide you want to delete a preset, it's simple—just open the New dialog, choose the preset you want to delete from the Preset pop-up menu, and then click on the Delete Preset button. A warning dialog will appear asking you to confirm the delete. Click on Yes, and it's gone!

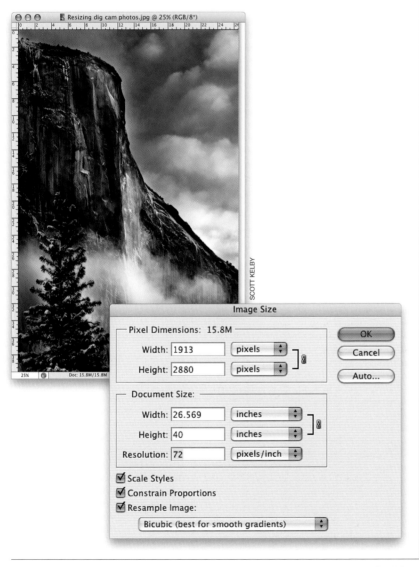

Resizing Digital Camera Photos

If you're used to resizing scans, you'll find that resizing images from digital cameras is a bit different, primarily because scanners create high-res scans (usually 300 ppi or more), but the default settings for many digital cameras produce an image that is large in physical dimensions, but lower in pixels-per-inch (usually 72 ppi). The trick is to decrease the physical size of your digital camera image (and increase its resolution) without losing any of its quality. Here's the trick:

Step One:
Open the digital camera image that you want to resize. Press Command-R (PC: Ctrl-R) to make Photoshop's rulers visible. As you can see from the rulers, the photo is nearly 27" wide by 40" high.

Step Two:
Go under the Image menu and choose Image Size (or press Command-Option-I [PC: Ctrl-Alt-I]) to bring up the Image Size dialog. Under the Document Size section, the Resolution setting is 72 ppi. A resolution of 72 ppi is considered "low resolution" and is ideal for photos that will only be viewed onscreen (such as Web graphics, slide shows, and so on), but it's too low to get high-quality results from a color inkjet printer, color laser printer, or for use on a printing press.

Continued

Step Three:

If we plan to output this photo to any printing device, it's pretty clear that we'll need to increase the resolution to get good results. I wish we could just type in the resolution we'd like it to be in the Resolution field (such as 200 or 300 ppi), but unfortunately this "resampling" makes our low-res photo appear soft (blurry) and pixelated. That's why we need to turn off the Resample Image checkbox (it's on by default). That way, when we type in a Resolution setting that we need, Photoshop automatically adjusts the Width and Height of the image down in the exact same proportion. As your Width and Height come down (with Resample Image turned off), your Resolution goes up. Best of all, there's absolutely no loss of quality. Pretty cool!

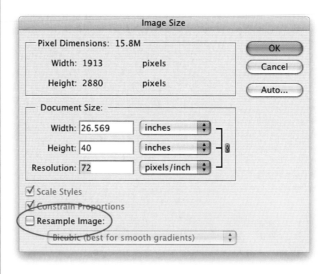

Step Four:

Here I've turned off Resample Image and I entered 150 in the Resolution field for output to a color inkjet printer. (I know, you probably think you need a lot more resolution, but you usually don't.) This resized my image to almost 13x19", so with a little bit of cropping I can easily output a 13x19" print (which happens to be the maximum output size for my Epson Stylus Photo R2400—perfect!).

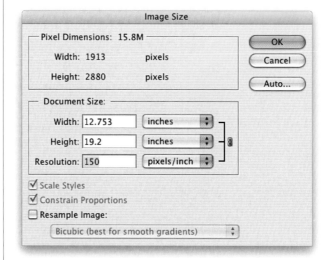

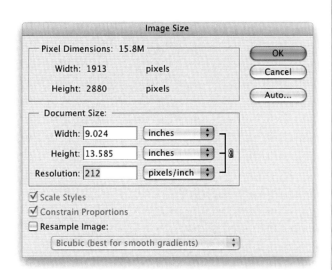

Step Five:

Here's the Image Size dialog for our source photo, and this time I've increased the Resolution setting to 212 ppi for output to a printing press. (Again, you don't need nearly as much resolution as you'd think.) As you can see, the Width of my image is no longer 27"—it's now just over 9". The Height is no longer 40"—now it's just over 13".

Step Six:

When you click OK, you won't see the image window change at all—it will appear at the exact same size onscreen—but look at the rulers. You can see that it's now about 9" wide by about 13.5" high. Resizing using this technique does three big things: (1) it gets your physical dimensions down to size (the photo now fits easily on an 11x17" sheet); (2) it increases the resolution enough so you can output this image on a printing press; and (3) you haven't softened, blurred, or pixelated the image in any way—the quality remains the same—all because you turned off Resample Image. *Note:* Do not turn off Resample Image for images that you scan on a scanner—they start as high-res images in the first place. Turning Resample Image off is only for photos taken with a digital camera.

Resizing the Smart Way (Using Smart Objects)

If you think there's even a slight chance that you'll need to upsize a photo you previously downsized, then you are going to love Smart Objects. Without getting all tech-geeky on you, when you choose to import your photo as a Smart Object, it embeds the original photo directly into the document itself. So when you go to resize an image you had downsized, it calls upon the original embedded photo so the image doesn't become all pixelated and soft when sized upward. Here's how to take advantage of Smart Objects for resizing:

Step One:

Open a new document in whatever size and resolution you'd like (in my example, I created a wide letter-sized document at 11x8"). To import a photo as a Smart Object, you don't open a photo. Instead, you go under the File menu and choose Place (as shown here). This is the simple key to making your photo a Smart Object—use the Place command rather than opening the photo and dragging into another document.

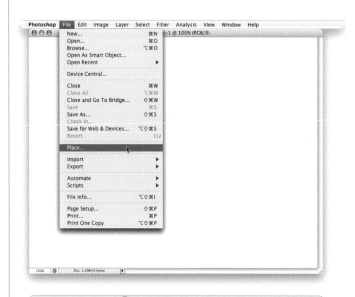

Step Two:

When you choose Place (as we did in Step One), your photo appears with a bounding box around it and a large X over the photo (as seen here). Press-and-hold the Shift key (to keep your resizing proportional), grab a corner point, and drag inward to shrink your photo down in size (as shown here). Press Return (PC: Enter) to lock in your resizing.

SCOTT KELBY

Step Three:

If you look in the Layers panel, you'll see a visual cue that your imported photo has become a Smart Object, and that's the little page icon that appears in the bottom-right corner of your layer's thumbnail (shown circled here in red). Go ahead and duplicate that layer by pressing Command-J (PC: Ctrl-J). The cool thing about duplicating a Smart Object is that your duplicate is linked to your original Smart Object, so things you do to the original affect the duplicate (you'll see why this is so cool later).

Step Four:

Now press Command-T (PC: Ctrl-T) to bring up Free Transform, press-and-hold the Shift key, grab any corner point, and drag outward to resize the photo up in size until that small duplicate photo fills the entire image area (as shown here). (*Note:* If you drag your corner point off the edge, you can press Command-0 [zero; PC: Ctrl-0] to zoom out and see it again.) When it fills the entire image area, press Return (PC: Enter) to lock in your resizing. As you can see here, the photo still looks crisp and sharp, but that's only because it's a Smart Object. If you had tried to resize a photo in any other format (JPEG, TIFF, PSD, even a RAW photo), the photo would be so soft and pixelated that you just wouldn't use it.

Step Five:

In the Layers panel, drag this duplicate layer behind your original photo layer, then lower the Opacity of this layer to 30% (as shown here), creating the back-screened look seen here.

Continued

Step Six:

Now that we've come this far, we might as well finish things off, eh? In the Layers panel, click on the top layer (the original photo layer) and then choose Drop Shadow from the Add a Layer Style pop-up menu at the bottom of the panel (although there are some limitations to what you can do to Smart Object layers, you can add layer styles like the drop shadow with no problem). When the Layer Style dialog appears (a close-up of part of it is shown here), increase the Size to 16 to make the shadow softer, then lower the Opacity to around 50% to make it lighter, as shown here in the inset, then click OK.

Step Seven:

In the Layers panel, click on the full-size background image layer. You can't convert the photo to black and white while it's still a Smart Object (unless of course, you placed a RAW photo as a Smart Object, which you do by using the Place command and clicking OK in the Camera Raw dialog, or by opening it in Camera Raw and Shift-clicking on the Open Image button). So, to get around that limitation, press D to set your Foreground color to black, then choose Gradient Map from the Create New Adjustment Layer pop-up menu (as shown here). This makes the full-size photo on the layer below it appear in black and white (as seen here).

Step Eight:

It looks like the smaller photo might look good with a thick black stroke around the photo, so click on the original photo layer again (the one on top), but this time choose Stroke from the Add a Layer Style pop-up menu. This brings up the Stroke Options section of the Layer Style dialog (a close-up is shown in the inset). Set the Size to 3, click on the red Color swatch and change the stroke color to black, then set the Position to Inside from the pop-up menu. Setting it to Inside makes the corners square rather than their default look, which is rounded.

Step Nine:

The last step is pretty easy—adding some type. I love this particular font for wedding albums (and a host of other uses). It's called Satisfaction, and I found it at MyFonts.com, where it cost $20 (it's actually only $12 if you don't buy the Open Type version with extra ligature characters, but I'm just a sucker for that kind of stuff, so I paid the $20, but to me, it's worth every penny!). Now, the layout is complete at this point, and we were able to upsize a photo that we had originally sized down, and the photo remained perfectly sharp and crisp (go ahead and save a copy of this file with all the layers intact), but I promised to show you something especially cool about Smart Objects and the advantage of duplicating a Smart Object, so...here goes.

Continued

Step 10:

As long as you saved the original layered file from last week's wedding, you can use it as a template for the next wedding you shoot. For example, let's say a week or so goes by and you shoot a different wedding. Open the layered template file (the one you saved near the end of Step Nine). Then go to the Layers panel, and Control-click (PC: Right-click) on the original Smart Object layer, just to the right of the layer's name. When the contextual menu appears, choose Replace Contents, as shown here. A standard Open dialog will appear (you won't need to use the Place command now, because your photo is already a Smart Object). Find the photo you'd like to use from your current wedding (this time, we're choosing a photo taken in RAW format).

Step 11:

Since this is a RAW photo, it first opens in the Camera Raw dialog (as seen here) so you can make any necessary adjustments. When you're done tweaking the photo, click the OK button (as shown here).

Step 12:

The previous photo is now replaced with your new photo, and because you duplicated the original layer to create your background layer, it gets automatically replaced as well (as seen here). In our example, the RAW photo I imported was physically larger in size than the original photo, so when the smaller photo appeared, it was larger than the one it replaced. I pressed Command-T (PC: Ctrl-T) to bring up Free Transform, then I held the Shift key, grabbed a corner point, dragged inward to scale the photo down in size (as seen here), and pressed Return (PC: Enter) to lock in the change. This took all of 15 seconds.

Step 13:

One last thing: in the Layers panel, double-click directly on the Smart Object thumbnail and the photo reopens immediately in Camera Raw so you can easily edit your RAW Smart Object photo (another advantage of using RAW). So, if you're thinking this all seems pretty amazing—you're right— and if you're thinking, "I'll use nothing but Smart Objects from now on" there is a downside you should know about. The main downside is that because it embeds the full original photo (including RAW photos) directly into your layered document, your file sizes can become quite large quickly, and generally speaking when your document file sizes get big, Photoshop can get somewhat slower. Just thought you should know both the good and the potentially not as good (like the spin I put in there—*not as good*? I should have been in politics).

Automated Saving and Resizing

Back when Photoshop CS was fairly new, Russell Preston Brown (Adobe's in-house evangelist and Photoshop madman) introduced a pretty slick little utility called Dr. Brown's Image Processor, which would let you take a folder full of images and save them in various formats (for example, it could open a PSD file and automatically make a JPEG and a TIFF from it, and resize each along the way). It became a cult hit, and so in CS2, an updated version of it was included (but sadly, they dropped the "Dr. Brown's" part, which I always thought gave it its charm).

Step One:

Go under the File menu, under Scripts, and choose Image Processor. By the way, if you're working in Adobe Bridge (rather than Photoshop), you can Command-click (PC: Ctrl-click) on all the photos you want to apply the Image Processor to, then go under the Tools menu, under Photoshop, and choose Image Processor. That way, when the Image Processor opens, it already has those photos pegged for processing. Sweet!

Step Two:

When the Image Processor dialog opens, the first thing you have to do is choose the folder of photos you want it to "do its thing" to by clicking on the Select Folder button, then navigating to the folder you want and clicking Choose (PC: OK). If you already have some photos open in Photoshop, you can click on the Use Open Images radio button (or if you choose Image Processor from Bridge, the Select Folder button won't be there at all—instead it will list how many photos you have selected in Bridge). Then, in the second section, decide whether you want the new copies to be saved in the same folder or copied into a different folder. No big whoop (that's a technical term).

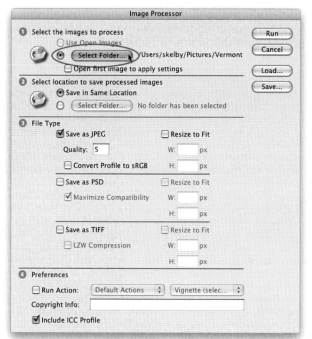

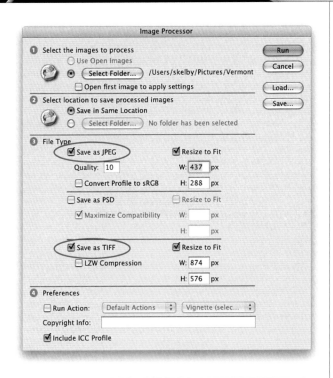

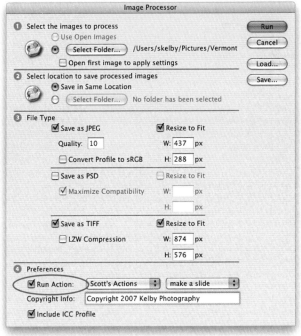

Step Three:

The third section is where the fun begins. This is where you decide how many copies of your original you're going to wind up with, and in what format. If you turn on the checkboxes for Save as JPEG, Save as PSD, and Save as TIFF, you're going to create three new copies of each photo. If you turn on the Resize to Fit checkboxes (and enter a size in the Width and Height fields), your copies will be resized too (in the example shown here, I chose a small JPEG of each file, then a larger TIFF, so in my folder I'd find one small JPEG and one larger TIFF for every file in my original folder).

Step Four:

In the fourth section, if you've created an action that you want applied to your copies, you can also have that happen automatically. Just turn on the Run Action checkbox, then from the pop-up menus choose which action you want to run. If you want to automatically embed your copyright info into these copies, type your info in the Copyright Info field. Lastly, there's a checkbox that lets you decide whether to include an ICC profile in each image or not (of course, I'm going to try to convince you to include the profile, because I wrote a whole chapter on how to set up color management in Photoshop [Chapter 5]). Click the Run button, sit back, and let it "do its thing," and before you know it, you'll have nice, clean copies aplenty.

Rule-Breaking Resizing for Poster-Sized Prints

This is a resizing technique I learned from my friend (and world-famous nature photographer) Vincent Versace. His poster-sized prints (24x36") always look so sharp and crisp—but we're both shooting with the same 6-megapixel camera—so I had to ask him his secret. I figured he was using some scaling plug-in, but he said he does the whole thing in Photoshop. My thanks to Vinny for sharing his simple, yet brilliant technique with me, so I could share it with you.

Step One:

Open the photo you want to resize, then go under the Image menu and choose Image Size. By the way, in Photoshop CS2 Adobe finally added a keyboard shortcut to get to the Image Size dialog: Command-Option-I (PC: Ctrl-Alt-I).

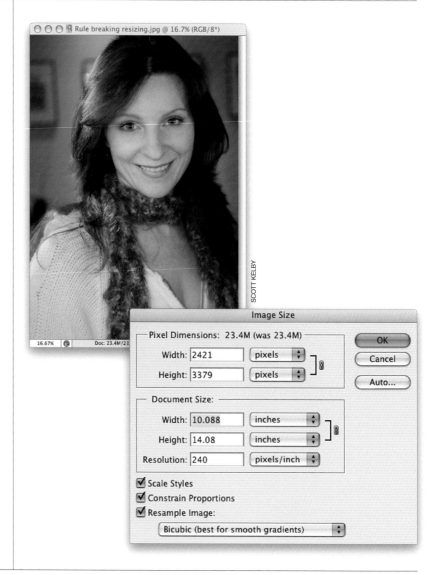

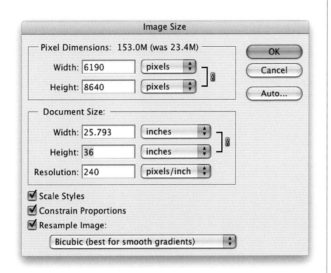

Step Two:

Type in the dimensions you want as your final print size. The original height for my 6-megapixel image is just a hair over 14", so when I type 36" for the Height, the Width field will automatically adjust to just over 25" (the Width and Height are linked proportionally by default—adjust one and the other adjusts in kind; here I'll have to crop my width down to 24"). Of course, not all images scale perfectly, so depending on how many megapixels your camera is, you may not be able to get exactly 24" (and in fact, you may not want to go that big. But if you do, you might need to enter more than 36" to make your width reach 24", and then you can go back and crop your height down to 36" [see the "Cropping to a Specific Size" technique earlier in this chapter]).

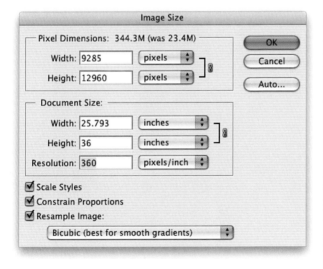

Step Three:

Once your size is in place, you'll need to adjust your resolution upward, so go to the Resolution field and enter 360. Now, you know and I know that this goes against every tried-and-true rule of resolution, and breaks the never-just-type-in-a-higher-number-with-the-Resample-Image-checkbox-turned-on rule that we all live and die by, but stick with me on this one—you've got to try it to believe it. So, type it in, grit your teeth, but don't click OK yet.

Continued

Step Four:

Back in Photoshop CS, Adobe introduced some new sampling algorithms for resizing images. According to Vincent's research, the key to this resizing technique is to not use the sampling method Adobe recommends (which is Bicubic Smoother), and instead to choose Bicubic Sharper in the Resample Image pop-up menu, which actually provides better results—so much so that Vincent claims that the printed results are not only just as good, but perhaps better than those produced by the expensive, fancy-schmancy upsizing plug-ins.

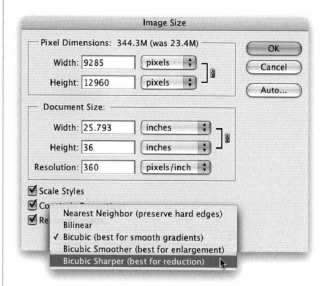

Step Five:

I've tried this technique numerous times, and I have to say—the results are pretty stunning. But don't take my word for it—click OK, print it out, and see for yourself. Here's the final image resized to 24x36" (you can see the size in the rulers by pressing Command-R [PC: Ctrl-R]).

There's a different set of rules we use for maintaining as much quality as possible when making an image smaller, and there are a couple of different ways to do just that (we'll cover the two main ones here). Luckily, maintaining image quality is much easier when sizing down than when scaling up (in fact, photos often look dramatically better—and sharper—when scaled down, especially if you follow these guidelines).

Making Your Photos Smaller (Downsizing)

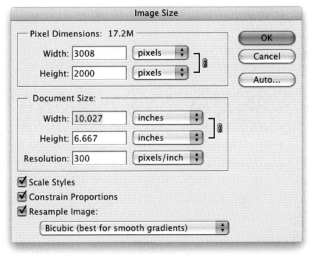

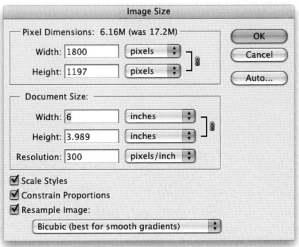

Downsizing photos where the resolution is already 300 ppi: Although earlier we discussed how to change image size if your digital camera gives you 72-ppi images with large physical dimensions (like 24x42" deep), what do you do if your camera gives you 300-ppi images at smaller physical dimensions (like a 10x6" at 300 ppi)? Basically, you turn on Resample Image (in the Image Size dialog under the Image menu), then simply type in the desired size (in this example, we want a 6x4" final image size), and click OK (don't change the Resolution setting, just click OK). The image will be scaled down to size, and the resolution will remain at 300 ppi. IMPORTANT: When you scale down using this method, it's likely that the image will soften a little bit, so after scaling you'll want to apply the Unsharp Mask filter to bring back any sharpness lost in the resizing (go to Chapter 11 to see what settings to use).

Continued

Making one photo smaller without shrinking the whole document:
If you're working with more than one image in the same document, you'll resize a bit differently. To scale down a photo on a layer, first click on that photo's layer in the Layers panel, then press Command-T (PC: Ctrl-T) to bring up Free Transform. Press-and-hold the Shift key (to keep the photo proportional), grab a corner point, and drag inward. When it looks good, press Return (PC: Enter). If the image looks softer after resizing it, apply the Unsharp Mask filter.

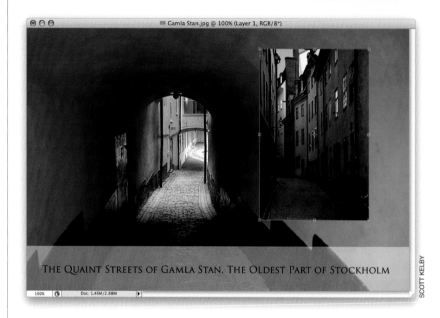

TIP: If you're resizing a photo on a layer using Free Transform and you can't reach the handles (because the edges of your photo extend outside the image area), just press Command-0 (PC: Ctrl-0), and your window will automatically resize so you can reach all the handles—no matter how far outside your image area they once were. Two things: (1) This only works once you have Free Transform active, and (2) it's Command-0—that's the number zero, not the letter O.

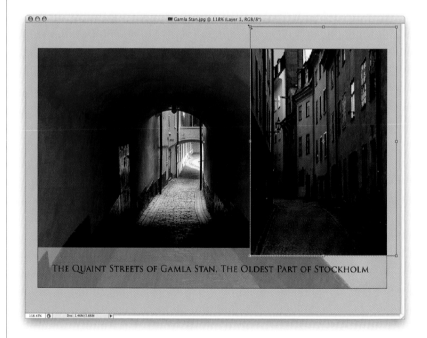

SCOTT KELBY

Resizing problems when dragging between documents:

This one gets a lot of people, because at first glance it just doesn't make sense. You have two documents, approximately the same size, side-by-side onscreen. But when you drag a 72-ppi photo (a close-up of a piano here) onto a 300-ppi document (Untitled-1), the photo appears really small. Why? Simply put—resolution. Although the documents appear to be the same size, they're not. The tip-off that you're not really seeing them at the same size is found in each photo's title bar. Here, the piano image is displayed at 100%, but the Untitled-1 document is displayed at only 25%. So, to get more predictable results, make sure both documents are at the same viewing size and resolution (check in the Image Size dialog under the Image menu).

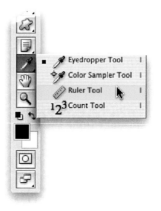

Straightening Crooked Photos

If you hand-held your camera for most of your shots rather than using a tripod, you can be sure that some of your photos are going to come out a bit crooked. Here's a quick way to straighten them accurately in just a few short steps:

Step One:
Open the photo that needs straightening. Choose the Ruler tool from Photoshop's Toolbox (it looks like a little ruler, and it's hidden behind the Eyedropper tool, so just click-and-hold for a moment on the Eyedropper tool until the Ruler tool appears in the flyout menu).

Step Two:
Try to find something in your photo that you think is supposed to be straight or relatively straight (the tops of the ridge on the right, in this example). Click-and-drag the Ruler tool horizontally along this straight edge in your photo, starting from the left and extending to the right. As soon as you drag the tool, you can see the angle of the line displayed in the Info palette (found under the Window menu) and up in the Options Bar, but you can ignore them both because Photoshop is already taking note of the angle and placing that info where you'll need it in the next step.

Step Three:
Go under the Image menu, under Rotate Canvas, choose Arbitrary, and the Rotate Canvas dialog will appear. Photoshop has already entered the proper angle of rotation you'll need to straighten the image (based on your measurement), and it even sets whether the image should be rotated clockwise or counterclockwise.

Step Four:
All you have to do now is click OK, and your photo will be perfectly straightened (check out the ridge in the photo shown here—it's now nice and straight).

Step Five:
After the image is straightened, you might have to re-crop it to remove the extra white canvas space showing around the corners of your photo, so press C to switch to the Crop tool, drag out a cropping border, and press the Return (PC: Enter) key.

TIP: When you use the Ruler tool, the line it draws stays on your photo until you rotate the image. If you want to clear the measurement and remove the line it drew on your image, click on the Clear button in the Options Bar.

Automated Cropping and Straightening

Since nearly everybody (digital or not) has a shoebox full of family photos up in the attic, I wanted to include a tutorial on the Crop and Straighten Photos automation. Its name is a bit misleading, because it does much more—it lets you scan multiple photos at one time (on your flatbed scanner), then it straightens every photo, and places each into its own separate window (saving you the trouble).

Step One:
Place as many photos as will fit at one time on the scanning bed of your desktop scanner and scan them in. They'll all appear in one large document in Photoshop. As you can see, these photos were crooked when placed on the scanning bed, so naturally they appear crooked in the Photoshop document.

SCOTT KELBY

Step Two:
Go under the File menu, under Automate, and choose Crop and Straighten Photos.

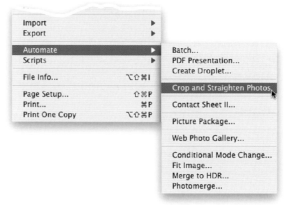

Step Three:
No dialog will appear. Instead, Photoshop will look for straight edges in your photos, straighten the photos, and copy each into its own separate window.

TIP: If you've scanned a number of photos, but decide you only want certain ones to be cropped and placed into their own separate documents, just put a selection around those photos using any selection tool (pressing-and-holding the Shift key to add to your selection) before you choose Crop and Straighten Photos. The photos in your selection must be contiguous or Photoshop will crop all of them.

Continued

Step Four:

This automation also works on single, crooked images. (Since the one shown here was taken with a digital camera, you're probably wondering how it got so crooked. I rotated it. Don't tell anybody.)

Step Five:

When you choose Crop and Straighten Photos, Photoshop will crop and straighten this one photo, but it still duplicates the image into a separate document. Hey, it's not perfect. Speaking of not perfect, it seems to work best when the photos you scan as a group have similar tonal qualities. The more varied the colors of the photos are, the harder time it seems to have straightening the images.

Exposure: 1/8s | Focal Length: 125mm | Aperture Value: ƒ/2.8

Fit to Print
step-by-step printing and color management

In the last version of this book, this chapter was simply called color management, when in reality it was pretty much a chapter on printing, because if you're not printing, who really cares if you're color managed, right? What you see onscreen is what you get—you don't have to match it to anything. But once you start printing, all heck breaks loose. (*Note:* I didn't want to use the word "heck" there, but my editor is "with child" and I didn't want to startle her.) The two are very closely tied together, and maybe that's why much of Photoshop's color management takes place in the Print dialog itself. So why did I change the name of this chapter? It's because I would get letters from people asking, "Why didn't you include a chapter about printing?" I would write them back and say, "I did—it's the color management

chapter," and they'd write back and say, "I didn't read that chapter because I didn't want to learn about color management, I wanted to learn about printing." Then I would write back, "But don't you want the prints that come out of your printer to match what you see onscreen?" And they would write back, "I don't use a screen because I'm Amish" and then I would write back, "Then how did you send this email?" And I would never hear from them again. Anyway, because Adobe made a number of enhancements and advances to printing in CS3, I thought I'd give this chapter a more descriptive subtitle (as seen above). The chapter name, "Fit to Print," is from John Mann's album *Hands in the Pavement*. It's actually a pretty good song—ya know, for a song about printing and color management.

Configuring Your Camera to Match Photoshop's Color Space

Although there are entire books written on the subject of color management in Photoshop, in this chapter we're going to focus on just one thing—getting what comes out of your color inkjet printer to match what you see onscreen. That's what it's all about, and if you follow the steps in this chapter, you'll get prints that match your screen. Now, I'm not going into the theory of color management, or CMYK soft proofing, or printing to multiple network printers, etc. It's just you, your computer, and your color inkjet printer. That, my friends, we can do.

Step One:

If you want to get consistent color from your camera to Photoshop to your printer, you'll want everybody speaking the same language, right? That's why if you shoot in either JPEG, TIFF, or JPEG+ RAW, I'm recommending that you change your camera's color space from its default sRGB (which is a color space designed for images only shown on the Web) to Adobe RGB (1998), which is probably the most popular color space used by photographers whose final image will come from a color inkjet printer. Now, if you only shoot in RAW, you can skip this because you'll assign the color space later in Photoshop's Camera Raw dialog, but otherwise, do it now. As an example, here's how to set up a Nikon D200 to tag your photos with the Adobe RGB (1998) color profile. First, click the Menu button on the back of your camera.

Nikon D200

Step Two:

When the menu appears, use the round multi selector on the back to go to the Shooting menu, and then in that menu, choose Color Space (as shown here) by pressing the Right Arrow on the multi selector.

Step Three:
This brings up the Color Space menu (shown here). Use the Down Arrow on the multi selector to choose Adobe RGB (as shown here), and then press the Right Arrow on the multi selector to lock in your change.

Step Four:
Now when you look in the Shooting menu, you should see the word "Adobe" to the right of Color Space, which lets you know that Adobe RGB (1998) is your camera's color space. So now you've taken your first step towards color consistency.

Setting up other cameras:
I just showed the simple color space setup for a Nikon D200, however if you've got a Canon digital camera (like the popular Canon 30D), it's pretty simple to configure, too: Just like with the Nikons, you go under the Shooting menu, and use the Quick Control dial to scroll down to Color Space. Press the center Set button to edit the color space, then choose Adobe RGB (as shown here) and press Set again to lock in your choice.

Note: Most dSLRs from Nikon and Canon work fairly similarly (although the menus may be slightly different), but if you're not shooting Nikon or Canon, it's time to dig up your owner's manual (or download it from the manufacturer's website) to find out how to make the switch to Adobe RGB (1998).

Configuring Photoshop for Adobe RGB (1998)

Once your camera's set to the right color space, it's time to set up Photoshop that way. In Photoshop 5.5, when Adobe (and the world) was totally absorbed with Web design, they switched Photoshop's default color space to sRGB (which some pros refer to as "stupid RGB"), which is fine for photos on the Web, but your printer can print a wider range of color (particularly in the blues and greens). So, if you work in sRGB, you're essentially leaving those rich vivid colors on the table. That's why we change our color space to Adobe RGB (1998), which is better for prints.

Step One:
Before we do this, I just want to reiterate that you only want to make this change if your final print will be output to your own color inkjet. If you're sending your images out to an outside lab for prints, you should probably stay in sRGB—both in the camera and in Photoshop—as most labs are set up to handle sRGB files. Your best bet: ask your lab which color space they prefer. Okay, now on to Photoshop: go under the Edit menu and choose Color Settings (as shown here).

Step Two:
This brings up the Color Settings dialog. By default, it uses a group of settings called "North America General Purpose 2." Now, does anything about the phrase "General Purpose" sound like it would be a good space for pro photographers? Didn't think so. The tip-off is that under Working Spaces, the RGB space is set to sRGB IEC61966–2.1 (which is the long-hand technical name for what we simply call sRGB, also sometimes referred to as "stupid RGB"). In short, you don't want to use this group of settings. They're for goobers—not for you (unless of course, you are a goober, which I doubt because you bought this book, and they don't sell this book to goobers. It's in each bookstore's contract).

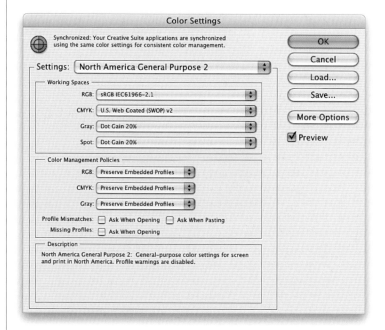

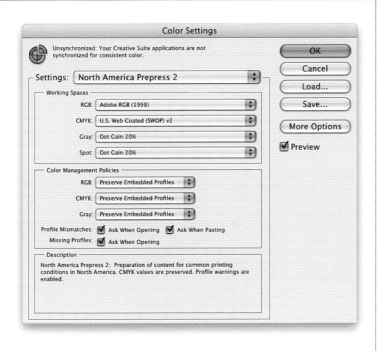

Step Three:

To get a preset group of settings that's better for photographers, from the Settings pop-up menu, choose North America Prepress 2. Don't let it throw you that we're using prepress settings here—they work great for color inkjet printing because it uses the Adobe RGB (1998) color space. It also sets up the appropriate warning dialogs to help you keep your color management plan in action when opening photos from outside sources or other cameras (more on this on the next page).

TIP: If you're using Adobe Photoshop Lightroom for your printing, instead of printing from here in Photoshop CS3, you might want to change your RGB working space to ProPhoto RGB, which is the native color space for Lightroom. That way, when you export a file from Lightroom over to Photoshop, make edits in Photoshop, and then save back to Lightroom, everything stays in the same consistent color space.

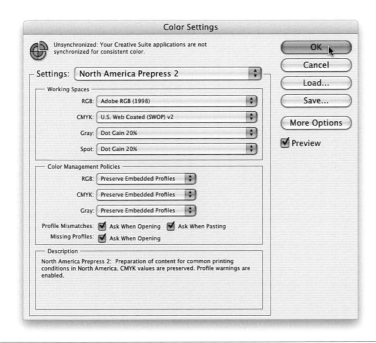

Step Four:

Before you click OK, just for fun, temporarily change the Settings pop-up menu to North America Web/Internet. You'll see that the RGB working space changes back to sRGB. That's because sRGB is best suited for Web design. Makes you stop and think, doesn't it? Now, switch back to North America Prepress 2, click OK, and Photoshop is configured with Adobe RGB (1998) as your RGB working space. However, you probably still want to know about the warnings you turned on, right?

Continued

Step Five:

About those warnings that help you keep your color management on track: Let's say you open a JPEG photo, and your camera was set to shoot in Adobe RGB (1998), and your Photoshop is set the same way. The two color spaces match, so no warnings appear. But, if you open a JPEG photo you took six months ago, it will probably still be in sRGB, which doesn't match your Photoshop working space. That's a mismatch, so you'd get the warning dialog shown here, telling you this. Luckily it gives you the choice of how to handle it. I recommend converting that document's colors to your current working space (as shown here).

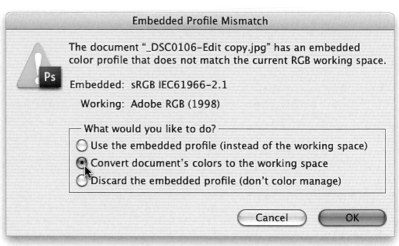

Step Six:

You can have Photoshop do this conversion automatically anytime it finds a mismatch. Just reopen the Color Settings dialog, and under Color Management Policies, in the RGB pop-up menu, change your default setting to Convert to Working RGB (as shown here). For Profile Mismatches, turn off the Ask When Opening checkbox. Now when you open sRGB photos, they will automatically update to match your current working space. Nice!

Step Seven:

Okay, so what if a friend emails you a photo, you open it in Photoshop, and the photo doesn't have any color profile at all? Well, once that photo is open in Photoshop, you can convert that "untagged" image to Adobe RGB (1998) by going under the Edit menu and choosing Assign Profile. When the Assign Profile dialog appears, click on the Profile radio button, ensure Adobe RGB (1998) is selected in the pop-up menu, then click OK.

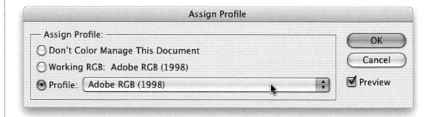

To have any hope of getting what comes out of your color inkjet printer to match what you see onscreen, you absolutely, positively have to calibrate your monitor. It's the cornerstone of color management, and there are two ways to do it: (1) buy a hardware calibration sensor that calibrates your monitor precisely; or (2) use the free built-in system software calibration, which is better than nothing, but not by much since you're just "eyeing" it. We'll start with the freebie calibration, but if you're serious about this stuff, turn to the next technique.

Calibrating Your Monitor (The Lame Built-In Freebie Method)

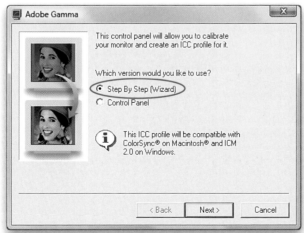

Freebie Calibration:
First, we'll look at the worst-case scenario: you're broke (you spent all available funds on the CS3 upgrade), so you'll have to go with the free built-in system software calibration. Macintosh computers have calibration built into the system, but Windows PCs use a separate utility from Adobe called Adobe Gamma, so we'll start with that, and then we'll do the Mac freebie calibration. To get to Adobe Gamma on your Windows Vista PC, go to C:\Program Files\Common Files\Adobe\ Calibration and double-click on the Adobe Gamma.cpl file. In Windows XP, from the Start menu, go to the Control Panel and double-click on Adobe Gamma. *Note:* If Adobe Gamma didn't load, you may have to manually copy the files from the Goodies\ Software\Adobe Gamma folder on the installation CD to the Calibration folder.

Step One (PC):
This brings up the Adobe Gamma dialog. Choose Step By Step (Wizard), which will lead you through the steps for creating a pretty lame calibration profile. (Hey, I can't help it—that's what it does. Do you really want me to sugarcoat it? Okay, how's this? "It will lead you through the steps for proper calibration" [cringe].) *Note:* Results will vary depending on whether your monitor is a CRT, LCD, etc.

Continued

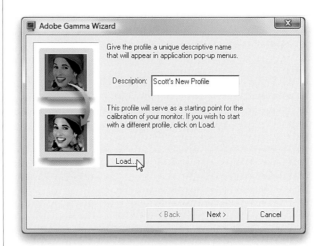

Step Two (PC):

Click the Next button and you'll be asked to name the profile you're about to create. Now, it's possible that when you first hooked up your monitor a manufacturer's profile was installed at the same time. Although that canned factory profile won't do the trick, it can save you some time because it will automatically answer some of the questions in the dialog, so it's worth a look to see if you have one. Click on the Load button, then navigate your way to the ICC profiles in your system (you should be directed to them by default). If you see a profile with your monitor's name, click on it and then click Open to load that profile. Click Next again.

Step Three (PC):

From here on out, you'll be prompted with various directions (some with little square graphics with sliders beneath them). It asks you to move the sliders and then judge how the colors look. This is the very essence of the term "eyeing it," and it's why pros avoid this method. Everyone sees color and tone differently, and we're all viewing these test squares under different lighting conditions, etc., so it's highly subjective. But hey—it's free.

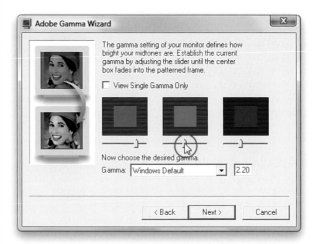

Step Four (PC):

The questions will continue (along the lines of the Spanish Inquisition) until it completes the calibration process, and then it offers you a before and after. You can pretty much ignore the Carmen Miranda before/after photo—that's just for looks—your before and after will be nothing like that, but after you're prompted to save your profile, you're done.

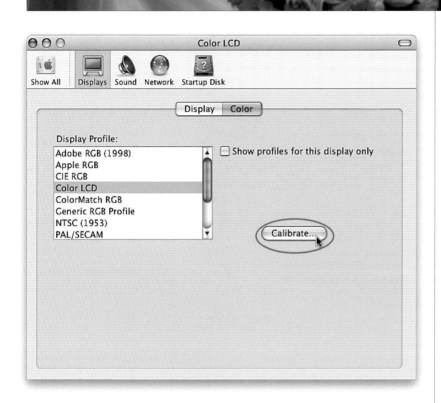

Step One (Mac):

Now for the freebie calibration on the Macintosh: To find Apple's built-in monitor calibration software, go under the Apple menu and choose System Preferences. In the System Preferences dialog, click on the Displays preferences, and when the options appear, click on the Color tab. When the Color options appear, click on the Calibrate button to bring up the Display Calibrator Assistant window (shown in the next step).

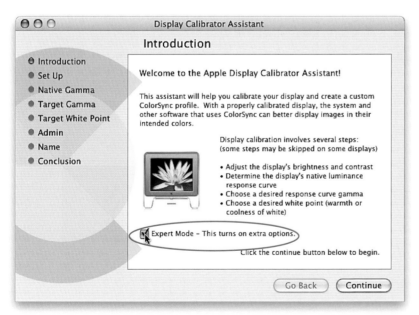

Step Two (Mac):

Now, at first this seems like a standard Welcome screen, so you'll probably be expecting to just click the Continue button, but don't do that until you turn on the Expert Mode checkbox. I know what you're thinking: "But I'm not an expert!" Don't worry, within a few minutes you'll be within the top 5% of all photographers who have knowledge of monitor calibration, because sadly most never calibrate their monitor. So turn on the checkbox and click the Continue button with the full confidence that you're about to enter an elite cadre of highly calibrated individuals (whatever that means).

Continued

Step Three (Mac):

The first section has you go through a series of five different windows, and each window will ask you to perform a simple matching test using a slider. It's a no-brainer, as Apple tells you exactly what to do in each of these five windows (it's actually the same for all five windows, so once you've read the first window's instructions, you're pretty much set). So, just follow Apple's easy instructions to get through these five windows, then I'll join you right after.

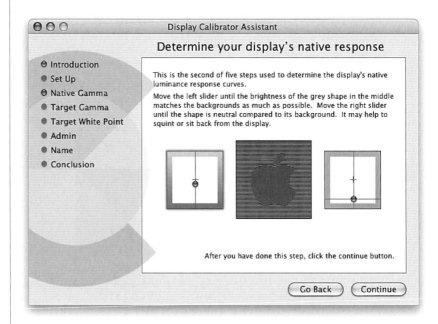

Step Four (Mac):

Okay, so you survived the "five native response windows of death." Amazingly easy, wasn't it? (It even borders on fun.) Well, believe it or not, that's the hard part—the rest could be done by your 5-year-old, provided you have a 5-year-old (if not, you can rent one from Apple's website). So here we are at a screen asking you to select a target gamma (basically, you're choosing a contrast setting here). Apple pretty much tells you "it is best to use the Mac Standard gamma of 1.8," but it has no idea that you're a photographer and need something better. Most digital imaging pros I know recommend setting your gamma to 2.2 (the PC Standard), which creates a richer contrast onscreen (which tends to make you open the shadows up when editing, which is generally a good thing detail-wise). Drag the slider to PC Standard and see if you agree, then click Continue.

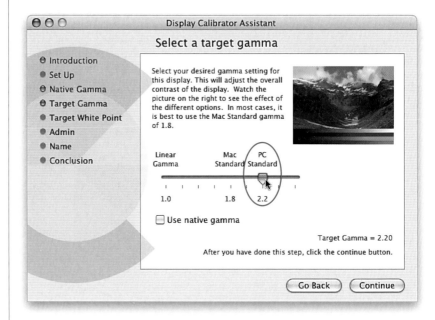

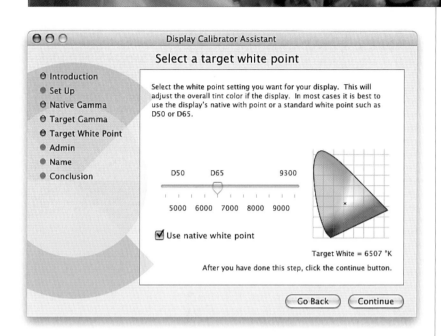

Step Five (Mac):

Now it asks you to select a white point. I use D65 (around 6500 Kelvin, in case you care). Why? That's what most of the pros use, because it delivers a nice, clean white point without the yellowish tint that occurs when using lower temperature settings. With the slider set at D65, you can click the Continue button. The next window just asks if you're sharing your computer with other users, so I'm skipping that window, because if you are, you'll turn on the checkbox; if you're not, you won't. Snore.

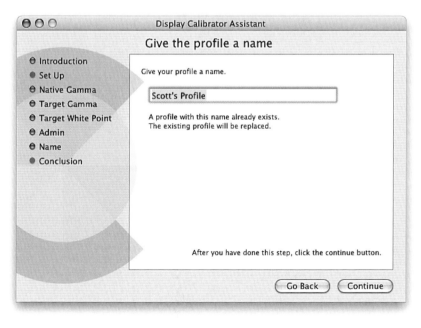

Step Six (Mac):

When you click Continue again, you'll be greeted with a window that lets you name your profile. Type in the name you want for your profile, and click the Continue button. The last window (which there's no real reason to show here) just sums up the choices you've made, so if you made some egregious mistake, you could click the Go Back button, but seriously, what kind of huge mistake could you have made that would show up at this point? Exactly. So click the Done button and you've created a semi-accurate profile for your monitor (hey, don't complain—it's free calibration). Now, you don't have to do anything in Photoshop for it to recognize this new profile—it happens automatically (in other words, "Photoshop just knows." Eerie, ain't it?).

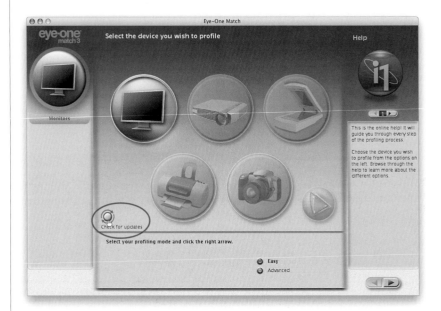

The Right Way to Calibrate Your Monitor (Hardware Calibration)

Hardware calibration is definitely the preferred method of monitor calibration (in fact, I don't know of a single pro using the freebie software-only method). With hardware calibration, it's measuring your actual monitor and building an accurate profile for the exact monitor you're using, and yes—it makes that big a difference. I now use X-Rite's Eye-One Display 2 (after hearing so many friends rave about it), and I have to say—I'm very impressed. It's become popular with pros thanks to the sheer quality of its profiles, its ease-of-use, and affordability (around $230 street).

Step One:

You start by installing the Eye-One Match 3 software from the CD that comes with it (the current version was 3.6.1 as of the writing of this book. However, once you launch Match 3 for the first time, I recommend clicking the Check for Updates button [as shown here] to have it check for a newer version, just in case). Once the latest version is installed, plug the Eye-One Display into your computer's USB port, then relaunch the software to bring up the main window (seen here). You do two things here: (1) you choose which device to profile (in this case, a monitor), and (2) you choose your profiling mode (where you choose between Easy or Advanced. If this is your first time using a hardware calibrator, I recommend clicking the Easy radio button).

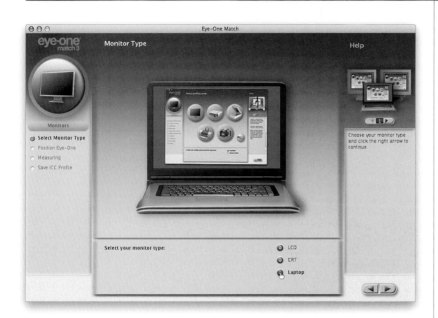

Step Two:

After choosing Easy, press the Right Arrow button in the bottom right, and the window you see here will appear. Here you just tell the software which type of monitor you have: an LCD (a flat-panel monitor), a CRT (a glass monitor with a tube), or a laptop (which is what I'm using, so I clicked on Laptop, as shown here), then press the Right Arrow button again.

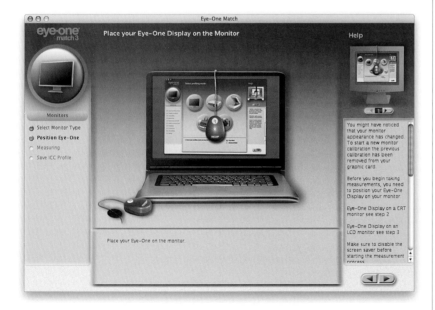

Step Three:

The next screen asks you to Place Your Eye-One Display on the Monitor, which means you drape the sensor over your monitor so the Eye-One Display sits flat against your monitor and the cord hangs over the back. The sensor comes with a counterweight you can attach to the cord, so you can position the sensor approximately in the center of your screen without it slipping down. There is a built-in suction cup for use on CRT monitors.

Continued

Step Four:

Once the sensor is in position (this takes all of about 20 seconds) click the Right Arrow key, sit back, and relax. You'll see the software conduct a series of onscreen tests, using gray and white rectangles and various color swatches, as shown here. (*Note:* Be careful not to watch these onscreen tests while listening to Jimi Hendrix's "Are you Experienced," because before you know it you'll be on your way to Canada in a psychedelic VW Microbus with only an acoustic guitar and a hand-drawn map to a campus protest. Hey, I've seen it happen.)

Step Five:

This testing only goes on for around six or seven minutes (at least, that's all it took for my laptop), then it's done. It does let you see a before and after (using the buttons on the bottom), and you'll probably be shocked when you see the before/after results (most people are amazed at how blue or red their screen was every day, yet they never noticed). Once you've compared your before and after, click the Finish Calibration button and that's it—your monitor is accurately profiled, and it even installs the profile for you and then quits. It should be called "Too Easy" mode.

When you buy a color inkjet printer and install the printer driver that comes with it, it basically lets Photoshop know what kind of printer is being used, and that's about it. But to get pro-quality results, you need a profile for your printer based on the exact type of paper you'll be printing on. Most inkjet paper manufacturers now create custom profiles for their papers, and you can usually download them free from their websites. Does this really make that big a difference? Ask any pro. Here's how to find and install your custom profiles:

The Other Secret to Getting Pro-Quality Prints That Match Your Screen

Step One:

Your first step is to go to the website of the company that makes the paper you're going to be printing on and search for their downloadable color profiles for your printer. I use the term "search" because they're usually not in a really obvious place. I use two Epson printers—a Stylus Photo R2400 and a Stylus Pro 3800—and I generally print on Epson paper. When I installed the 3800's printer driver, I was tickled to find that it also installed custom color profiles for all Epson papers (this is rare), but my R2400 (like most printers) doesn't. So, the first stop would be Epson's website, where you'd click on the Drivers & Support link (as shown here). *Note:* Even if you're not an Epson user, still follow along (you'll see why).

Continued

Step Two:

Once you get to Drivers & Support, find your particular printer in the list. Click on that link, and on the next page, click on Drivers & Downloads (choose Windows or Macintosh). On that page is a note linking you to the printer's Premium ICC Profiles page. Here's what Epson says right there about these free profiles: "In most cases, these custom ICC profiles will provide more accurate color and black and white reproduction than with the standard profiles already shipping with every printer." So, click on that Premium ICC Profiles link.

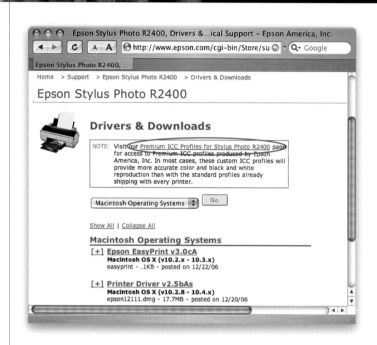

Step Three:

When you click that link, a page appears with a list of Mac and Windows ICC profiles for Epson's papers and printers. I primarily print on two papers: (1) Epson's Premium Luster Photo paper, and (2) Epson's Velvet Fine Art paper. So, I'd download the ICC profiles for the Glossy Papers (as shown here), and the Fine Art Papers Matte (at the bottom of the window). They download onto your computer, and you just double-click the installer for each one, and they're added to your list of profiles in Photoshop (I'll show how to choose them in the Print dialog a little later). That's it—you download them, double-click to install, and they'll be waiting for you in Photoshop's print dialog. Easy enough. But what if you're not using Epson paper? Or if you have a different printer, like a Canon or an HP?

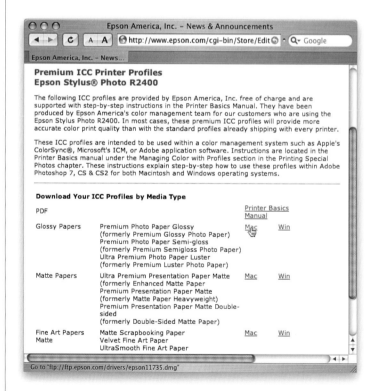

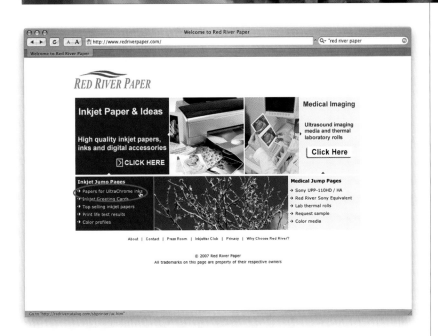

Step Four:

We'll tackle the different paper issue first (because they're tied together). I mentioned earlier that I usually print on Epson papers. I say usually because sometimes I want a final print that fits in a 16x20" standard pre-made frame, without having to cut or trim the photo. In those cases, I use Red River Paper's 16x20" Ultra Satin Pro instead (which is very much like Epson's Premium Luster, but it's already pre-cut to 16x20"). So, even though you're printing on an Epson printer, now you'd go to Red River Paper's site (www.redriverpaper.com) to find their color profiles for the Epson 3800. (Remember, profiles come from the company that makes the paper.) On the Red River Paper homepage is a link for Papers for UltraChrome Inks (which are Epson's inks), so click on that.

Step Five:

Once you click that link, things get easier, because on the right side of Red River's Epson UltraChrome Inks page is a clear, direct link—with a color graphic no less—right to their free downloadable color profiles (as seen here). Making profiles easy to find like this is extremely rare (it's almost too easy—it must be a trap, right?). So, click on that Color Profiles link and it takes you right to the profiles for Epson printers, as seen in Step Six (how sweet is that?)

Continued

Step Six:

Under the section named Epson Wide Format, there's a direct link to the Epson Pro 3800 (as shown here), but did you also notice that there are ICC Color profiles for the Canon printers, as well? See, the process is the same for other printers, but be aware: although HP and Canon now both make pro-quality photo printers, Epson has had the pro market to itself for quite a while, so while Epson profiles are created by most major paper manufacturers, you may not always find paper profiles for HP and Canon printers. As you can see at Red River, they widely support Epson, and some Canon profiles are there too—but there's nothing for HP yet. That doesn't mean this won't change, but as of the writing of this book, that's the reality. Speaking of change—the look and navigation of websites change pretty regularly, so if these sites look different when you visit them, don't freak out. Okay, you can freak out, but just a little.

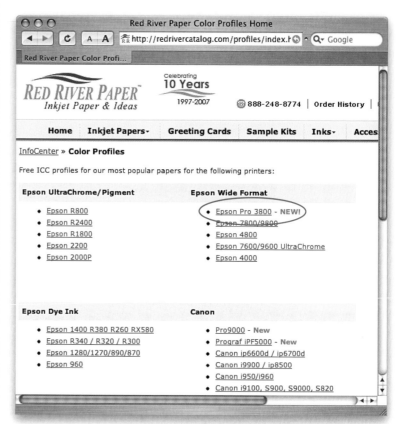

Step Seven:

Although profiles from Epson's website come with an installer, in Red River's case (and in the case of many other paper manufacturers), you just get the profile (shown here) and instructions, so you install it yourself (don't worry—it's easy). On a PC, just Right-click on the profile and choose Install Profile. Easy enough. (*Note:* If you're using Windows XP and this doesn't work, you'll have to drag the profile into the Profiles folder itself. It's at C:\Windows\system32\spool\drivers\color.) On a Mac, go to your hard disk, open your Library folder, and open your Color-Sync folder, where you'll see a Profiles folder. Just drag the file in there and you're set (in Photoshop CS3 you don't even have to restart Photoshop—it automatically updates).

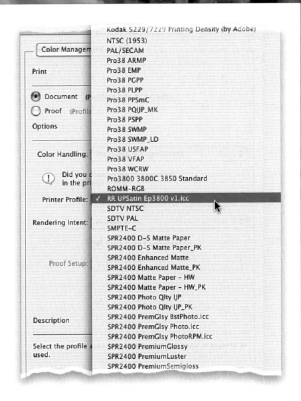

Step Eight:

Now, you'll access your profile by choosing Print from Photoshop's File menu. In the Print dialog, change the Color Handling pop-up menu to Photoshop Manages Color. Then, click on the Printer Profile pop-up menu, and your new color profile(s) will appear (as shown here). In our example, I'm printing to an Epson 3800 using Red River's Ultra Pro Satin paper, so that's what I'm choosing here as my printer profile (it's named RR UPSatin Ep3800 v1.icc). More on using these color profiles later in this chapter.

TIP: You can also pay an outside service to create a custom profile for your printer. You print a test sheet (which they provide), overnight it to them, and they'll use an expensive colorimeter to measure your test print and create a custom profile. The catch: it's only good for that printer, on that paper, with that ink. If anything changes, your custom profile is just about worthless. Of course, you could do your own personal printer profiling (using something like one of X-Rite's Eye-One Pro packages) so you can re-profile each time you change paper or inks. It's really determined by your fussiness/time/money factor (if you know what I mean).

Making the Print (Finally, It All Comes Together)

Okay, you've set your camera to Adobe RGB (1998); you've hardware calibrated your monitor (or at the very least—you "eyed it"); you've set up Photoshop to use Adobe RGB (1998); and you've set it up so any photos you bring in that are not in Adobe RGB (1998) will automatically be converted to Adobe RGB (1998). You've even downloaded a printer profile for the exact printer model and style of paper you're printing on. In short—you're there. Luckily, you only have to do all that stuff once—now we can just sit back and print. Well, pretty much.

Step One:
Go under Photoshop's File menu and choose Print (as shown here). In previous versions of Photoshop, to access the color management features for printing you had to choose Print with Preview, but in CS3, we're happily down to just one simple command—Print!

Step Two:
When the Print dialog appears, let's choose your printer and paper size first. Near the top of the center column, you'll see a Page Setup button. Click on it to bring up the Page Setup dialog (shown here). Choose the printer you want to print to from the Format For pop-up menu (on a PC, you'll have to choose it from the Printer pop-up menu before clicking Page Setup), and then from the Paper Size pop-up menu (found on the Paper tab on a PC) choose your paper size (in this case, a 16x20" sheet). You can choose your page orientation here if you want, but you can also choose this later in Photoshop's Print dialog. Leave the Scale at 100% (you can change that later), and click OK to return to the Print dialog.

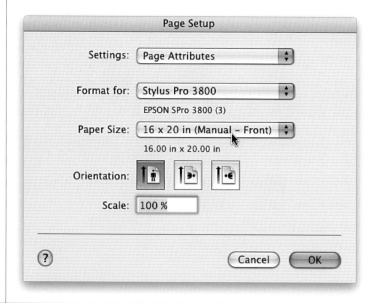

SCOTT KELBY

Step Three:
In the Print dialog, at the top of the far-right column, make sure Color Management is selected from the pop-up menu (as shown here). Then, at the top of the center column, choose your Printer from the pop-up menu (even though you chose it in the Page Setup dialog, you may have to choose it again from here).

Step Four:
From the Color Handling pop-up menu, choose Photoshop Manages Colors (as shown here) so we can use the color profile we downloaded for our printer and paper combination, which will give us the best possible match. Here's the thing: by default the Color Handling is set up to have your printer manage colors. You really only want to choose this if you weren't able to download the printer/paper profile for your printer. So, basically having your printer manage colors is your back-up plan. It's not your first choice, but today's printers have gotten to the point that if you have to go with this, it still does a decent job (that wasn't the case just a few years ago—if you didn't have a color profile, you didn't have a chance at getting a pro-quality print).

Continued

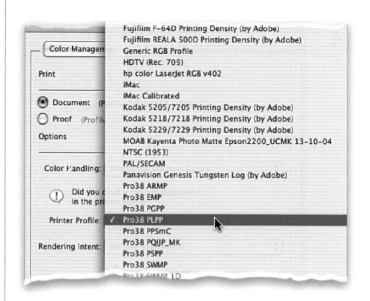

Step Five:

After you've selected Photoshop Manages Colors, you'll need to choose your profile from the Printer Profile pop-up menu. I'm going to be printing to an Epson Stylus Pro 3800 printer using Epson's Premium Luster paper, so I'll choose the printer/paper profile that matches my printer and my paper (as I mentioned in the previous technique, the Epson 3800 came with color profiles for Epson papers already installed, but Epson does their best to give these color profiles names designed to appeal to people who decipher encrypted code for the NSA. So, for the 3800 on Premium Luster, I'd choose Pro38 PLPP). Doing this optimizes the color to give the best possible color print on that printer using that paper.

Step Six:

Lastly, you'll need to choose the Rendering Intent. There are four choices here, but only two I recommend: either Relative Colorimetric (which is the default setting) or Perceptual. Here's the thing: I've had printers where I got the best looking prints with my Rendering Intent set to Perceptual, but currently, on my Epson Stylus Pro 3800, I get better results when it's set to Relative Colorimetric. So, which one gives the best results for your printer? I recommend printing a photo once using Perceptual, then print the same print using Relative Colorimetric, and when you compare the two, you'll know.

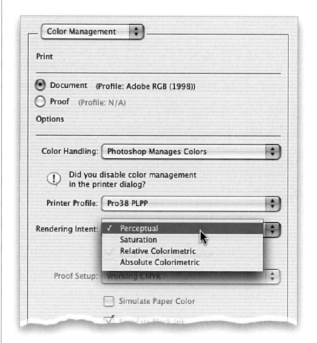

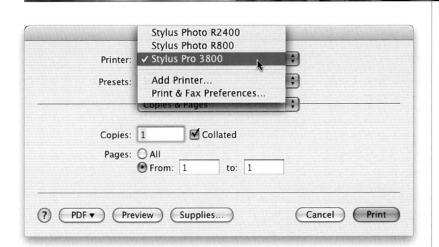

Step Seven:

Lastly, before you click the Print button, just make sure the Black Point Compensation checkbox is turned on (it should be by default). When you're printing photographic images (like we are here), this option helps maintain more detail and color in the shadow areas of your photos. Now click the Print button, and when you do, another Print dialog will appear—your print driver's dialog. Choose your printer from the Printer pop-up menu, as shown here (yes, this is the third time you've chosen your printer). The example shown here is from a Mac running Mac OS X. On a Windows PC, choose your printer from the Name pop-up menu, and then click on the Properties button to choose from your printer's options.

Step Eight:

Click on the Copies & Pages pop-up menu to reveal a list of all the printer options you can choose from. There are two critical changes we need to make here. First, choose Print Settings (as shown here) so we can configure the printer to give us the best-quality prints.

WARNING: From this point on, what appears in the Copies & Pages pop-up menu is contingent on your printer's options. You may or may not be able to access these same settings, so you may need to view each option to find the settings you need to adjust. If you're using a Windows PC, after you click on the Properties button, you may have to click on the Advanced tab or an Advanced button in your printer's Properties dialog to be able to choose from similar settings.

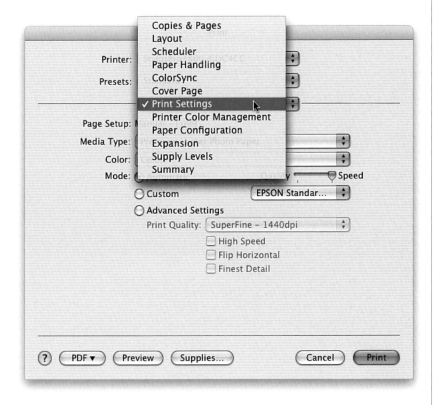

Continued

Step Nine:

Once you choose Print Settings, and those options appear, choose the type of paper you'll be printing on from the Media Type pop-up menu (as shown here). In our example, I'm printing on Premium Luster Photo Paper. *Note:* The Premium Luster Photo Paper is my favorite overall Epson paper for color and black-and-white prints. My second favorite is their Velvet Fine Art Paper, which I use when I want more of a painterly watercolor look and feel. It works really nicely for the right kind of photos because the paper has a lot of texture, so your photos look softer. Try it for shots of flowers, nature, soft landscapes, and any shot where tack-sharp focus is not the goal. Velvet Fine Art Paper is also a very forgiving paper when your photo is slightly out of focus.

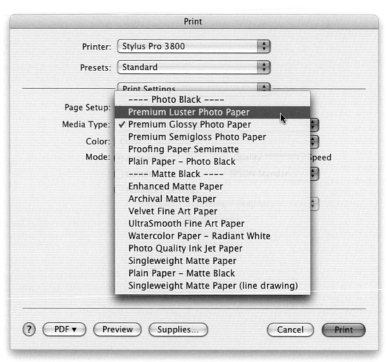

Step 10:

Under the Mode section, click on Advanced Settings. (On a PC, choose Custom and click on the Advanced button.) Choose your Print Quality from the pop-up menu. I used to choose Super-Photo - 2880 dpi because I wanted to get the highest possible quality, but I feel the trade-off between time and ink usage vs. the difference in quality (which is fairly negligible in most cases, if visible at all) isn't worth it, so now I choose SuperFine - 1440 dpi, which creates a wonderful quality print without waiting around all day. The only reason I might bump up to 2880 is if the photo I just printed has some visible banding, or I see a problem that I hope a higher printing dpi might fix, but thankfully that is rare. Again, this is one of those things to test with your own printer: print the same image on similar paper, once at 1440, once at 2880, and see if you spot a distinct difference.

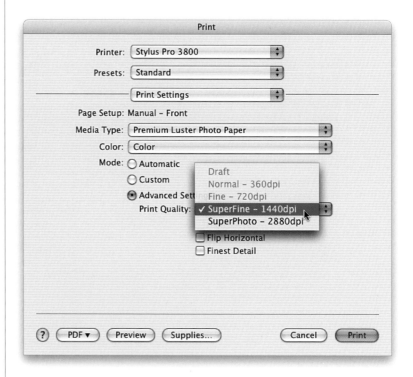

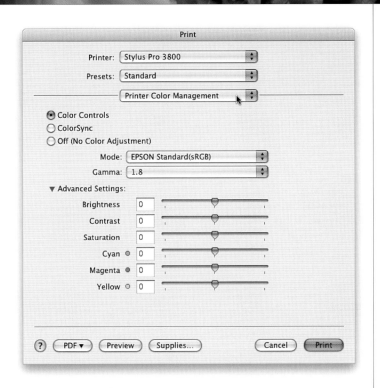

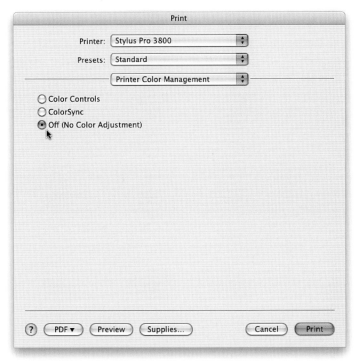

Step 11:

This next change, turning off the printer's color management, is critical. You do this by choosing Printer Color Management from that third pop-up menu to make the Color Management options visible (on a PC, they are in the same Advanced dialog). Then, ignore these very tempting-looking settings (the Mode pop-up menu, Gamma pop-up menu, and lots of fun-looking sliders that are just begging you to mess with them—but don't do it). Those controls are evil. So why did we come here in the first place? To turn this junk off—just click on the Off (No Color Adjustment) radio button (as shown in the next step).

Step 12:

When you select Off (No Color Adjustment), thankfully all that tempting stuff is immediately hidden from view, because now the printer's color management features are turned off. You want no color adjustment from your printer—you're letting Photoshop manage your color instead. Now you're ready to hit the Print button to get prints that match your screen, as you've color managed your photo from beginning to end.

WARNING: If you're printing to a color inkjet printer, don't ever convert your photo to CMYK format (even though you may be tempted to because your printer uses cyan, magenta, yellow, and black inks). The conversion from RGB to CMYK inks happens within the printer itself, and if you do it first in Photoshop, your printer will attempt to convert it again in the printer, and your printed colors will be way off.

Photo by Scott Kelby   Exposure: 1/20s   Focal Length: 220mm   Aperture Value: ƒ/4.0

Local Color
color correction secrets

In previous editions of the book, I pretty much used up all the good titles for this chapter. I already used "True Colors" (my personal favorite title, inspired by the Cindy Lauper song), and up to this point I have skillfully avoided using Chicago's "Color My World" as a title. By the time I got to the CS2 version of the book, I was already running out of decent names, so I had to go with "The Color of Money" (from the movie of the same name), which admittedly was kind of lame. So this time I dug a little deeper and found a movie called *Local Color*, made back in 1977, that starred Jane Campbell, Bob Herron, and Temmie Brodkey, among others. If none of those people sound familiar, it's probably because you didn't see *Local Color*, which was the story of a young boy in a small village who only had Photoshop 5.5 and used only Brightness/Contrast for his tonal corrections. This made the other children laugh at him, and recalibrate his monitor to crazy colors when he was off selling his handmade trinkets to the American tourists who would visit his tiny village. Then one day, he met a kind American tourist (we'll call him Señor Willmore), who was getting on his air-conditioned tour bus when he stopped and looked back at the uncalibrated little boy, and tossed him an X-Rite Eye-One Display 2 hardware calibrator. The little boy's eyes filled with joy as he ran back to his 25 Mhz Macintosh Quadra, opened the box, took out the USB cable, and started to connect the calibrator, but then he realized his old Mac Quadra didn't have a USB port, and he cried and cried, then the movie ended. It was a really sad movie. No wonder you didn't see it.

Two Things to Do Before You Color Correct Anything

Before we correct even a single photo, there are two quick little changes we need to make in Photoshop to get better, more accurate results. The first is to change how the Eyedropper tool measures color, and the second is to get a neutral gray background behind your photos so your background doesn't affect how you color correct your photos. Although it's just two simple changes, don't underestimate their impact—this is important stuff.

Step One:

Go to the Toolbox and click on the Eyedropper tool (or just press the letter I). If you look up in the Options Bar, you'll see that the default Sample Size setting for this tool is Point Sample. The problem with this setting is it gives you a reading from just one individual pixel, rather than giving you an average of the area where you're clicking (which is much more accurate for color correction purposes). To fix this, go up to the Options Bar, and change the Sample Size pop-up menu to 3 by 3 Average (as shown here). By the way, if you're working on super-high-resolution images, in CS3 Adobe added larger sampling areas, like 5x5, 11x11, 31x31, and on up to 101x101.

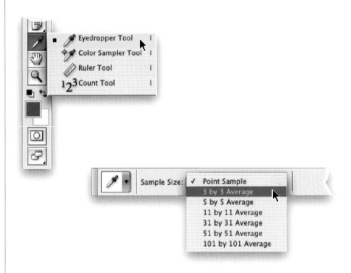

Step Two:

Although having a colorful desktop background is fine when we're working in Photoshop, you'll rarely find a professional doing color correction with a colorful desktop background because it changes how you perceive color (and that will influence how you color correct your photos). Ideally, you'd use a neutral gray background, and to get one, just press the letter F once. This centers your photo onscreen with a neutral gray background behind it. To return to regular mode, press the letter F three more times. Okay, now you're ready.

SCOTT KELBY

As far as digital technology has come, there's still one thing that digital cameras won't do: give you perfect color every time. In fact, if they gave us perfect color 50% of the time, that would be incredible; but unfortunately, every digital camera (and every scanner) sneaks in some kind of color cast in your image. Generally, it's a red cast, but depending on the camera, it could be blue. Either way, you can be pretty sure there's a cast. (Think of it this way: if there weren't, the term "color correction" wouldn't be used.) Here's how to get your color in line:

Color Correcting Digital Camera Images

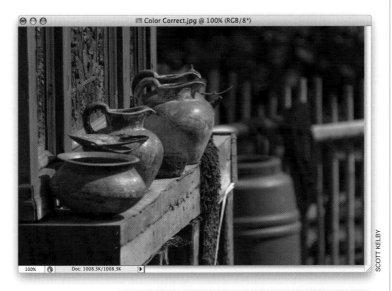

Step One:
Open the RGB photo you want to color correct. (The photo shown here doesn't look all that bad, but as we go through the correction process, you'll see that, like most photos, it really needed a correction.)

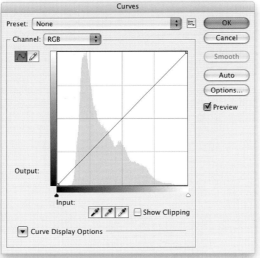

Step Two:
Go under the Image menu, under Adjustments, and choose Curves (or press Command-M [PC: Ctrl-M]). Curves is the hands-down choice of professionals for correcting color because it gives you a greater level of control than other tools, like Levels, where you pretty much are limited to just three adjustment sliders. The Curves dialog may look intimidating at first, but the technique you're going to learn here requires no previous knowledge of Curves, and it's so easy, you'll be correcting photos using Curves immediately.

Continued

Step Three:

First, we need to set some preferences in the Curves dialog so we'll get the results we want when color correcting. We'll start by setting a target color for our shadow areas. To set this preference, in the Curves dialog, double-click on the black Eyedropper tool (the Eyedroppers are found below the center of the curve grid, and the shadow Eyedropper is the first Eyedropper from the left [the one half-filled with black], as shown here).

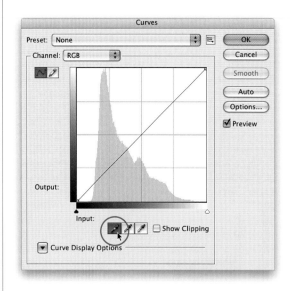

Step Four:

When you double-click on that shadow Eyedropper, it brings up the Color Picker asking you to select your target shadow color. This is where you'll enter some new RGB numbers that will help remove any color casts your camera introduced in the shadow areas of your photo. We're going to enter values in the R, G, and B (Red, Green, and Blue) fields of this dialog (the Red field is highlighted here).

For R, enter 10
For G, enter 10
For B, enter 10

Now click OK to save these numbers as your target shadow settings. Because these figures are evenly balanced (they're all the same number) it helps ensure that your shadow areas won't have too much of one color (which is exactly what causes a color cast—too much of one color), and by using 10 we get dark shadows while still maintaining shadow detail in our prints.

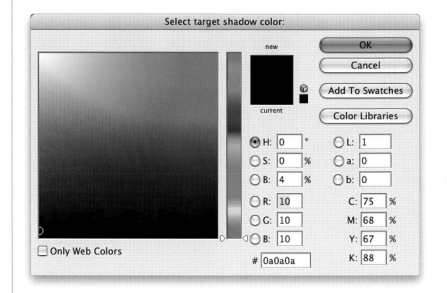

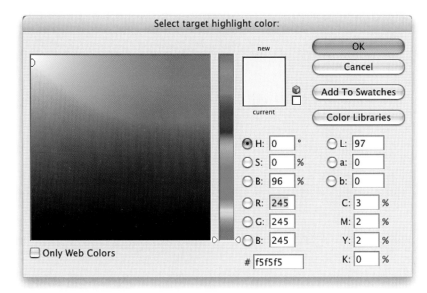

Step Five:

Now we'll set a preference to make our highlight areas neutral. Double-click on the white Eyedropper (the third of the three Eyedroppers at the bottom of the Curves dialog). The Color Picker will appear asking you to Select Target Highlight Color. Click in the R field, and then enter these values (*Note:* To move from field to field, just press the Tab key):

For R, enter 245
For G, enter 245
For B, enter 245

Click OK to set those values as your highlight target.

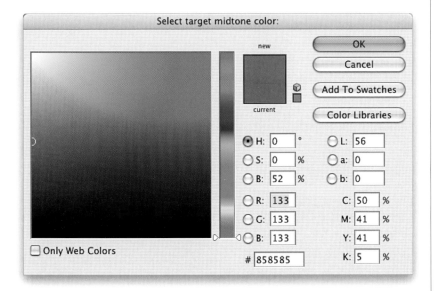

Step Six:

Now, set your midtone preference. You know the drill: Double-click on the midtone Eyedropper (the middle of the three Eyedroppers) so you can Select Target Midtone Color. Enter these values in the RGB fields:

For R, enter 133
For G, enter 133
For B, enter 133

Then click OK to set those values as your midtone target. That's it—you've done all the hard work. The rest from here on out is pretty easy.

Continued

Step Seven:

If you still have the Curves dialog open, click OK to exit it for now, and you'll get a warning dialog asking you if you want to Save the New Target Colors as Defaults. Click Yes (as shown here), and from this point on, you won't have to enter these values each time you correct a photo, because they'll already be entered for you—they're now the default settings. So, the next time you color correct a photo, you can skip these seven steps and go straight to the correcting.

Step Eight:

Okay, now that you've entered your preferences (target colors) in the Curves dialog, you're going to use these same Curves Eyedropper tools (shown here) to do most of your color correction work. In a nutshell, here's what you'll do with those three Eyedroppers:

(1) Find something in your photo that you know is supposed to be the color black. If you can't find something black, find the darkest area in your photo and convert that area to your target shadow color by clicking on that area once with the shadow Eyedropper.

(2) Find something in your photo that you know is supposed to be the color white. If you can't find something white, find the brightest area in your photo and convert that area to your target highlight color by clicking on that area once with the highlight Eyedropper.

(3) Find a neutral gray area in your photo and convert that to your target midtone color by clicking on that area once with the midtone Eyedropper.

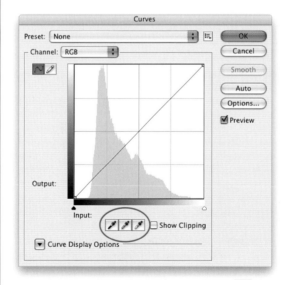

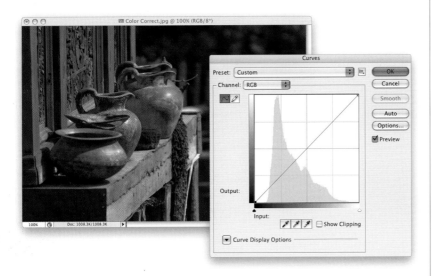

Step Nine:

Let's start by setting the shadows first, so press Command-M (PC: Ctrl-M) to bring back up the Curves dialog (shown here). Now, your job is to look at the photo and find something that's supposed to be the color black. In most photos, this won't be a problem—you'll see a dark area of shadows (like behind the pots and pitchers in this photo), or a black car tire, or someone wearing a black shirt, etc., and in those cases it's no sweat. But, if you can't find something that's supposed to be the color black, then you can have Photoshop show you exactly where the darkest part of the photo is.

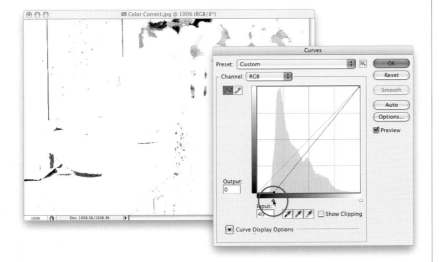

Step 10:

There are two sliders directly under the curve grid that can help you. Press-and-hold the Option (PC: Alt) key and click on the left (Shadow) slider, and your image area turns solid white (as seen here). As you drag slider to the right (while still holding that Option/Alt key down), the first areas that appear onscreen are the darkest parts of your photo. That's Photoshop telling you exactly where to click, so remember where those areas are (in this case, it's the shadow under the first pot on the left).

Continued

Step 11:

Now that you know where your shadow area is, drag that Shadow slider back to the left, and release the Option (PC: Alt) key. Now, click on the shadow Eyedropper, move out over your photo (while the Curves dialog is still open), and click once on that shadow area. In this case, click on the shadows below that first pot from the left (as shown here), and it converts your shadow areas to a neutral shadow color, and the color cast is removed from the shadow areas (compare this photo with the one in Step Nine and you'll see the difference this one click makes).

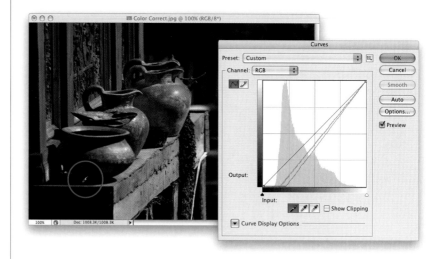

TIP: When you click in that shadow area, three new lines appear in your curve, showing how the Red, Green, and Blue channels were affected by your move. This is a new feature in CS3, and although some users love it, some find it really distracting. If you'd like those channel lines turned off, just click on the triangle next to Curve Display Options at the bottom left of the Curves dialog, then turn off the checkbox for Channel Overlays (as shown here).

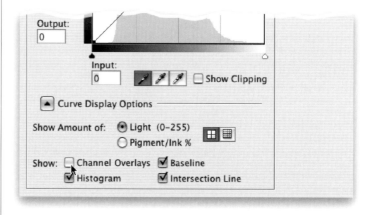

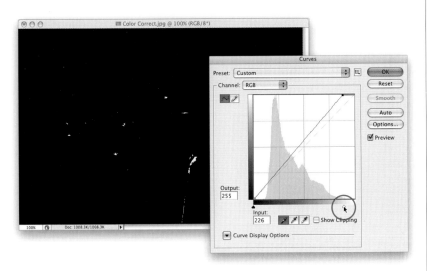

Step 12:

Now, on to setting the highlight point. Your job: find something that's supposed to be the color white. Again, this is usually pretty easy, but if you can't find something white, you can use the same trick you just learned to have Photoshop show you where the lightest part of your photo is. Press-and-hold the Option (PC: Alt) key, but this time drag the far-right slider to the left. The screen turns black (as shown here), and as you drag to the left the first white areas that appear are the lightest parts of your image.

Step 13:

Now that you know where your highlight area is, drag that Highlight slider back all the way to the right, and release the Option (PC: Alt) key. Now, click on the highlight Eyedropper, move out over your photo, and click once on that highlight area. I try and look for a white area that has some detail (rather than clicking on what's called a specular highlight, which is a blown out highlight area with no detail, like the sun, or a bright sun reflection on a chrome car bumper, etc.). In this case, I clicked on the white painted area to the right of the dark blue netting (as shown here), and that makes your highlight areas neutral and removes any color cast in your highlights (we're only two clicks into this correction, and look how much better the photo already looks).

Continued

Step 14:

Now for your third click—finding something that's supposed to be a neutral gray. This one's a little trickier, because not every photo has a neutral gray area, and the Curves dialog doesn't have a "find the gray" trick like it does for shadows and highlights, but never fear—there's a project coming up in this chapter that shows you a way to find that neutral area every time. In the example we're working on, finding an area that's supposed to be a neutral gray isn't a problem—you can click on the edge of the large vase on the ground (as I did here). It neutralizes the color cast in the midtones, and as you can see here, it removed that lingering reddish color cast that was still there after neutralizing the highlights and shadows.

Step 15:

Before you click OK, you're going to use Curves to increase the overall contrast in the photo (in fact, it's the best way to increase contrast in Photoshop). Plus, it's easy: (1) first, click once right in the very center of the grid to add a point; (2) then, click above and to the right of the center, right along the line, where the gray grid lines intersect with the diagonal line; and (3) add one more point on the line, where the lines intersect at the bottom quarter (as shown here).

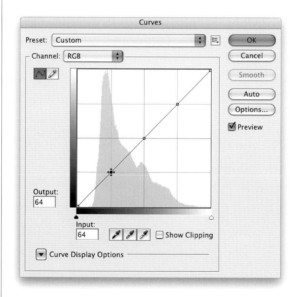

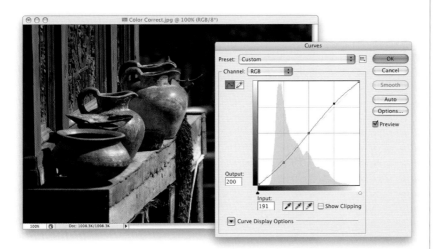

Step 16:

Now, while the bottom-left point is selected, press the Down Arrow key on your keyboard eight or nine times, to move that point of the curve downward, which increases the contrast in the shadow areas. Then, click on the top-right point, but now press the Up Arrow key on your keyboard eight or nine times, to increase the contrast in the highlights. Moving the top point up and the bottom point down like this steepens the curve and adds more contrast. Now you can click OK, and you're done.

Before

After

Drag-and-Drop Instant Color Correction

This is a wonderful timesaving trick for quickly correcting an entire group of photos that have similar lighting. It's ideal for studio shots, where the lighting conditions are controlled, but works equally well for outdoor shots, or really any situation where the lighting for your group of shots is fairly consistent. Once you try this, you'll use it again and again.

Step One:

First, here's a tip within a step: If you're opening a group of photos from Adobe Bridge CS3, you don't have to open them one by one. Just press-and-hold the Command (PC: Ctrl) key and click on all the photos you want to open. (If all your photos are consecutive, press-and-hold the Shift key and click on the first and last photo in the window to select them all.) Then, double-click on any one of your selected photos and the images will open in Photoshop. So now that you know that tip, go ahead and open at least three or four images, just to get started.

Step Two:

At the bottom of the Layers panel, there's an icon with a pop-up menu for adding adjustment layers (it's the half-white/half-black circle icon). Click on it and choose Curves. There are a number of advantages to having this correction applied as a layer, as you'll soon see, but the main advantage is that you can edit or delete this tonal adjustment at any time while you're working, plus you can save this adjustment with your file as a layer.

Step Three:
When you choose this adjustment layer, the regular Curves dialog appears, just like always. Go ahead and make your corrections to your topmost open image, just as you did in the previous tutorial (setting highlights, midtones, shadows, etc.). When your correction looks good, click OK.

TIP: In Photoshop CS3, Adobe greatly improved the results you get from the Brightness/Contrast controls (Adobe must have realized that despite all efforts to get people to stop using it, and use Curves or Levels instead, many people were still using it). Now the controls actually maintain better highlight and shadow detail, and the Contrast slider now gives you more of an S-curve contrast like you'd get using Curves, so it's much improved. However, if you liked the old way it worked (please tell me you didn't like the old way), you can return to the old method by turning on the Use Legacy checkbox, and the two sliders will then make everything look yucky and awful again—just like before.

Step Four:
In the Layers panel, you'll see that a new Curves 1 adjustment layer was created (if you can't read the Layers panel, expand its width by clicking-and-dragging on the very bottom-right corner of the panel). Because you applied this correction as an adjustment layer, you can treat this adjustment just like a regular layer, right? Right! So now we'll apply this Curves adjustment to your other open images.

Continued

Step Five:

Since Photoshop lets you drag-and-drop layers between open documents, go to the Layers panel and simply drag this layer right onto one of your other open photos. That photo will instantly have the same correction applied to it. This technique works because you're correcting photos that share similar lighting conditions. Need to correct 12 photos? Just drag-and-drop it 12 times (making it the fastest correction in town!). In the example shown here, I've dragged-and-dropped that Curves adjustment layer onto one of the other open photos.

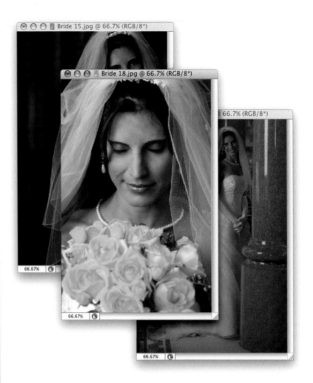

Step Six:

Okay, what if one of the "dragged corrections" doesn't look right? That's the beauty of adjustment layers; just double-click directly on the adjustment layer thumbnail for that photo and the Curves dialog will reappear with the last settings you applied still in place. You can then adjust this individual photo separately from the rest. Try this dragging-and-dropping-adjustment-layers trick once, and you'll use it again and again to save time when correcting a digital roll with similar lighting conditions.

If you're shooting in a studio, whether it be portraits or products, there's a technique you can use that makes the color-correction process so easy that you'll be able to train laboratory test rats to correct photos for you. In the back of this book, I've included a color swatch card (it's perforated so you can easily tear it out). After you get your studio lighting set the way you want it, and you're ready to start shooting, just put this swatch card into your shot (just once) and take the shot. What does this do for you? You'll see.

Studio Portrait Correction Made Simple

Step One:
When you're ready to start shooting and the lighting is set the way you want it, tear out the swatch card from the back of this book and place it within your shot (if you're shooting a portrait, have the subject hold the card for you), and then take the shot. After you've got one shot with the swatch card, you can remove it and continue with the rest of your shoot.

Step Two:
When you open the first photo taken in your studio session, you'll see the swatch card in the photo. By having a card that's pure white, neutral gray, and pure black in your photo, you no longer have to try to determine which area of your photo is supposed to be black (to set the shadows), which area is supposed to be gray (to set the midtones), or which area is supposed to be white (to set the highlights). They're right there in the card.

Continued

Step Three:

Press Command-M (PC: Ctrl-M) to bring up the Curves dialog. Click the black Eyedropper on the black panel of the card to set the shadows (as shown here), then click the middle gray Eyedropper on the darker gray panel to set the midtones.

Step Four:

Finally, click the white Eyedropper on the white panel to set the highlights, and the photo will nearly correct itself. No guessing, no Threshold adjustment layers, no using the Info palette to determine the darkest areas of the image—now you know exactly which part of that image should be black and which should be white. Once you have the Curves setting for the first image, you can correct the rest of the photos using the exact same curve: Just open the next photo and press Command-Option-M (PC: Ctrl-Alt-M) to apply the exact same curve to this photo that you did to the swatch card photo. Or, you can use the drag-and-drop color-correction method I showed in the previous tutorial.

Finding a neutral midtone while color correcting has always been kind of tricky. Well, it was until Dave Cross, who works with me as Senior Developer of Education for the National Association of Photoshop Professionals (NAPP), came into my office one day to show me his amazing trick for finding right where the midtones live in just about any image. When he showed me, I immediately blacked out. After I came to, I begged Dave to let me share his very slick trick in my book, and being the friendly Canadian he is, he obliged.

Dave's Amazing Trick for Finding a Neutral Gray

Step One:
Open any color photo, and click on the Create a New Layer icon at the bottom of the Layers panel to create a new blank layer. Then, go under the Edit menu and choose Fill. When the Fill dialog appears, in the Contents section, under the Use pop-up menu, choose 50% Gray (as shown here).

Step Two:
When you click OK, it fills your layer with (you guessed it) 50% gray (you can see the gray thumbnail for Layer 1 in the Layers panel shown here). Now, go to the Layers panel and change the blend mode of this layer to Difference (as shown here). Changing the layer blend mode to Difference doesn't do much for the look of your photo (as you can see here), but don't worry—it's only temporary.

Continued

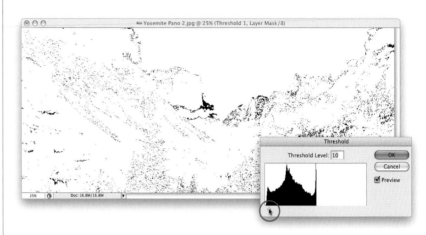

Step Three:

Choose Threshold from the Create New Adjustment Layer pop-up menu at the bottom of the Layers panel. When the dialog appears, drag the slider all the way to the left (your photo will turn completely white). Now, slowly drag the slider back to the right, and the first areas that appear in black are the neutral midtones. In the center of this photo is a decent-sized area of black, so that will be our midtone correction point. To help you remember exactly where that area is, hold the Shift key, move your cursor out over that spot, and click once to add a Color Sampler tool point just as a reminder. Then click the Cancel button in the Threshold dialog.

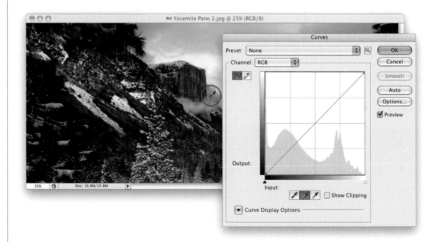

Step Four:

Now that your midtone point is marked, go back to the Layers panel and drag the 50% gray layer onto the Trash icon to delete it (it already did its job, so you can get rid of it). You'll see your full-color photo again. Now, press Command-M (PC: Ctrl-M) to open Curves, get the midtones Eyedropper (it's the middle Eyedropper), and click directly on that Color Sampler point (shown circled in red here).

Step Five:
That's it; you've found the neutral midtones and corrected any color cast within them (in this case, it removed the red color cast, and made the trees look greener). So, will this trick work every time? It works most of the time, but you will run across photos that just don't have a neutral midtone, so you'll have to either not correct the midtones or go back to what we used to do—guess.

Adjusting RGB Flesh Tones

So what do you do if you've used Curves to properly set the highlights, midtones, and shadows, but the flesh tones in your photo still look too red? Try this quick trick that works great for getting your flesh tones in line by removing the excess red.

Step One:

Open a photo that you've corrected using the Curves technique shown earlier in this chapter. If the whole image appears too red, skip this step and go on to Step Three. However, if it's just the flesh-tone areas that appear too red, press L to get the Lasso tool and make a selection around all the flesh-tone areas in your photo. Press-and-hold the Shift key to add other flesh-tone areas to the selection, such as arms, hands, legs, etc., or press-and-hold the Option (PC: Alt) key to subtract from your selection. This can be a really loose selection like the one shown in Step Two (which doesn't include her ears or neck).

Step Two:

Go under the Select menu, under Modify and choose Feather. Enter a Feather Radius of 3 pixels (as shown here), and then click OK. By adding this feather, you're softening the edges of your selection, which will keep you from having a hard, visible edge show up where you made your adjustment.

TIP: Once you've made a selection of the flesh-tone areas, you might find it easier if you hide the selection border from view (that makes it easier to see what you're correcting) by pressing Command-H (PC: Ctrl-H).

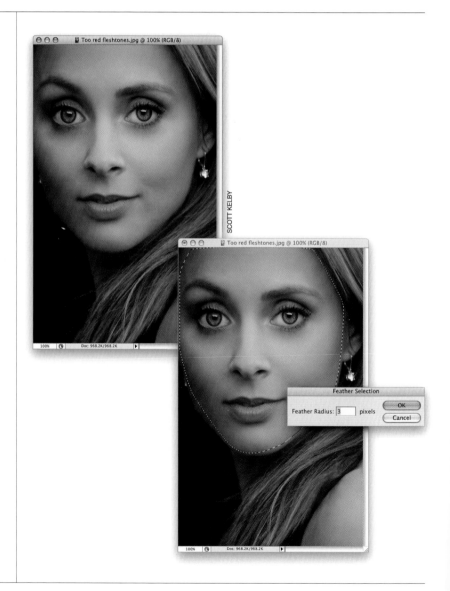

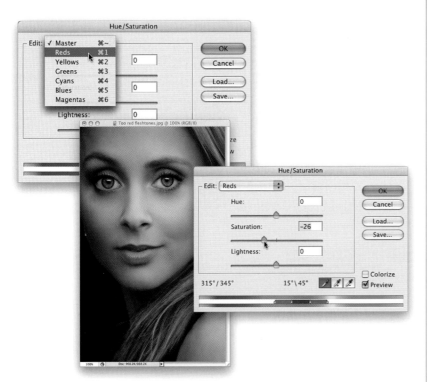

Step Three:

Go under the Image menu, under Adjustments, and choose Hue/ Saturation. When the dialog appears, click-and-hold on the Edit pop-up menu and choose Reds, so you're only adjusting the reds in your photo in your selected areas (if you put a selection around just the flesh tones).

Step Four:

The rest is easy—you're simply going to reduce the amount of saturation so the flesh tones appear more natural. Drag the Saturation slider to the left to reduce the amount of red. You'll be able to see the effect of removing the red as you lower the Saturation slider. When it looks good to you, click OK in the dialog, and then press Command-D (PC: Ctrl-D) to Deselect, completing the technique.

Before

After

Color Correcting One Problem Area Fast!

This particular technique really comes in handy when shooting outdoor scenes, because it lets you enhance the color in one particular area of the photo (like the sky or water), while leaving the rest of the photo untouched. Real estate photographers often use this trick when shooting home exteriors to make it look like the sky was bright and sunny when they took the shot (even though the weather doesn't always cooperate). Here you'll use the technique to make the grayish sky look blue.

Step One:
Open an image containing an area of color that you would like to enhance. In this example, we want to make the sky blue (rather than gray). Go to the Layers panel and choose Color Balance from the Create New Adjustment Layer pop-up menu at the bottom of the panel (it's the half-white/half-black circle icon, fourth from the left). A new adjustment layer named Color Balance 1 will be added to your Layers panel, but the name will probably be cut off by default. If you want to see the layer's name, you'll have to widen your Layers panel by clicking-and-dragging its bottom-right corner.

Step Two:
When the Color Balance dialog appears, drag the top slider to the left toward Cyan to add some bright blue into your sky, and then drag the bottom slider to the right toward Blue until the sky looks as blue as you'd like it. When the sky looks good to you, click OK. When you do this, the entire photo (hills, mountains, and all) will have a heavy blue cast to it.

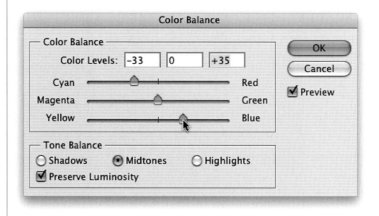

Step Three:

Press Command-I (PC: Ctrl-I) to fill your adjustment layer's mask with black, as shown here (you're just inverting the mask, which was white, so now it's black). This solid black mask hides the blue and cyan adjustments you made in the Color Balance dialog, so now the sky looks gray again.

Step Four:

Now you'll reveal parts of the blue/cyan Color Balance adjustment layer using the Brush tool. Make sure your Foreground color is white. Press B to switch to the Brush tool, and then in the Options Bar, click on the thumbnail to the right of the word "Brush" and choose a large, soft-edged brush from the Brush Picker. Begin painting over the sky and as you paint, the blue version is revealed. If you make a mistake (like painting over the ground), press the X key to toggle your Foreground to black, and the original color will reappear where you paint.

Before

After

Keeping Great Color When You Email or Post Photos to the Web

Email applications (and nearly all Web browsers) don't support color management. So, if you're working in Adobe RGB (1998) or ProPhoto RGB as your Photoshop color space, when you email your photos or post them on the Web, they probably look like %$*# (with the colors all desaturated and flat-looking). Ah, if only there was a trick that would let anyone you email (or anybody who sees your photos on the Web) see your photos pretty much the same way you do in Photoshop (of course, there is—I just wish I knew it. Kidding!) Here ya go:

Step One:
To convert this photo for the proper color space for emailing or posting to the Web, go under the Edit menu and choose Convert to Profile. This brings up the Convert to Profile dialog (shown here). The Source Space at the top shows you the current color space your photo is in (if you're working in Adobe RGB [1998], like in this example, that's what you'll see here). For your Destination Space (what you're converting to), choose sRGB IEC61966-2.1 from the Profile pop-up menu (as shown here) and click OK. That's it—it's ready to go.

Step Two:
One quick way to ensure that your photo has been converted to sRGB is to look at the window's title bar. If you've got Photoshop's color space set to Adobe RGB (1998), which is pretty typical for photographers, and you just converted this photo to a different color space (sRGB), then you have a "profile mismatch." So, you should see an asterisk right after (RGB/8) in the title bar (like this: RGB/8*), which is Photoshop's way of letting you know that your photo is one space, and Photoshop is in another. In this case, that's a good thing.

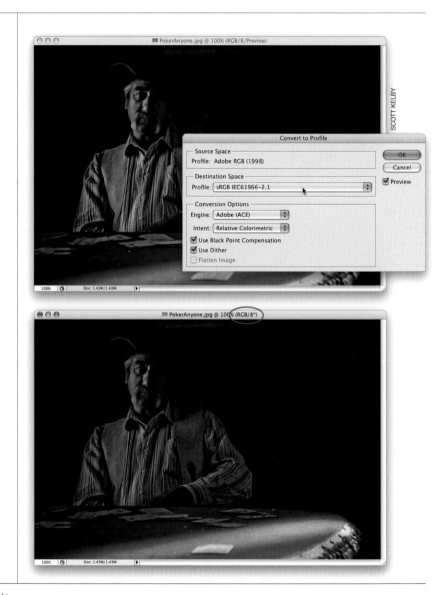

Exposure: 1/400s | Focal Length: 280mm | Aperture Value: ƒ/4.5

Black & White World
how to create stunning b&w images

If you search the iTunes Store for "Black & White" you will be stunned at how many songs are named exactly that—"Black & White." In fact, if I just wanted to stay with the chapter title "Black & White" (like I did back in the CS2 book), then I'd be pretty much covered until about Photoshop CS46. However, for some reason I was drawn to "Black and White World" by Elvis Costello. I almost went with "Black Widow" by Mötley Crüe, but I noticed that the song was tagged with the iTunes Store "Clean" icon, which means there must also be an "Explicit" version, too. Now, you know, and I know, that when you search for "Black Widow" on the iTunes Store, you're going to listen to the explicit version, right? See, I knew it! And I'm sure that explicit version is laden with words so naughty that you'd normally have to listen to an Andrew Dice Clay show just to keep up, but somehow

when Vince Neil sings them, they don't sound as naughty. They sound beautiful, and melodic, with meaning, texture, and a certain poetic charm to them. Aw, who am I trying to kid? It's super-dirty naughtiness, but you don't even care. You know why? Because you're a photographer, which means that at least one time in your career you did a client shoot where some setting in the camera was horribly wrong, but you didn't realize it until you opened the images later in Photoshop. It was at that moment you learned that the entire shoot was done with your camera set to JPEG Basic mode, with your image size set to Small. Right then you started screaming expletives that would make Snoop Dogg wash your mouth out with soap. So, the next time this happens, just pop in that Crüe song and let Vince do the cussing on your behalf. Apparently, he's quite comfortable with it.

The Lightness Channel Method

If you've ever converted a color photo to black and white by going under the Image menu, under Mode, and choosing Grayscale, my guess is the very next thing you did was look for a better method, because that method produces the flattest, lamest, blahest (insert your own "est" adjective here) B&W photo ever. Since the beginning of Photoshop time, we've been looking for a better way. I'm starting here with the easiest method, which uses the Lightness channel from Lab color mode, and gives a better black and white on even its worst day.

Step One:
Open the color photo that you want to convert to grayscale using the Lightness channel method. Now, you might want to duplicate this photo (under the Image menu, just choose Duplicate), and go ahead and convert this duplicate to black and white by going under the Image menu, under Mode, and choosing Grayscale. That way, you have a reference of how flat and uninspired this B&W conversion can be.

Step Two:
Go under the Image menu, under Mode, and choose Lab Color to convert your RGB photo into Lab color mode. You won't see a visual difference between the RGB photo and the Lab color photo—the difference is in the channels that make up your color photo (as you'll see in a moment).

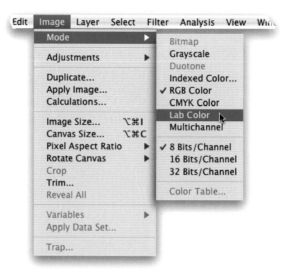

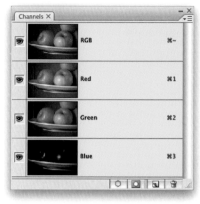

Regular RGB image

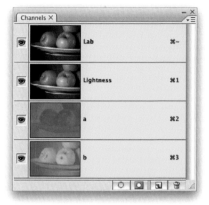

Converted to Lab color

Step Three:
Go to the Channels panel (found under the Window menu), and you'll see that your photo is no longer made up of a Red, a Green, and a Blue channel. Instead, the luminosity (detail) of the photo has been separated from the color data, which now resides in two channels named "a" and "b." That luminosity is called the Lightness channel in Lab color mode, and it generally has lots of nice highlight detail, so it makes a pretty attractive starting place for making a B&W conversion.

Step Four:
Click on the Lightness channel in the Channels panel to make it active. Now you're seeing just the Lightness channel, and as you can see here—it doesn't look too bad. A little light maybe, but it's not totally flat and lifeless like the conversion you did to the duplicate photo in Step One.

Continued

Step Five:

Now, go under the Image menu, under Mode, and choose Grayscale (it's okay to do this now, because clicking on that Lightness channel has already told Photoshop what you're going to use for your B&W photo). Photoshop will bring up a warning dialog (seen here) asking if you want to discard the other channels (the two color channels—"a" and "b"— and your full-color Lab channel). Click OK. If you look in the Channels panel, you'll now see only a Gray channel.

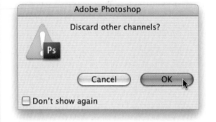

Step Six:

Take a look at your B&W photo now, and see if you think it's too light (which is fairly likely) or too dark (which can also be the case, depending on the photo). If it's too light, go to the Layers panel, click on the Background layer, and then press Command-J (PC: Ctrl-J) to duplicate the Background layer. To make this layer darker, change the layer blend mode to Multiply (as shown here). In our example, changing that top layer to Multiply mode made the photo a bit too dark, but don't sweat it—it's just a starting point.

Note: If your photo looks too dark, then instead you'd switch the layer blend mode from Normal to Screen, and you'd see the photo become much lighter.

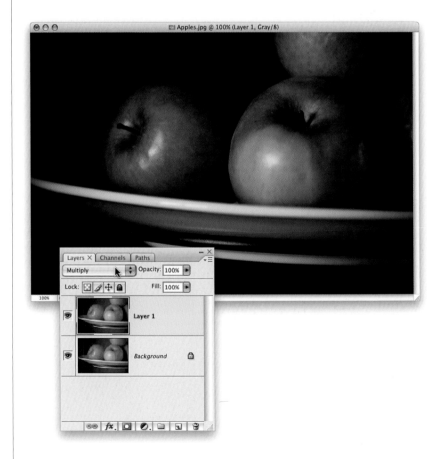

Step Seven:

This is where you get to "dial in" your ideal B&W tone. Just lower the Opacity of your Multiply layer in the Layers panel until you have the tonal balance you've been looking for (as shown here, where I lowered the Opacity to 65%, which gave me richer shadows to complement my nice highlights from the Lightness channel we used earlier). Besides being just plain easy, this Lab color method gives you more control and depth than just converting to Grayscale mode ever could (as seen below).

Standard grayscale conversion

Lab color Lightness channel conversion

Using CS3's New Black & White Converter

The Channel Mixer had become quite popular for creating B&W conversions, because you could control the amount of the Red, Green, and Blue channels separately, since it never left RGB mode (it just removed the color). In CS3, there's now a dedicated tool for B&W conversions, and while it's probably better than the Channel Mixer (it adds sliders for adjusting Magenta, Yellow, and Cyan), and it's more fun to use, I still feel I can get better, more predictable results using some of the other methods in this chapter. Give it a try and see what you think.

Step One:

Open the color photo you want to convert to black and white. Choose Black & White from the Create New Adjustment Layer pop-up menu at the bottom of the Layers panel (it's the half-black/half-white circle icon). Black & White is also found under the Image menu, under Adjustments; however, by applying it as an adjustment layer, it's non-destructive (you can edit your conversion later, paint [mask] over parts that you don't want black and white, lower the opacity for a faded-color look, or you can delete the adjustment layer, and return to your full-color photo).

Step Two:

When the Black and White dialog opens, it applies its default B&W conversion (seen here), which isn't nearly as flat a conversion as you'd get by going under the Image menu, under Mode, and choosing Grayscale, but it's not a real great starting point either. If you notice, the percentage of each group of two colors (Reds and Yellows for example) adds up to 100%. That's fine if your goal is to maintain the same brightness in the photo, but most photographers want that rich high-contrast B&W look, which means your numbers will probably add up to more than 100%. Don't let that freak you out.

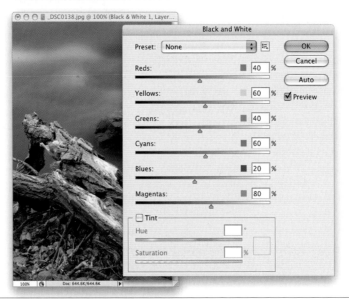

Step Three:

At the top of the Black and White dialog, there's a pop-up menu with presets put there by Adobe (as shown here). Go ahead and give these a try and see what you think (my guess is you'll think they're pretty lame. In fact, I haven't found one of those presets that looks good for any photo I've applied it to, but hey, that's just me). I think the real advantage of the Preset pop-up menu is saving your own custom presets. If you come up with a combination and you'd like to add your custom preset to this pop-up menu, just click on that little square icon to the immediate right of the Preset pop-up menu and choose Save Preset. Then give your preset a name, and it will now appear in this pop-up menu.

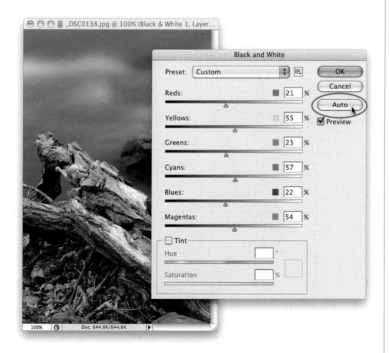

Step Four:

After you've tried the presets, choose None from the top of the Preset pop-up menu to return to the default B&W conversion. Luckily, there is an Auto button (shown circled in red here), which does an auto-B&W conversion. I think it tends to give better results than the default conversion or any of the presets, so go ahead and click on it, and use it as a starting point for your conversion (of course, you could just click Auto and be done with it, but you're really not one of those "Auto" people, are you? I didn't think so. You're a tweaker, aren't you? I knew it—I knew it! Okay, then you'll really love the next step, because it's the most fun part of this process).

Continued

Step Five:

Since you're now seeing the photo in black and white, it's a little challenging figuring out which color slider will affect which area, and that's one of the problems with the old Channel Mixer—it was somewhat of a guessing game. Just like here, you could toggle the Preview checkbox on and off, and you could peek at the color photo for a moment, so you could make an educated guess as to which color would adjust what in your B&W photo. Thankfully, there's a better way: move your cursor outside the Black and White dialog, and go out over the area in your photo you want to adjust (as shown here). Now click-and-drag to the left to darken the area where you're at, or click-and-drag to the right to lighten that area. Your cursor knows which colors are below it, and it moves just the color sliders that would affect that particular area. Very slick.

Step Six:

So, that's what you'll do from here on out. This is the way I work with this Black and White dialog all the time. The only difference is, once I see which slider is adjusting the colors where I clicked, I sometimes go over and manually drag that slider a little just to tweak it, as shown here. Also, sometimes you'll drag left (or right), and the change will be very subtle. In those cases, I go straight to the slider itself and drag it all the way to the left, then back all the way to right. That way I can clearly see which areas in the photo are being adjusted, and whether it's worth even bothering with. I think the photo looks better here, after dragging in different parts of it, and as you can see, some of the numbers add up to more than 100%. Yet, I'm still able to sleep at night.

Step Seven:

So far the advantages over the Channel Mixer are: (1) being able to save presets, (2) the Auto conversion button, (3) there are three more sliders of control—not just Red, Green, and Blue, and (4) you can interactively adjust areas by clicking-and-dragging your cursor left or right directly on the photo. The final advantage over the Channel Mixer is the ability to apply a tint for an instant duotone effect. Just turn on the Tint checkbox at the bottom-left corner of the dialog, and it applies a tint to your photo. By default, the Saturation amount is set pretty high, so just drag the Saturation slider to the left to reduce the amount of saturation until it looks about right (as shown here). So, although it's not my favorite B&W conversion method, it does have its advantages over the Channel Mixer alone.

Standard grayscale conversion

CS3's new Black & White conversion

Step Five:

Once you're back at this Gradient Editor dialog, and your color stop is now gray, you can drag that middle gray stop around to adjust the tone of your image (as shown here). What's weird is you drag the opposite way that the gradient shows. For example, to darken the photo, you drag to the right, toward the white end of the gradient, and to lighten the photo, you drag left toward the dark end. Freaky, I know. One other thing: unlike almost every other slider in all of Photoshop, as you drag that color stop, you *do not* get a live preview of what's happening—you have to release the mouse button and then it shows you the results of your dragging. Click OK twice, and you're done.

Step Six:

Here's one of the two variations I talked about in the introduction for this technique: just go to the Layers panel and lower the Opacity of your Gradient Map adjustment layer to 80%. This bleeds back in a little of the color, and gives a really nice subtle "wash" effect (compare this slightly-colored photo with the full-color photo in Step One, and you'll see what I mean. It's kinda nice, isn't it? Okay, now raise it back up to 100% for the second variation, which is also a second version of your B&W conversion.

Step Seven:

For this version, go to the Layers panel and click on the Background layer, which is still in color. If you remove the color from that Background layer, you'd get a somewhat different conversion, right? Right! So, once you've clicked on the Background layer, press Command-Shift-U (PC: Ctrl-Shift-U), which is the shortcut for the Desaturate command (it's found under the Image menu, under Adjustments). This removes the color and gives you a different look (although the change is fairly subtle with this photo, with some photos it's pretty dramatic—it just depends on the photo). But, either way, wouldn't you rather choose between two B&W conversions and then pick your favorite? If you don't like this other look, just press Command-Z (PC: Ctrl-Z) to Undo it.

Regular grayscale conversion

Scott's high-contrast B&W conversion

Regular grayscale conversion

B&W conversion using Calculations

I taught a week-long hands-on class last year at the Santa Fe Workshops out in Santa Fe, New Mexico (by the way, it's an incredibly well-run training experience— highly recommended), and my students learned a number of techniques for converting to black and white. However, by the end of the week, my students were shooting exclusively in RAW, and once I showed this simple B&W conversion in Camera Raw, this is pretty much all they used. Of course, in CS3, you can now use Camera Raw on JPEG and TIFF photos, too—so here ya go!

Black and White in Camera Raw

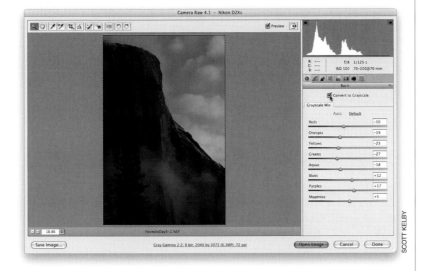

Step One:

Open the RAW color photo you want to convert. When the Camera Raw dialog opens, go to the HSL/Grayscale panel and turn on the Convert to Grayscale checkbox, as shown here. This gives a pretty flat-looking conversion, but you're only about three sliders away from a great conversion. (*Note:* If you're not shooting in RAW, you can still open your JPEG or TIFF photos in Camera Raw, just choose Open [PC: Open As] from Photoshop's File Menu, then navigate to the JPEG or TIFF you want to open. When you find the photo, click on it, then from the Format [PC: Open As] pop-up menu choose Camera Raw and your photo will open in Adobe Camera Raw, as seen here. Of course, this actually is a RAW photo, but you get the idea, right? Cool.)

Step Two:

Go back to the Basic panel and drag the Exposure slider as far to the right as you can without clipping any highlights. To do that, turn on the highlight clipping warning by clicking once on the top-right triangle up in the histogram. While you're dragging the slider to the right, if any part of your photo turns red—stop! Then drag the Recovery slider to the right to recover those clipped highlights (as shown here).

Continued

Step Three:

Now go to the Blacks slider and drag to the right to make the shadow areas really nice and rich. It's okay if you clip a little of the shadow areas—just make sure they're not areas of critical detail. In our example, the shadow clipping mostly occurs in the shadowy crevices on the face of the mountain, and in the darkest shadow areas of the tree in the foreground, so I'm not losing enough to worry about. Remember—clipping by itself isn't a bad thing—as long as it's not a critical detail area.

Step Four:

Lastly, to add that little bit of "pop" to our photo, click on the second icon on the top right of the dialog to go to the Tone Curve panel. Click on the Point tab and then choose Strong Contrast from the Curve pop-up menu (as shown here). It doesn't get much easier than that! Now, if you wanted to tweak this curve a little bit more, you could click once on the second from top point in the curve, then press the Up Arrow key on your keyboard a few times to make the highlight part of the curve a little steeper, which makes the whole photo appear more contrasty (remember—the steeper the curve, the more contrast it creates). You can add even more contrast by clicking on the second to bottom point, and pressing the Down Arrow key a few times. Lastly, if your highlights start to get blown out, click on the Parametric tab, then drag the Lights slider to the left a little bit. Now click Open Image, and you're done.

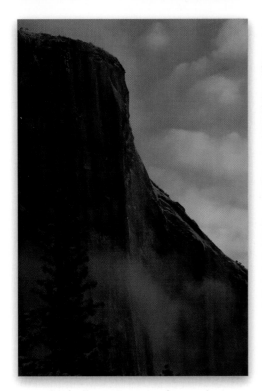

Regular Camera Raw grayscale conversion *High-contrast Camera Raw B&W conversion*

Photo by Scott Kelby

Exposure: 1/160s | Focal Length: 17mm | Aperture Value: ƒ/2.8

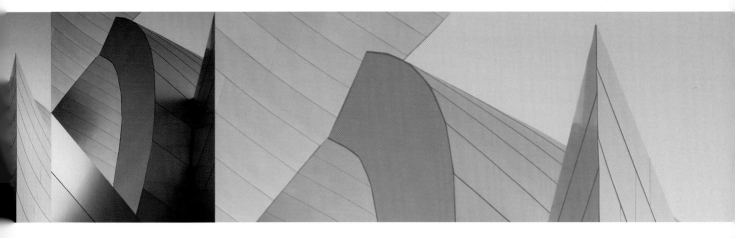

99 Problems
dealing with common digital image problems

Yo, we got some Jay-Z up in the house (that's my sad attempt at trying to sound "street." Seriously, is there nothing sadder than some 40-something guy trying to sound like he's 17 because he's trying to appeal to a demographic with huge amounts of disposable income? That's exactly why I would never stoop to those tactics. Yo dog, I just ain't all that)! Anyway, his song "99 Problems" is actually a pretty decent song, even though when I watched the video in Apple's iTunes, a lot of the words had been blanked out (there were gaps in the vocals—his mouth was moving, but you couldn't hear what he was saying). For example, at one point he says, "In my rear view mirror is…" and then the next few phrases are blanked out. So, I guess we're to form our own conclusions about what Jay-Z was seeing in his rear view mirror. You know what I think he was seeing? I think it was probably a billboard advertising a local dry cleaner, and they had one of those "Spring Cleaning" specials where you get like 20% off when they clean your comforters, blankets, or quilts, and you know they really have to give a pretty decent discount like that because it's already spring, and you won't be using that stuff again until next fall, but then it will be full price, so it's probably good if you take advantage of that discount now. Anyway, I'll bet Jay-Z saw something like that, and since they weren't paying Jay-Z a promotional fee, he wasn't going to give the name of the dry cleaner out—or their special offer—without "gettin' some bank" (dig my street lingo), right? So, in the studio, they probably blanked out that part. Yeah, that's probably what it was. Yo!

Fixing Color in Indoor Shots

You can shoot outside all day and be getting shots that look just great, but step indoors and everything changes. The culprit is Auto white balance (the default setting on digital cameras, and most people never change from this default). With Auto white balance, shooting indoors (like the interior shot shown below) you get what you see here—a photo that looks way too yellow (or if I had shot in an office, where the standard is fluorescent lighting, it would be too blue). You don't have to reach for Curves to fix this—it's simple in Camera Raw (even for JPEGs).

Step One:
Here's the interior photo, taken under standard household lighting (called "tungsten lighting" by photographers, people who sell home lighting for a living, and people who are seriously geeky). In our example, the photo was shot in RAW format, so when you open the photo from Adobe Bridge (or wherever), it opens in the Camera Raw dialog (shown here). Now, you can use Camera Raw to process your JPEG photos (as you'll see in Step Four), but adjusting white balance is one area where you get better results from RAW than from JPEG (as you'll soon see).

Step Two:
Since you took the shot indoors (under tungsten lighting) and you shot in RAW, you can take the easy way out and simply choose Tungsten from the White Balance pop-up menu (as shown here). Just look at the immediate difference (the counters are white again!). By the way, if you had changed your camera's White Balance setting to Tungsten before you took the shot, you wouldn't even be reading this page, so it's worth it to get it right in the camera, rather than having to waste time fixing it later in Photoshop. Hey, I'm sorry—this is "tough love."

Step Three:

After you choose Tungsten, see if the ceiling in the top-right side of the photo doesn't look a little red to you (it did to me). Luckily, that's easy to fix—just go to the Tint slider and drag slowly to the left (as shown here) away from magenta until the reddish look disappears. By the way, if for some reason choosing the Tungsten preset in Camera Raw doesn't look good, then instead set the White Balance pop-up menu back to As Shot, and just drag the Temperature slider to the left until the yellowing goes away.

Step Four:

If you shot in JPEG, to use Camera Raw to adjust your white balance, in the Open (PC: Open As) dialog choose Camera Raw from the Format (PC: Open As) pop-up menu. The problem is there is no Tungsten preset for JPEGs or TIFFs—just As Shot and Auto (neither of which looks good for this photo). So, all you can do is either try to find a neutral gray and click on it with the Eyedropper tool (I didn't have much luck), or you can drag the Temperature slider to the left until the yellowing goes away, and if the reddish look persists, you can drag the Tint slider to the left a little bit. This was as close as I was able to come with a JPEG (you can see on the next page the advantage of RAW in this instance).

Continued

Before

After (adjusting the white balance in Camera Raw)

JPEG (after adjusting the white balance in Camera Raw)

When Your Subject Is in the Shadows

We all wind up shooting subjects that are backlit (where the sun is behind your subject). That's because our eyes automatically adjust to the situation and we see the subject just fine in our viewfinder. The problem is our cameras aren't nearly as sophisticated as our eyes are, so you're almost guaranteed to get some shots where the subject is way too dark when you open them in Photoshop. That's why Shadow/Highlight rocks, and here you'll learn how easy it is to use, and a cool CS3-only trick at the end that makes it non-destructive and totally editable.

Step One:

Open a photo containing shadow or highlight areas that need adjusting (in this case, it's a photo of the Valley of the Gods out in Utah). In this example, the light is coming from the left of the rocks, and I'm standing behind the rocks shooting into the shadow areas, so ideally we'd like to open up the shadows on this side. The other problem is the sky is pretty washed out, so I'd like to darken the sky by pulling back the highlights. That's when you reach for Shadow/Highlight—it's found under the Image menu, under Adjustments (as shown here).

Continued

Step Two:

Adobe knows that if you're choosing Shadow/Highlight, you probably have a problem in the shadow areas. That's why by default, it's set to open up (lighten) the shadow areas in your photo by 50% (as seen here). Here's the thing: to me, that 50% default setting seems like too much lightening (look at the photo shown here), so the first thing I do is lower the Shadows Amount until it looks better. There's another problem with opening the shadows 50% or more—it looks a bit fake, and your photos tend to look "milky" and overadjusted. To get around that, turn on the Show More Options checkbox, as shown here.

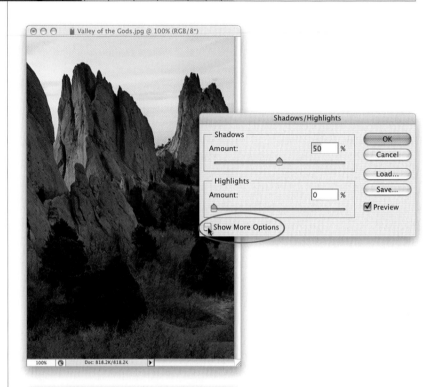

Step Three:

This brings up an expanded version of the dialog (as shown here). I have a little formula that I use that usually gives me the opened up shadow areas I need, without looking totally fake. First, I lower the Amount to somewhere between 25% and 35%, as shown here (the final amount depends on the individual photo—I start at 25% and drag up a little to see if I can get away with 35%). Then, I drag the Shadows Radius slider to the right to between 160 and 190, which smoothes out the effect even more.

TIP: If you find a setting you like better than the default 50% Shadows Amount setting, dial in that setting, then click the Save As Defaults button in the bottom-left corner of the dialog.

Step Four:

Now that the shadows are opened up (and look reasonably realistic), you can work on the highlights. In most cases, you'll only be working on one or the other—the shadows or the highlights, but not both. It takes someone special to actually take a photo that is so wrong on every level that it needs both areas adjusted. So, to pull back (darken) the highlights in the sky, you go to the Highlights section and drag the Amount slider to the right (as shown here). This darkens the highlights, which is good, but in our case it also introduced a new problem—a white glow around the edges of the rocks. Luckily, that's easy enough to fix.

Step Five:

To get rid of those white halos around the edges of the rocks, in the Highlights section drag the Radius slider all the way to the left (as shown here), and the halos are gone. By the way, before we move on, here's what the Tonal Width, Radius, and Adjustments sliders actually do: If you're tweaking shadows, lowering the Tonal Width lets you affect only the darkest shadow areas; increasing it affects a wider range of shadows. Increase it a bunch, and it'll start to affect the midtones as well. It works similarly for the highlights. The Radius amount determines how many pixels each adjustment affects, so to affect a wider range of pixels, increase the amount. If you increase the shadow detail, the colors may become too saturated. If that's the case, reduce the Color Correction amount (which basically only affects the area you're adjusting). You can also adjust the contrast in the midtones using the Midtone Contrast slider.

Continued

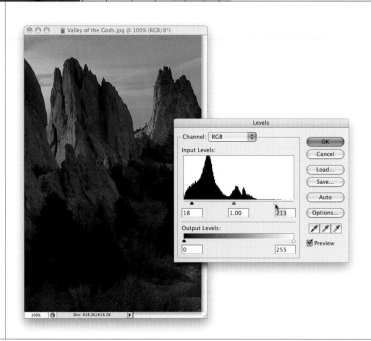

Step Six:

Go ahead and click OK to apply your Shadow/Highlight edits. Lastly, press Command-L (PC: Ctrl-L) to bring up Levels, which we'll use to add some contrast back into the photo and saturate the colors a bit. So, when the Levels dialog appears, grab the Highlights slider (on the far right under the histogram), and drag it to the left to brighten the highlights (as shown here). Then drag the Shadows slider (the black triangle on the far left) to the right to darken the shadows, and click OK to get the final image shown below.

Before

After (opening up the shadows, pulling back the highlights, and making a simple Levels adjustment)

Step Seven:

Okay, remember that cool CS3-only trick I mentioned in the intro? Well, here it is: I'm going to show you a way that you can apply the Highlight/Shadow as a totally editable, non-destructive Smart Filter, even though it's not a filter (oh yeah, baby—this sounds sa-weet!!!). There are two prep steps, but you only have to do this first prep step if your photo is a standard 8-bit image (so if it's a 16-bit RAW photo, you can skip #1): (1) Go under the Image menu, under Mode, and choose 16-Bits/Channel. The look of your photo won't change, but we have to be in 16-bit for this trick to work. Then, (2) go under the Filter menu and choose Convert for Smart Filters (as shown here), which basically turns your photo into a Smart Object.

Step Eight:

Now, just like before, go under the Image menu, under Adjustments, and you'll see that every adjustment is grayed-out but one—Shadow/Highlight—so go ahead and choose it (as shown here). This brings up the regular Shadows/Highlights dialog just like always, and you can go ahead and adjust the photo using the techniques you learned on the previous pages, then click OK. This is where everything changes.

Continued

15-Second Fix for Under- or Overexposed Photos

This is a tonal correction for people who don't like making tonal corrections (more than 60 million Americans suffer from the paralyzing fear of MTC [Making Tonal Corrections]). Since this technique requires no knowledge of Levels or Curves, it's very popular, and even though it's incredibly simple to perform, it does a pretty incredible job of fixing both underexposed and overexposed photos, and the only difference between the two is one simple change.

Step One:

We'll start by fixing a dark, underexposed photo, and once you learn this technique, the overexposed fix is almost the same (with just one small change). This photo was taken on a pure white background (which gives you an idea of how underexposed this shot really is). The first step is just to duplicate the Background layer (as seen here) by dragging it onto the Create a New Layer icon at the bottom of the Layers panel.

Step Two:

On this new layer, change the layer blend mode at the top of the Layers panel from Normal to Screen to lighten the entire photo (as shown here).

SCOTT KELBY

Step Three:
If the photo is still too dark, press Command-J (PC: Ctrl-J) to duplicate this Screen layer, which makes the photo that much lighter again. In this case, adding a third layer helped, but it also made it look slightly overexposed on her right cheek. So, lower the opacity of this layer (as shown here) to "dial in" the perfect amount of lightening (the opacity lets you choose anything between the full brightness of this third layer (at 100%) and no Screen layer at all (at 0%). Once the photo looks properly exposed, choose Flatten Image from the Layers panel's flyout menu.

Before

After (using two Screen blend mode layers)

Continued

Step Four:

Now, for an overexposed photo you pretty much do the same thing: you start by duplicating the Background layer (as shown here), so it's exactly the same thus far.

Step Five:

The only difference in the technique is that instead of choosing Screen mode (which makes things lighter), you choose Multiply, which makes the image darker (as shown here). Even just adding one Multiply layer looks dramatically better. In the After example shown on the next page, I duplicated the Multiply layer (for a total of three layers) to get the face of the watch dark enough, but that's all I did. So, the next time you run across a photo that's too light or too dark, give these two 15-second fixes a try. By the way, these techniques are particularly handy when you're working on restoring old scanned family photos.

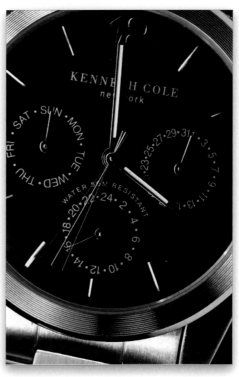

Before

After (using two Multiply blend mode layers)

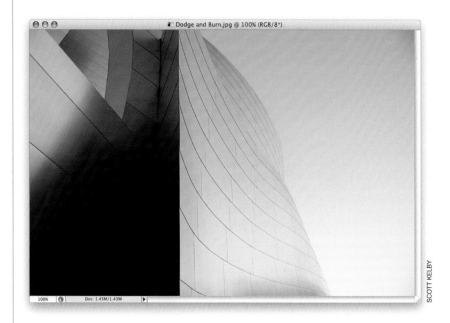

Dodging and Burning Done Right

If you've ever used Photoshop's Dodge and Burn tools, you already know how lame they are. That's why the pros choose this method instead—it gives a level of control that the Dodge and Burn tools just don't offer, and best of all, it doesn't "bruise the pixels." (That's Photoshop-speak for: it doesn't mess up your original image data while you're editing.)

Step One:

In this photo, the light simply didn't fall where we wish it had. So, here we're going to burn (darken) the areas that we wish were darker (like the sky and the bright area on the far left that's drawing your eye away from the right side of the building, which is where we want the viewer to look, and we'll probably darken that up a bit, too), and then we're going to dodge (lighten) just the shadow areas to the left of the center, to bring back some detail in that area. Basically, we're just going to rearrange how the light is falling on our photo.

Step Two:

Go to the Layers panel, and from the panel's flyout menu, choose New Layer to access the New Layer dialog (seen here). You can also Option-click (PC: Alt-click) on the Create a New Layer icon instead to bring up this same dialog. When the New Layer dialog appears, change the Mode to Overlay, then right below it, turn on the check-box for Fill with Overlay-Neutral Color (50% Gray), as shown here. This option is normally grayed out, but when you choose Overlay mode first, this checkbox becomes available. Now click OK.

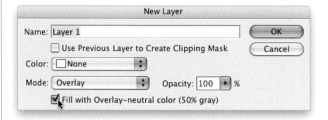

Step Three:

This creates a new layer (filled with 50% gray) above your Background layer. (When you fill a layer with 50% gray and change the blend mode to Overlay, Photoshop ignores the color. You'll see a gray thumbnail in the Layers panel, but the layer will appear transparent in your image window.)

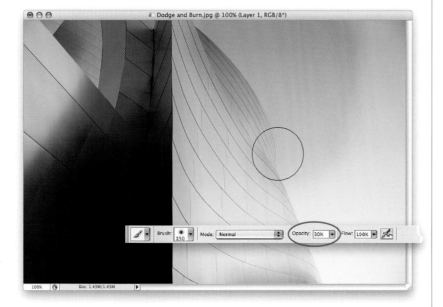

Step Four:

Press B to get the Brush tool, then up in the Options Bar, click on the thumbnail to the right of the word "Brush" and choose a medium, soft-edged brush from the Brush Picker. Now, lower the Brush tool's Opacity to approximately 30% (shown circled here in red). Press the letter D to set your Foreground color to black, then paint over the areas that you want to burn (darken). In this case, paint over the sky and the right side of the building. As you paint, in the Layers panel you'll see dark strokes appear in the thumbnail of your gray transparent layer, but on your photo you'll see those areas simply getting darker (as shown here).

Continued

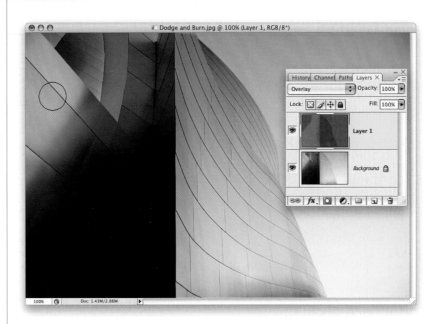

Step Five:

If the darkening isn't as intense as you'd like, just release the mouse button and click-and-paint right over the same area again. Because you're dodging at a low brush opacity setting, the light areas will build up as you paint multiple strokes. (I painted over the sky two times, and the right side of the building three times. I also painted over the top left twice to darken it, and give you the new, balanced lighting you see here.) *Note:* If the darkening appears too intense, try lowering the Opacity of the Brush tool to 20% up in the Options Bar.

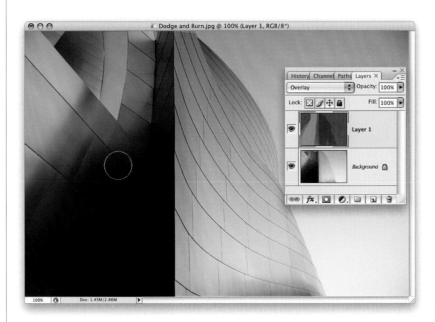

Step Six:

Now press the letter X to set your Foreground color to white, and paint over those shadow areas on the far left to lighten them up. If you look in the Layers panel, you'll see that your Overlay layer has all sorts of white, gray, and black strokes over it.

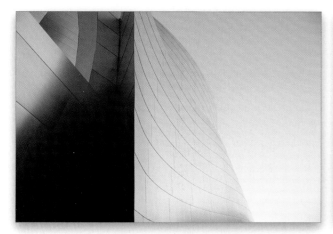

Before (with the sky too light, the right side of the building too light, the top left too bright, and the shadows on the left side of the building too dark)

After (with the sky and building on the right darkened, the top-left side of the building darkened, and the shadows opened up on the left side of the building)

Instant Red-Eye Removal

When I see a digital camera with the flash mounted directly above the lens, I think, "Hey, there's a red-eye maker." If you're a pro, you probably don't have to deal with this as much, because your flash probably isn't mounted directly above your lens—you're using bounce flash, using off-camera wireless flash, using studio strobes, or one of a dozen other techniques that avoid red eye. But even when the pros pick up a point-and-shoot camera, red eye can find them (it senses fear). Here's the quick "I-just-want-it-gone" technique for getting rid of red eye fast.

Step One:
Open a photo where the subject has red eye (this is a photo of my buddy Larry Becker's son, Reed).

Step Two:
Press Z to get the Zoom tool and zoom in on the eyes by clicking-and-dragging out a rectangle around them. Now get the Red Eye tool from the Toolbox (it's nested under the Spot Healing Brush, or you can press Shift-J until you get the tool).

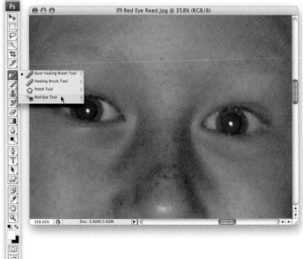

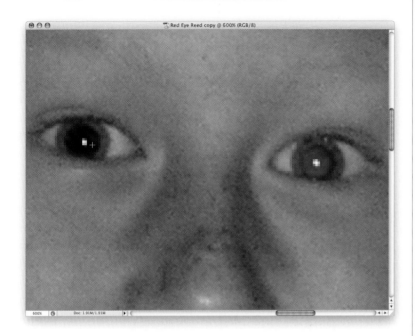

Step Three:

Tools don't get much easier to use than this—just click it once on the red area of the eye, and in just a second or two the red is gone (as shown here, where I just clicked it in the red area of his left eye). Think of it as a "Red Eye Magic Wand" because it automatically selects all the red area with just one click. Now, what do you do if you click in the red area, and you don't like the results? Well, there are two controls that can help you tweak the performance of the Red Eye tool: Pupil Size and Darken Amount (you find both of these in the Options Bar).

Step Four:

Think of the Pupil Size control like you would the Threshold setting for the Magic Wand tool—the higher the amount, the more colors it will select. So if your first try doesn't select all the red, increase the Pupil Size. The Darken Amount basically determines how dark the color is that replaces the red eye. The default setting of 50% gives you a very dark gray pupil. If you want a pure black pupil, just increase the amount. To complete the retouch, just click the Red Eye tool once in the right eye (you did the left eye earlier). Press Command-0 (zero; PC: Ctrl-0) to fit your image onscreen, and you'll have the red-eye retouched photo you see here.

Fixing Reflections in Glasses

I get more requests for how to fix this problem than probably all the rest combined. The reason is it's so darn hard to fix. If you're lucky, you get to spend an hour or more desperately cloning. In many cases, you're just stuck with it. However, if you're smart, you'll invest an extra 30 seconds while shooting to take one shot with the glasses off (or ideally, one "glasses off" shot for each new pose). Do that, and Photoshop will make this fix absolutely simple. If this sounds like a pain, then you've never spent an hour desperately cloning away a reflection.

Step One:
Before we get into this, make sure you read the short intro up top here first, or you're going to wonder what's going on in Step Two. Okay, here's a photo of my buddy Matt Kloskowski that I took at a restaurant in New York.

Step Two:
I could see right away that we were going to have a reflection in his glasses, so I told him after the shot not to move his head, but just to reach up and remove his glasses. I was surprised at how well Matt did this (totally kidding. Matt's actually very good at removing his glasses, his wedding ring, etc. Still kidding. Just a joke, etc.). Get the Move tool (V), press-and-hold the Shift key, and click-and-drag the "no glasses" shot on top of the "glasses" photo.

Step Three:
Holding the Shift key will help get the alignment of the two layers somewhat close, but in this case, it's still off by a bit because Matt is very unstable. Either that, or it's because I was hand-holding the shot (I like to think it was the unstable thing). Anyway, for this to work, the two photos have to be lined up with each other right on the money, and in CS3, Photoshop will do it for you. You start by going to the Layers panel, clicking on the Background layer, then pressing-and-holding the Command (PC: Ctrl) key and clicking on Layer 1 to select them both (you can see they're both highlighted here). Then go under the Edit menu and choose Auto-Align Layers (if that function is grayed out, it's because you don't have both layers selected). When the dialog appears, leave it set to Auto and just click OK.

Step Four:
A little progress bar will appear telling you that it's aligning the selected layers based on their content, and within a few seconds the two layers will be precisely lined up (as shown here. Of course, it's hard for you to tell they're precisely lined up unless you've downloaded these two photos and checked it yourself. What? You didn't know you could download these same photos and follow along? That's only because you skipped the Unexpected Q&A Section at the front of the book). Okay, now you'll need to hide the top layer by clicking on the little Eye icon to the left of the layer, then click once on the Background layer (as shown here). Now you're seeing the original shot, with the reflection in the glasses.

Continued

Step Five:

You're going to need to select the inside area of both lenses, and you can use whichever selection tool you're most comfortable with (like the Magnetic Lasso tool perhaps), but for a job like this, I think the Pen tool is perfect. If you choose to go the Pen tool route, get the Pen tool (P), then go up to the Options Bar and click on the second icon from the left (so it just draws a path). Then click the Pen tool once on a lower part of one of the glass lenses, move your cursor over to the left, and click, hold, and drag slightly to the left (as shown here). This draws a slightly curved path between the two points (the farther you drag after clicking, the more the curve bends).

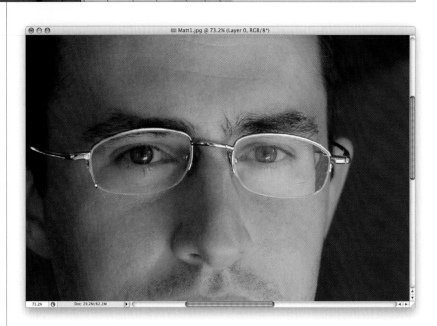

Step Six:

So basically, that's how it works—you move a little further along the lens, click, hold, and drag. Move again—click, hold, and drag, and continue this as you're basically going to trace around the lens with a path. When you get back to the point where you started, a little circle appears in the bottom-right corner of your Pen tool's icon letting you know you've come "full circle." Click on that point to close your path. Now do the same thing to the other lens. Once you've gotten paths drawn around both lenses, press Command-Return (PC: Ctrl-Enter) to turn your paths into a selection (as shown here). Remember, you don't have to do this using the Pen tool—use any selection tool(s) you're comfortable with.

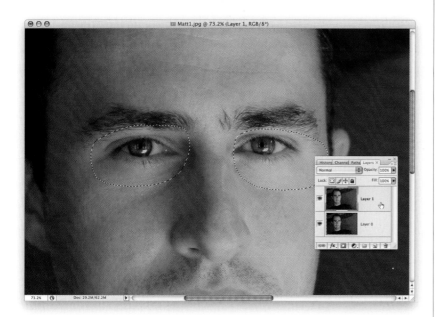

Step Seven:
After your selection is in place, make the top layer visible again (seen here) by clicking in the first column on the Layers panel where the Eye icon used to be. Then, click on the top layer to select it.

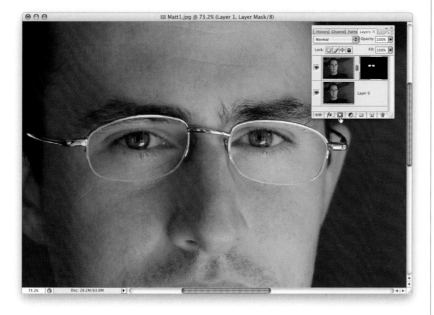

Step Eight:
To complete the effect, just click the Add Layer Mask icon at the bottom of the Layers panel (as shown here) and the eyes from the top layer replace the eyes from the original glasses layer, and your reflection problems are gone. Better yet—it not only fixed the reflection, it also fixed the fall-off that makes a person's eyes look smaller (take a look at the eyes and area around the eyes in the before/after shown on the next page. See how you can see the side of Matt's face in the Before photo, but that's fixed in the After photo? It's two fixes in one).

Continued

Before (notice the reflection—most visible in the right eye—and note how you can see the side of his face in the right eye lens)

After (the reflection is gone, as is the fall-off caused by prescription glasses)

The CS3 Secret to Fixing Group Shots

Group shots are always a challenge because without a doubt somebody in the group will be totally hammered (at least, that's been the experience with my family. You know I'm kidding, right?). Okay, the real problem is that in group photos there's always one or more people who blinked at just the wrong time, or forgot to smile, or weren't looking at the camera, etc. Of course, you could just take their expression from another frame and combine it with this one, but that takes a lot of work. Well, at least it did before CS3's Auto Blend feature. This thing rocks!

Step One:

Here's a promo photo of the band Big Electric Cat, which plays at the Photoshop World Conference & Expo and is made up of employees and friends of the National Association of Photoshop Professionals (including yours truly on keyboards). This was actually a test shot so I could check the lighting (which was coming from two wireless Nikon SB-800 strobes). The guy in the light blue shirt is a friend of the drummer (he's a percussionist himself), and he's standing in for me since I'm taking the photo. The problem here is Felix, the bass player (sitting), is turned away from the camera and Tony, the guitar player (up front right), is looking away from the camera.

Step Two:

Of course, with group shots you take as many shots as the group will endure, and luckily in the very next frame there was a great shot of Tony, and Felix wasn't turned away. So, the idea is to take Felix and Tony from this shot, and combine it with the previous photo, where Scotty the drummer and his stand-in buddy looked good (well, they had that tough "I'm-in-a-band" look. Well, as tough a look as guys our age can have, which is not very).

Continued

Step Three:

Start by dragging the two photos into the same document: get the Move tool (V), press-and-hold the Shift key, and click-and-drag one photo over onto the other (it will appear as its own layer in the other document, as you can see in the Layers panel shown here). Now, you'll need to convert the Background layer into a regular layer, so go to the Layers panel and double-click directly on the Background layer. This brings up the New Layer dialog (shown here), which by default renames your Background layer as Layer 0. Just click OK and it's now a regular ol' Photoshop layer.

TIP: In this case, the photos lined up pretty well because I took the shots on a tripod, but if you're hand-holding, you might want to select both layers and choose Auto-Align Layers from the Edit menu first, to have Photoshop CS3 align the two layers for you.

Step Four:

The next two steps couldn't be easier: First, in the Layers panel hide Layer 0 from view by clicking on the little Eye icon to the left of the layer. Then click on Layer 1. Now, get the Rectangular Marquee tool (M) and draw a rectangular selection over the parts of this layer that don't look good (in other words, you're going to delete everything you don't want to keep—so put a selection around the two guys on the left) and hit the Delete (PC: Backspace) key. This leaves you with just the part of this layer you want to keep. Now, Deselect by pressing Command-D (PC: Ctrl-D).

Step Five:

Now hide that top layer from view, and make Layer 0 visible again by clicking once in the first column where the little Eye icon used to be. Click on Layer 0, then do the same thing—erase the two guys you don't want (in this case, you're putting a Rectangular Marquee selection around Felix turning away and Tony looking off in the distance), then press the Delete (PC: Backspace) key, so you have the image you see here. Now you can Deselect. The key thing to remember here is this: make sure these two layers overlap, because CS3 needs some overlapping area to do its blending (in other words, don't erase so much that there's any gap between the two layers—it's got to overlap. I'd shoot for a 20% overlap if you can).

Step Six:

Go to the Layers panel and make both layers visible (as seen here). Now, you have the right poses together, but you also have a very harsh seam moving right through the stand-in's arm, and look at the extra shadows that appear on the floor. It looks "pieced together" big time. Of course, you could add layer masks and try blending the edges yourself with the Brush tool, but that's what makes this technique so sweet: CS3 will do a brilliant job of all that for you—in just seconds.

Continued

Step Seven:

Here's the last step: select both layers in the Layers panel (click on one layer, press-and-hold the Command [PC: Ctrl] key, then click on the other layer to select it as well), then once both layers are selected, go under the Edit menu and choose Auto-Blend Layers (as shown here). That's it—in just seconds you have a perfectly smooth, seamless blend of the two photos, and Photoshop did all the hard work. You can see the before and after in the example below and look close—that seam is 100% gone! It does leave the layer masks that Auto-Blend Layers creates in place, just in case you want to tweak them, but I haven't come up with an instance where I needed to yet. Just choose Flatten Image from the Layers panel's flyout menu, and you're done.

Before (the two guys on the right are in bad poses—one turned away, one looking away)

After (the first photo is seamlessly blended with the second photo, replacing the two guys on the right with their better poses from a different frame)

If you wind up getting a little spot or speck on either your lens or your digital camera's sensor, that little spot is going to show up on every single photo you take. Of course, once you find out that you have the problem (when you zoom in on the photos in Photoshop), it's too late for that batch of photos (so if you took 240 shots at a dawn shoot that day, you have 240 spots in the same place on every photo). Here's how to remove the spot from one photo, and use that one repair to fix the other 239 automatically!

Fixing Spots or Sensor Dust on Multiple Photos at Once

SCOTT KELBY

Step One:

The first step is to open the shots that need a spot removal in Camera Raw (remember, they don't have to be shot in RAW to use Camera Raw. In CS3, you can open JPEGs and TIFFs in Camera Raw as well). In this example (shots from a sunrise shoot in North Carolina, and sure enough, there's a speck of dust on every single photo in the exact same spot), I shot in RAW, so in Bridge I selected all the photos, then pressed Command-R (PC: Ctrl-R) to open all of them in Camera Raw. The first-selected photo appears in the preview, and the rest of the open photos appear in the filmstrip along the left side.

Step Two:

Get the Zoom tool (Z) from up in Camera Raw's toolbar, and click-and-drag out a selection around the spot (it's just to the right of the center, and down a little bit) to zoom in so you can really see what we're dealing with. By the way, you'll be happy to know that while I did make these RAW photos available for you to download, I didn't put all 240 up there, or you'd be downloading somewhere around 4 gigs of photos. I just posted three shots, but I posted both the RAW versions (57.9 MB) and some smaller JPEG versions as well (only 348 KB).

Continued

Step Three:

Now all you have to do is fix this one photo, and all the rest will take care of themselves. You start by clicking on the Retouch tool (B) up in Camera Raw's toolbar. This pops down a little options section beneath the toolbar, but for something this easy, you're not even going to need to mess with anything there. Click-and-hold the tool's cursor in the center of your spot and drag outward to expand the size of the tool's "repair zone" (not its official name) until it's just a little bigger than the spot you want to retouch (as shown here).

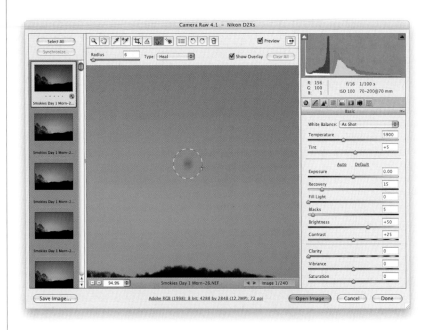

Step Four:

When you release the mouse button, Camera Raw removes the spot (as shown here) by sampling a nearby area (represented by the green circle, which appears as soon as you release the mouse button). If, for some reason, the repair looks funky (that's the official term by the way), you can try having Camera Raw do its sampling from a different area by dragging that green circle to a different area (you can drag it farther away from the red circle, closer to it, or drag it left, right, etc.). When you release the mouse button again, it resamples again and you see the results instantly. So, keep moving it until you get a result you're happy with. Luckily, this is easier than you'd think. *Note:* You can change the size of the circle manually, using the Radius slider up in the options section. Also, if the spot you're trying to fix is near the edge of another object in your photo, you might want to try Clone as your repair Type from the pop-up menu, rather than the default of Heal (found up in the options section).

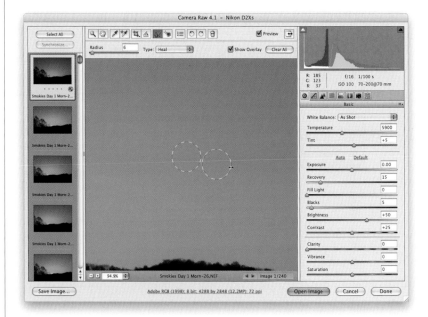

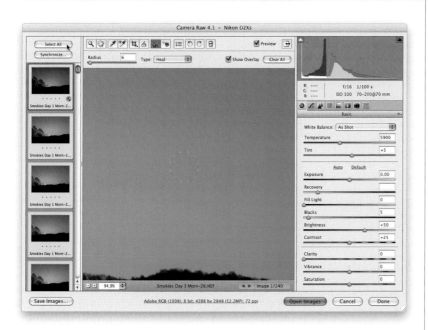

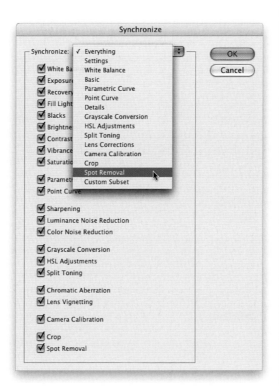

Step Five:

Okay, so you've fixed that one spot. Of course, if you have multiple spots, go and fix the next ones as well (it won't disturb your initially fixed spot), until all your spots have been healed. Now it's time to apply that fix to all the other photos in your batch (in our case, to the other 239 photos). You start by going to the top of the filmstrip on the left and clicking on the Select All button (as shown here) to select all the other photos (they all become highlighted in the filmstrip). Notice though, that photo you've been working on appears as the "most selected" photo (it stands out with a dark blue border around it). That's important because you're about to apply the changes you made to your "most selected" photo to the rest of your photos.

Step Six:

Now, just under the Select All button is a button labeled Synchronize. Click on that button to bring up the Synchronize dialog (shown here). By default, it wants to apply every Camera Raw edit possible to all your other photos, but you've only done a Spot Removal at this point, so from the pop-up menu at the top choose Spot Removal (as shown here).

Continued

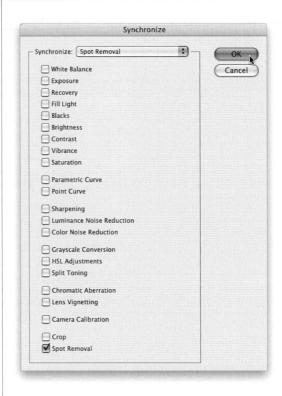

Step Seven:

Choosing Spot Removal turns off all the other Camera Raw edits (as shown here), leaving the only edit that will be applied to your other photos—Spot Removal. Now, you might ask yourself why we had to uncheck all that other stuff if all we've done is remove spots thus far? In this case, you're right—it really wouldn't hurt to leave them all on, but in many other cases removing spots won't have been the first thing you've done to your photos, and you don't want to undo any tonal edits, or cropping, or whatever you did previously, so it's just safer to get in the habit of choosing just the change you want applied. Now, click OK in the Synchronize dialog (as shown here).

Step Eight:

In just a few moments, your change is applied to all your photos. To check for yourself, click on any one of your other photos (in this case, I clicked on the third photo down), and if you look at the large preview in the center, you'll see the red and green circles are right there in place repairing that spot. In fact, they'll be there in every single photo. Sweet! Now, at this point I would click the Done button, and it will close Camera Raw and your spot removal changes will be stored with your files. If you click Open Images now, you'll be opening 240 images in Photoshop, and that may be kind of unwieldy. But hey—maybe that's what you want to do—who am I to judge how insane you are (kidding)?

Faces
retouching portraits

Okay, this one isn't a song title (well, there are a bunch of songs with the word "faces" in the title), this one is actually a band name. Well, at least part of a band name—it's my tribute to Rod Stewart and Faces (of course, when he got really big, he quickly dumped Faces and just became Rod Stewart, but that wasn't until he got ahold of some really strong mousse). That type of thing always happens, doesn't it? It even happened to me a long time ago. When I first started retouching portraits, I started a firm called Scott Kelby and the Ugly Pug Fixers, and I would go to local bars and nightclubs and retouch photos of the doorman, or bouncer, or bartender, etc., but then one night I got my big break when I was able to retouch the club owner himself (I still remember him to this day—his name was Nigel Buttocks). Anyway, he had this crack in his smile, and I was able to use a combination of Photoshop tools to seamlessly remove his crack, and he was so gassed about the results that he cut one—of his in-house staff of retouchers and made me his new headliner. I'll never forget walking back into my old studio for the last time. All the Ugly Pug Fixers were there, and they could tell by the look in my eyes it was over. But thankfully, we're still friends to this very day, and every once in a while I'll run across a really hideous portrait of someone, and I'll jump in my Porsche 911 Turbo and drive over to their small, dimly lit retouching studio, and we'll pull the image up on the screen, look at the person with all those facial imperfections, and we'll just laugh and laugh. Gosh I miss those days.

Removing Blemishes

When it comes to removing blemishes, acne, or any other imperfections on the skin, our goal is to maintain as much of the original skin texture as possible. That way, our retouch doesn't look pasty and obvious. There are a number of different techniques you can use, but after years of using them all, I believe this really is the best, most reliable, and easiest method out there.

Step One:
Open a photo containing some skin imperfections you want to remove (in this example, we're going to remove a series of little blemishes). Get the Zoom tool (Z) and zoom in on the area you want to retouch, then get the Healing Brush tool from the Toolbox (as shown here). You might be tempted to use the Spot Healing Brush tool, because it's so easy to use (and it's the default healing tool in the Toolbox), but don't fall for it. Although it does a pretty good job on its own, you can do better and work faster with the Healing Brush because you won't have to redo anything (and you generally will have a number of redos using the Spot Healing Brush). Besides, you only save one click using the Spot Healing Brush over the regular Healing Brush.

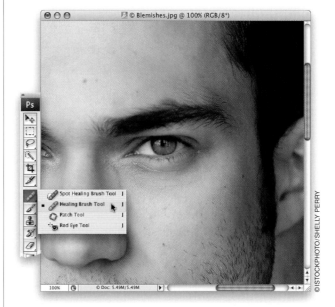

Step Two:
The key to using the Healing Brush correctly is to find an area of skin to sample that has a similar texture to the area you want to repair (this is different than the Clone Stamp tool, where you're looking for matching color and shading as well). Move your cursor over this "clean" area of skin, press-and-hold the Option (PC: Alt) key, and click once to sample that area. Your cursor will momentarily change to a target as you sample (as shown here).

Step Three:
Now, just move the Healing Brush directly over the blemish you want to remove and simply click. Don't paint—click. Once. That's it. That's the whole technique—BAM—the blemish is gone!

Continued

TIP: For the best results, use a brush size that is just a little bit larger than the blemish you want to remove (use the Left/Right Bracket keys on your keyboard [they're to the right of the letter P] to change brush sizes). Also, you don't have to worry about sampling an area right near where the blemish is—you can sample from another side of the face, even in the shadows—just choose a similar texture, that's the key.

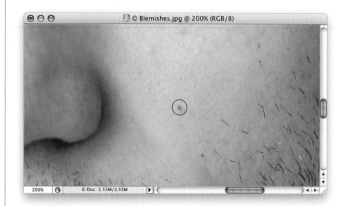

Before

After

This is another one of those techniques that takes just a moment to apply, but it can really make a huge difference in giving your subject a much thinner appearance where it counts most—the face. In the example shown in print here, the effect doesn't look that dramatic (because of the small size of the final example), but this is one where when you see it on your own screen at a larger size, you'll be absolutely amazed at the impact it has. Try it once, and you'll use it again and again.

Reducing a Double Chin

Step One:
Open the photo that you want to retouch, then get the Lasso tool (L) and draw a very loose selection around your subject's jaw and the lower part of the face on both sides (as shown here). This is one of those rare times where you don't need to apply a feather to hide the tracks of your retouch. In fact, in this case if you do apply a feather, it actually makes the retouch more obvious (which usually isn't the case).

Step Two:
Go under the Filter menu, under Distort, and choose Pinch. When the Pinch dialog appears, drag the slider down to just 15% (as shown here). You'll see a preview of how the effect looks right within the dialog, and to see a before and after, just take your cursor and click-and-hold right in the preview window to see the before. Then, to see the after, release the mouse button.

Continued

Step Three:

Press-and-hold the Option (PC: Alt) key and click once in an area near the eye that isn't affected by the dark circles. If the cheeks aren't too rosy (like the ones shown here), you can click to sample there (I did here), but more likely you'll click on (sample) an area just below the dark circles under the eyes. Now take that Clone Stamp tool and paint a stroke (from left to right) over the dark circles to lessen or remove them. It may take two or more strokes for the dark circles to pretty much disappear (go right, then back again to the left, and so on), so don't be afraid to go back over the same area if the first stroke didn't work. The photos below show the before and after of this 45-second retouch. I did have to go over each side about three to four times.

Before

After

Did ya notice the name of this one's not "Removing Wrinkles?" That's because unless your subject is around 29 years old, you're not removing their wrinkles, you're reducing their wrinkles—you're making them 10 years younger, not 40 years younger. He's how to reduce your subject's wrinkles anywhere from around 40% to around 70% (hey, most people would love to have 70% less wrinkles). Here's how to make your subjects look younger, without making them look like youngsters:

Reducing Wrinkles

Step One:
Open a photo you want to retouch, then from the Toolbox choose the Healing Brush (as shown here). Before you do anything, press Command-J (PC: Ctrl-J) to duplicate the Background layer, as you'll be doing all your retouching on this duplicate layer (this isn't just to make sure your retouch is non-destructive by applying it to its own layer, it's key to making this particular retouch realistic).

Step Two:
Move your cursor over a nearby area of non-wrinkled skin, press-and-hold the Option (PC: Alt) key, and click once on that area. This samples the texture of the area you're clicking on and uses it for the repair. I generally use the subject's cheek if it's smooth enough, and in this case I was able to find a nice smooth area on his left cheek (as shown here).

Continued

Step Three:
With the Healing Brush, paint a stroke over the wrinkles you want to remove (as shown here where I painted over the wrinkles just below his left eye).

Step Four:
When you first paint your stroke, for a moment the tones won't match and it'll look like a really obvious retouch, but a second or two later, the Healing Brush does its calculations and presents you with its final "magic" that seamlessly blends in the original texture, removing the wrinkle (as shown here).

TIP: For fixing problems like large wrinkles, you can also try the Healing Brush's sister tool (and a personal favorite of mine)—the Patch tool. It works like the Lasso tool—you just draw a loose selection completely around the wrinkle you want to remove. Then you click inside the selection and drag it to a clean area of skin. When you release the mouse button, it snaps back into position, and in a few seconds it repairs that area. Here's another cool thing: you can make a selection with any tool you'd like, and once the selection is in place, then switch to the Patch tool, drag that selected area, etc., just like you would if you had used the Patch tool from the beginning.

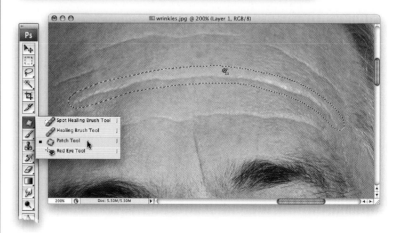

Step Five:

Once you've got the wrinkles under the eyes taken care of, move to other wrinkle areas (like the wrinkles on his forehead). Sample a clean nearby area (in this case, the skin right below the wrinkles), and paint over those wrinkles to remove them as well.

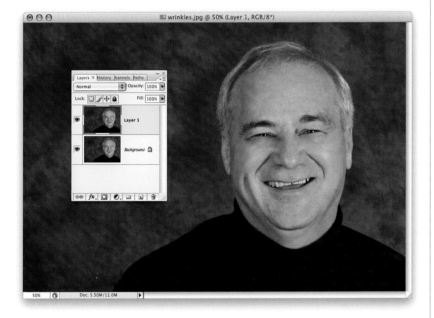

Step Six:

Continue this process until all the wrinkles you want to reduce have been completely removed. I know what you're thinking—I thought you said we were going to reduce them, not remove them. That's true, but for now, you've got to remove all traces of them, so finish this guy off (sorry to sound so *The Sopranos* on you. I meant, finish the rest of the retouch).

TIP: If you're just going to fix one or two wrinkles, you don't have to go through all of this—just do your healing right on the Background layer, but right after you paint a stroke with the Healing Brush, go under the Edit menu and choose Fade Healing Brush. There you can lower the Opacity setting (the amount of healing) after the fact.

Continued

Step Seven:

In the Layers panel, lower the healed layer's Opacity to 45% (as shown here) to bring back some of the original wrinkles. What you're really doing here is letting a small amount of the original photo (on the Background layer, with all its wrinkles still intact) show through. Keep lowering the Opacity until the wrinkles are visible but not nearly as prominent, so the photo looks much more realistic. Usually, I'll wind up with something between 40% and 70% but remember, if you reduce them too much, the client might like the way it looks when you first show it to him, but once he starts showing friends and family members (and they start snickering), he'll wish you hadn't reduced them so much. A 45% reduction in wrinkles is more significant than you'd think—just compare the before and after photos below. The wrinkles are still there (so your subject still looks like himself), but their depth has been reduced by enough that your subject looks 10 or more years younger.

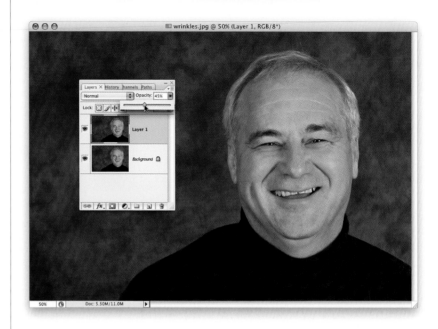

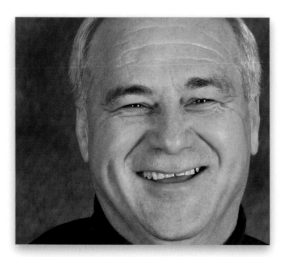

Before (visible wrinkles on forehead and under eyes)

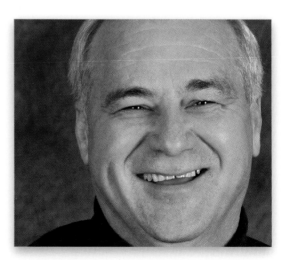

After (reducing wrinkles on forehead and under eyes)

This retouching technique has become incredibly popular in promo photos for Hollywood celebrities, and for pop and R&B CD covers. I'm not sure what the official name for it is, so I call it "Hollywood Highlights" (although it really enhances both the highlights and the shadows for a very dramatic effect). The effect is surprisingly easy, and yet it definitely has its own look and feel to it. Here's how it's done:

Hollywood Highlights

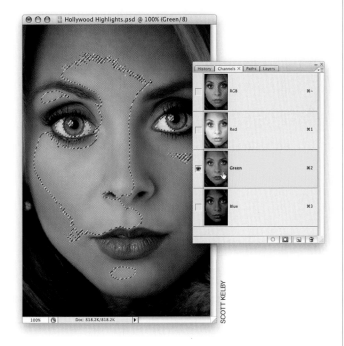

SCOTT KELBY

Step One:
Open the color photo you want to add the "Hollywood Highlights" effect to. Now go to the Channels panel (under the Window menu, choose Channels), and when it appears, look at each of the three grayscale channels individually by clicking on them one at a time. What you're looking for is the channel with the most overall contrast between light and dark. It's usually not going to be the Red channel in portraits (which is usually very bright because of the skin tones), so chances are it will be either the Green channel (which it is in this case), or the Blue channel (which in this case is really dark, so I didn't use it). Give each one a quick look and you'll see what I mean. Once you've determined which channel you're going to use, press-and-hold the Command (PC: Ctrl) key and in the Channels panel, click directly on that channel's thumbnail (in this case, the Green channel's thumbnail, as shown here) to load that channel as a selection. You can see the selection loaded in the image shown here.

Continued

Step Two:

Now, in the Channels panel click on the RGB channel (as shown here) to return to the full-color photo (this doesn't deselect your selection, which is good, because we want that selection still in place). Now, return to the Layers panel and click once on the Background layer to make it active. Your selection will still be in place on your Background layer.

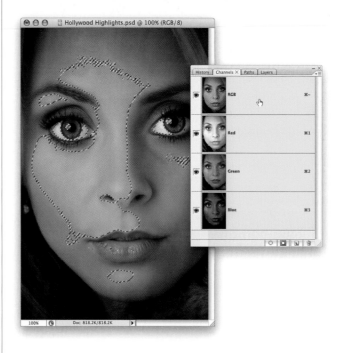

Step Three:

Press Command-J (PC: Ctrl-J) to put the selected area of your Background layer up on its own separate layer (as shown here). Doing that automatically deselects the selection. Now, change the blend mode of this layer to Screen (as shown here) to brighten the highlights in this layer.

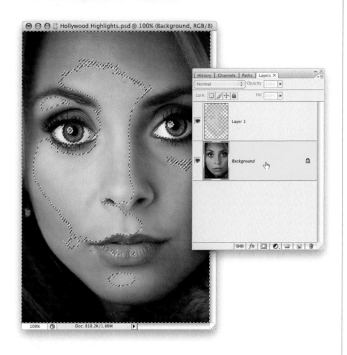

Step Four:
Press-and-hold the Command (PC: Ctrl) key again and click once on the thumbnail for that new layer you just created to reload it as a selection. This puts that same selection back in place. Now, click on the Background layer (as shown here), then press Command-Shift-I (PC: Ctrl-Shift-I) to Inverse your selection (you can also go up under the Select menu and choose Inverse, if you're charging by the hour).

Step Five:
Press Command-J (PC: Ctrl-J) to put this selected area up on its own separate layer (as shown here), which again deselects your selection, since now it's its own layer. So, basically, you've got one layer (Layer 1 in Screen mode) with the highlights of your contrast channel, and another layer (Layer 2 still in Normal mode) with the shadow areas of your contrast channel. Change the blend mode of this layer (Layer 2) to Multiply (as seen in the next step) to darken this layer.

Continued

Step Six:

Now what you're going to do is lower the Opacity of this Multiply layer until the shadows look good (nice and contrasty, but still good), then you'll switch to Layer 1 (the highlights layer in Screen mode) and lower it until it balances nicely with the shadows layer). There are no special percentages I can give you to dial in, because this is strictly a personal preference choice. I can tell you for this particular photo, I lowered the shadows layer to 60%, and the highlights layer to 80% because that's where I thought it looked good to me. You can see the before and after in the images shown below.

Before

After

If you've got a photo where a female subject has flat, boring-looking lips, and you want to add some of that Hollywood color and shine, then try these two techniques: the first (which I picked up from my buddy and *NAPP TV* co-host Dave Cross) enhances the color and shine factor, and the second technique really pumps up the highlights and adds even more shine and interest.

Enhancing Lips

Step One:
Start by taking the selection tool of your choice and putting a selection around just the lips (as seen here). To make the selection you see here, I used the Magnetic Lasso tool (press Shift-L until you have it), which worked great because the edges of the area to be selected were pretty well defined. Once the lips are selected, to help hide the tracks of our retouch, go under the Select menu, under Modify, and choose Feather. When the dialog appears, enter 1 pixel and click OK to soften the edges of our selection.

Step Two:
Press Command-J (PC: Ctrl-J) to copy the selected lips up onto their own separate layer (as seen here).

Continued

Step Three:

To add in our first level of depth and shine, go under the Filter menu, under Artistic, and choose Plastic Wrap. When the Plastic Wrap dialog appears (this filter actually appears within the larger Filter Gallery dialog, but don't let that throw you—you only have to move two sliders), set the Highlight Strength to 18 and increase the Detail amount to 14 to bring out that shine. You can see a preview of how this will look on the lips as you drag the sliders.

Step Four:

When you click OK it applies the Plastic Wrap filter effect to the lips. Of course, at this stage, it looks pretty darn stupid, but we'll fix that in the next step.

TIP: When you use the term "enhancing lips," a lot of people instantly think of making the lips larger. If you want to do that, just open the photo, then go under the Filter menu and choose Liquify. In the Liquify dialog, choose the fifth tool down in the Toolbox—the Bloat tool. Make your brush just a little bit larger than the lips, then don't paint—just click, once on the far-left side of the lips, once left of the center, once right of the center, and once on the far right (you're moving from left to right) to make them larger. Easy enough.

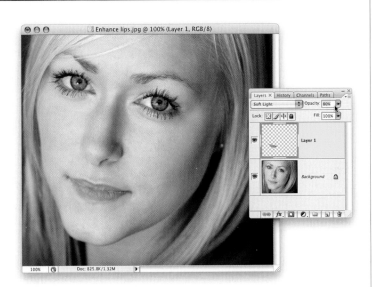

Step Five:
Go to the Layers panel and change the layer blend mode from Normal to Soft Light (as seen here). This blends the Plastic Wrap effect in with the original photo on the Background layer, gives the lips a little shine, makes the color richer, and gives the lips more detail. Now, if you really want that Hollywood shine, then try choosing Overlay mode instead of Soft Light (Soft Light is always the more subtle of the two). Whichever mode you choose, if the effect looks too intense, you can back off the intensity by lowering the Opacity setting of the lips layer, as shown here where I lowered the Soft Light layer to 80% opacity.

Step Six:
If you want to add that next level of shine, first go the Layer panels, press-and-hold the Command (PC: Ctrl) key, then click on the layer thumbnail for the lips layer to load it as a selection. Go under the Select menu and choose Color Range. When the Color Range dialog appears, choose Highlights from the Select pop-up menu up top (as shown here), and then click OK.

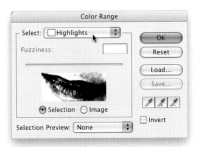

Step Seven:
This loads a selection of just the high-light areas of her lips (it only loads her lip highlights because you put a selection around the lip layer before you went to Color Range). You can see the highlights in her lips selected here.

Continued

Step Eight:

Press Command-J (PC: Ctrl-J) to put those selected highlights in her lips up on their own separate layer (as shown here). Now, to bring in the "lip gloss," change the layer blend mode of this layer to Color Dodge (as seen here). The lips are very glossy now, but in this particular case it seems like there's too much shine on the very bottom of her lip. To get rid of that excess bright area, first click on the Add Layer Mask icon at the bottom of the Layers panel (as shown here), then get the Brush tool (B), make sure your Foreground color is set to black, and just paint right over those lower areas of her lips to complete the effect (seen below).

Before

After

There are two techniques I use for whitening eyes, and I have to show you both, because if the first method creates some side effects (meaning, after you've brightened the eyes, they look red or have some other color cast that has been accentuated by the retouch), you can always fall back on the second method. They're both simple, and sometimes the final result is subtle, but not so subtle that you wouldn't take the 60 seconds it takes to do it. Remember, everyone is drawn to the eyes, so take a moment to make them look their very best.

Brightening and Whitening the Eyes

©ISTOCKPHOTO/MATT OLSEN

Step One:
Open the photo of the person whose eyes you want to brighten. Go to the Layers panel and choose Curves from the Create New Adjustment Layer pop-up menu at the bottom of the panel. When the Curves dialog appears, don't make any adjustments—just click OK. The reason we do this is in the next step we'll need to apply a layer blend mode to our photo to make it brighter, but duplicating the Background layer doubles our file size. So to keep our file size small (and Photoshop running faster), we use an adjustment layer instead, which still lets us use a blend mode, but without adding any file size or slowing us down.

Step Two:
When the Curves adjustment layer appears in your Layers panel, change the blend mode of this adjustment layer from Normal to Screen (as shown here). This will lighten the entire photo.

Continued

Step Three:

Now press Command-I (PC: Ctrl-I) to Invert the adjustment layer's layer mask, which fills it with black. This hides the lightening effect brought on by changing the blend mode to Screen. Press the letter X to switch your Foreground color to white, zoom in on the eyes, then press B to get the Brush tool.

Step Four:

Choose a very small, soft-edged brush from the Brush Picker, and begin painting over the eyes (as shown here, where I'm painting over the left eye). As you paint, these areas become much brighter because you're revealing the Screen adjustment layer you applied earlier. Now, you have to decide whether to paint over just the whites of the eyes, or over the whole eye itself (which I chose in this case). When you're done, the eyes will probably look too white (giving your subject a possessed look), so zoom back out so you can make a reasonable judgment, then lower the Opacity of this Curves adjustment layer to make the whitening more subtle and natural (I lowered it to around 70%) to complete the effect (shown below). Now, on to #2.

Before

After

©ISTOCKPHOTO

Step One:

I do this technique instead if the first one caused any of those side effects I talked about in the introduction. You start the same way, by creating an adjustment layer, but this time choose Levels (as shown here).

Step Two:

When the Levels dialog appears, brighten the entire photo by dragging the Input Levels highlights slider to the left, then drag the center midtones slider to the left as well, and keep a watch on how the eyes look while you're doing this. The rest of the photo will probably start to look blown out, but you're just concerned with the eyes, so ignore any other damage that's happening in other parts of the photo. If the eyes look brighter, but start to look washed out, then drag the Input Levels shadows slider to the right a little bit to bring back some saturation. When the eyes look good, click OK.

Continued

Step Three:

Now press Command-I (PC: Ctrl-I), to fill the layer mask with black, which once again hides the brighter layer behind that mask. Make sure your Foreground color is set to white, get the Brush tool (B), pick a small, soft-edged brush from the Brush Picker, and paint over the eyes (as shown here, where I'm painting over her left eye).

Step Four:

Sometimes even a simple Levels adjustment can create its own side effects; the main one being, it changes the color of the eye a bit. So, to get around that, simply change the blend mode of your adjustment layer to Luminosity. That way, it doesn't affect the color—only the brightness. Then lower the Opacity of this Levels adjustment layer until it looks natural (I went back to around 50% here, but anywhere between 50% and 60% looked good to me). The final retouch is shown below.

Before

After

Whitening Teeth

This really should be called "Removing Yellowing, Then Whitening Teeth" because almost everyone has some yellowing, so we remove that first before we move on to the whitening process. This is a simple technique, but the results have a big impact on the overall look of the portrait, which is why I do this to every portrait where the subject is smiling.

Step One:

Open the photo you need to retouch. Press L to switch to the Lasso tool, and carefully draw a selection around the teeth, being careful not to select any of the gums or lips (as shown here). Also, you might try using the Magnetic Lasso tool (nested beneath the Lasso tool), which works nicely for this—just click once at the base of a tooth to get started, then release the mouse button and trace loosely around the edge of the teeth and your selection will snap to the teeth. It may not do a perfect job, but it will usually do 90% of the job for you. Then you can get the regular Lasso tool, press-and-hold the Shift key, and add in any parts it missed.

Step Two:

Go under the Select menu, under Modify, and choose Feather. When the Feather Selection dialog appears, enter 1 pixel and click OK to smooth the edges of your selection. That way, you won't see a hard edge along the area you selected after you've whitened the teeth, which is a dead giveaway that the photo's been retouched.

Continued

Step Three:

Now go under the Image menu, under Adjustments, and choose Hue/Saturation. When the dialog appears, choose Yellows from the Edit pop-up menu at the top (as shown here). Then, drag the Saturation slider to the left to remove the yellowing from the teeth. In this case, we had to drag quite a ways to the left, but that won't normally be the case. In fact, usually if you drag too far, the teeth will start to look gray, so just keep an eye on the teeth as you drag.

Step Four:

Now that the yellowing is removed, switch the Edit pop-up menu back to Master, and drag the Lightness slider to the right (as shown here) to whiten and brighten the teeth. Be careful not to drag it too far or the retouch will be obvious. Click OK in the Hue/Saturation dialog to apply your changes, then press Command-D (PC: Ctrl-D) to Deselect and see your finished retouch.

Before

After

If you've ever had to deal with hot spots (shiny areas on your subject's face caused by uneven lighting or the flash reflecting off shiny surfaces, making your subject look as if he or she is sweating), you know they can be pretty tough to correct. That is, unless you know this trick.

Removing Hot Spots

Step One:
Open the photo that has hot spots that need to be toned down. Press Command-J (PC: Ctrl-J) to duplicate the Background layer and then press S to get the Clone Stamp tool from the Toolbox. In the Options Bar up top, change the Mode pop-up menu from Normal to Darken, and lower the Opacity to 40%. By changing the Mode to Darken, we'll only affect pixels that are lighter than the area we're sampling (those lighter pixels are the hot spots).

Step Two:
In the Options Bar, click on the thumbnail after the word "Brush" and choose a medium-sized, soft-edged brush from the Brush Picker. Then, press-and-hold the Option (PC: Alt) key and click once in a nearby area of clean skin (in other words, an area with no hot spots). This will be your sample area (or reference point) so Photoshop knows to affect only pixels that are lighter than this area. In the example shown here, I sampled the area just above the hot spots on his forehead.

Continued

Step Three:

Start gently painting over the hot-spot areas with the Clone Stamp tool, and as you do, the hot spots will fade away (as shown here, where I'm painting over the hot spots on his forehead). The cross-hair (plus sign) shows the area where I sampled, and the round brush shows where I'm painting. Because we've set the brush opacity so low, and set the mode to Darken, it just adds in the tone without destroying the detail or texture.

Step Four:

As you work on different hot spots, you'll have to resample (Option-click [PC: Alt-click]) on nearby areas of skin so the skin tone matches. For example, when you work on the hot spots on his left cheek (as shown here), sample an area of skin from that same cheek, if possible, where no hot spots exist. It's amazing what 60 seconds of hot-spot retouching can do for your image (as seen below).

Before

After

Although this technique has a number of steps, it's actually very simple to do and is worth every extra step, because it breaks away from the overly soft, porcelain-skin look that is just "so 2006" to give you that pro skin-softening look along with some of the original skin texture, which makes it much more realistic. This "keep some of the texture" look is totally "in" right now, so it's worth spending an extra two minutes. I also want to give credit to Ray 12, whose article last year on RetouchPro.com turned me on to the texture mask which I now use daily.

Advanced Skin Softening

Step One:
Start by pressing Command-J (PC: Ctrl-J) to duplicate the Background layer, as shown here. (See? I told you these steps were going to be easy.)

Step Two:
Go under the Filter menu, under Blur, and choose Gaussian Blur. For high-resolution photos (from a 6- to 10-megapixel camera), apply a 20-pixel blur, then click OK (for 12-megapixels or higher, try 25 pixels). This blurs the living daylights out of the photo (as seen here). Sure, it's blurry, but boy is her skin soft! (Okay, that was lame. Continue.)

Continued

Step Three:

In the Layers panel, lower the Opacity of this blurry layer to 50% (as shown here).

Step Four:

Press-and-hold the Option (PC: Alt) key and click once on the Add Layer Mask icon at the bottom of the Layers panel (as shown here). This adds a black layer mask to your blurry layer (seen here to the right of the top layer), and this black mask hides the blurry layer, so all you're seeing now is the original unblurred Background layer. The idea is to reveal the blurry layer just where you want it (on her skin), while avoiding all the detail areas (like her eyes, hair, clothing, eyebrows, nostrils, lips, jewelry, etc.).

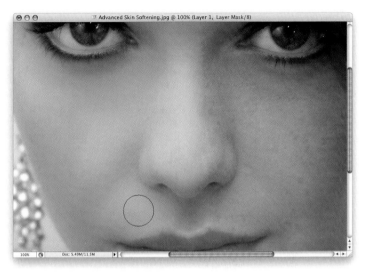

Step Five:

Get the Zoom tool (Z) and zoom in on her face. Then get the Brush tool (B), choose a medium-sized, soft-edged brush from the Brush Picker up in the Options Bar, and begin painting over her skin (as shown here). You're not actually painting over the photo—you're painting in white over that black mask, and as you paint, it reveals that part of the blurry layer. Remember the rule: don't paint over detail areas—avoid the eyes, hair, etc., as I mentioned earlier. In the example shown here, I have only painted over (softened) the left side of her face, so you can see the effect of the skin softening.

Step Six:

Continue painting on both sides of her face until you've carefully covered all the non-detail areas of her face. You'll have to vary the size of the brush to get under her nose, and carefully just below her left eyebrow.

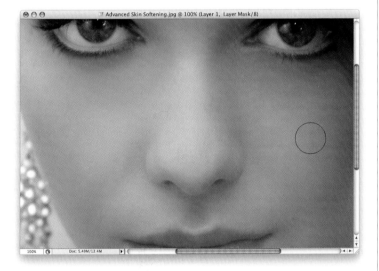

TIP: You can use the Bracket keys on the keyboard to change brush sizes—the Left Bracket key ([) makes the brush size smaller; the Right Bracket key (]) makes it larger. By the way, the Bracket keys are to the right of the letter P on your keyboard. Well, if you're using a U.S. English keyboard anyway.

Continued

Step 17:

So (and here's where the cool part is), you're going to dial in the exact amount of original skin texture you'd like visible by lowering the Opacity of this texture layer. The lower you make the Opacity, the less skin texture is visible. For this particular photo, lowering the Opacity to 50% looks like it gives about the right balance between softening and texture. Compare the before and after photos below. Also, the image at the very bottom of the page has only one additional change: I added the "Hollywood Highlights" effect from earlier in this chapter.

Before

After

*After (doing this technique and adding the
"Hollywood Highlights" effect from earlier in this chapter)*

TIP: In CS3, there is an alternate way to do this technique, and that is instead of duplicating the Background layer, blurring it, and adding a layer mask, you could convert the Background layer to a Smart Object, then apply a Smart Filter directly to that layer. The advantages are: (1) much smaller file sizes to deal with (in fact, nearly half), so on large high-resolution files, Photoshop will work a lot faster; and (2) you can always go back and change the amount of blur. Here's a quick step-by-step:

Step One:
Once you open the photo, go under the Filter menu, and choose Convert for Smart Filters (as shown top left). Now just add your Gaussian Blur like before (same settings, etc.) and when you click OK, it adds a Smart Filters sublayer below your Background layer, and then a thin sublayer bar under it reading "Gaussian Blur."

Step Two:
On the far right of the Gaussian Blur sublayer, double-click on the two adjustment bar icons and it brings up a Blending Options dialog. Lower the Opacity to 50% (which reduces the amount of blur by 50%, just like before), and click OK.

Step Three:
In the Layers panel, click on the thumbnail for the Smart Filters mask (as shown here), then press Command-I (PC: Ctrl-I) to fill the mask with black and hide the blurry layer (just like we did previously). Now you'll paint on the mask to reveal the blurry parts just like before, and the rest of the technique remains the same. If later you want to change the amount of blur, just double-click directly on the words "Gaussian Blur" and the dialog appears with your original settings.

Slimming and Trimming

This is an incredibly popular technique because it consistently works so well, and because just about everyone would like to look about 10–20 pounds thinner. I've never applied this technique to a photo and (a) been caught, or (b) not had the clients absolutely love the way they look. The hardest part of this technique may be not telling your clients you used it.

Step One:
Open the photo of the person that you want to put on a quick diet. Press Command-A (PC: Ctrl-A) to put a selection around the entire photo. Then press Command-T (PC: Ctrl-T) to bring up the Free Transform function. The Free Transform handles might be a little hard to reach, so press Command-0 (zero; PC: Ctrl-0), which resizes your window, making some of the gray canvas area around your photo visible, so you can easily reach all the handles (as seen here).

Step Two:
Grab the right-center handle and drag it horizontally toward the left to slim the subject. The farther you drag, the slimmer the person becomes. How far is too far (in other words, how far can you drag before people start looking like they've been retouched)? Look at the Width field in the Options Bar for a guide—you're pretty safe to drag inward to around 95%, as shown here, but depending on the person, I've dragged to as much as 92% without getting caught. In this case, let's try dragging over until it reads 93% (giving us a 7% reduction in width).

Step Three:

When your person looks "naturally" slimmer, press Return (PC: Enter) to lock in your transformation. Doing this transformation leaves you with some excess white canvas area on the right side of the photo, but luckily your original selection will still be in place (from back in Step One), so just go under the Image menu and choose Crop (as shown here) to remove the excess white space and crop your image down to size. Press Command-D (PC: Ctrl-D) to Deselect, and you're done! The before and after below show the original on the left, and a 7% thinner version on the right.

Before

After

Removing Love Handles

Here's another handy use for the Liquify filter—removing love handles. This time, we're using a tool we haven't used in this chapter before, but in the right instance (like this), it does an amazing job. Here's how to deal with those unsightly love handles in 60 seconds (or less), plus I added a little quick trick at the end for getting rid of any "poochiness" in the stomach ("poochiness" was not found in InDesign's spell checker, however you still knew what I was talking about, right?).

Step One:

Open a photo that needs to have a love handle repair. In the fitness-style photo shown here, only one side needs the retouch, so it's a really quick fix. Start by going under the Filter menu and choosing Liquify.

Step Two:

When the Liquify dialog appears, click on the Zoom tool at the bottom of the Toolbox on the left-hand side of the dialog. Then, click-and-drag out a selection around the area you want to work on to give you a close-up view for greater accuracy. Get the Push Left tool (as shown here) from the Toolbox (it's the sixth tool down from the top). Next, choose a medium size for your brush using the Left and Right Bracket keys (they're found to the right of the letter P on your keyboard).

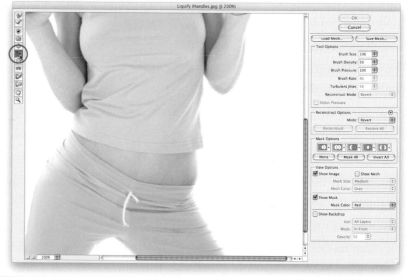

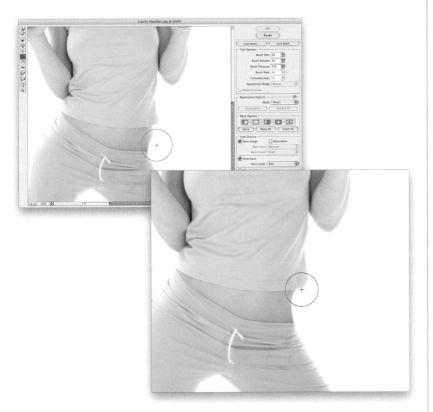

Step Three:

Now, start just below where her love handle starts and paint an upward stroke. As you do, the pixels will shift back in toward her body, removing the love handle as you paint. When you get up near her shirt, shrink your brush size way down so you can tuck that little area of skin in toward her shirt. I did fix one other little thing: once you fix the love handle, her stomach still looks a little "poochy," so I used the same technique we showed earlier for reducing the size of the nose—get the Pucker tool, choose a large brush size, and click three or four times over the center of her stomach, right where her skin meets the top of her pants. This just shrinks that poochiness right away. When you click OK, the love handle repair is complete. (*Note:* If you need to remove a love handle on the left side of the body, paint downward rather than upward. Why? That's just the way it works.)

Before

After

Exposure: 1/125s | Focal Length: 70mm | Aperture Value: ƒ/8.0

Special Delivery
special effects for photographers

The chapter title above is actually the name of a band. I ran across their song "Love Broke" as I was searching in Apple's iTunes Store under the word "Special." Of course, iTunes came up with songs from bands like .38 Special, as well as a band called The Specials, but somehow in the midst of all this, another title caught my eye. The song was named "Specinal" (which is either a typo, or a very clever misspelling of Special designed to throw off authors using iTunes as a research tool for naming chapters), but it wasn't the name of the song that drew me to it, it was the name of the band—Dufus. That's right, they named their band Dufus. Now, I'm not entirely sure, but the name Dufus might not be the best name for attracting members of the opposite sex (if you can, indeed, determine what that would be). I mean, imagine the following conversa-

tion between the bass player for Dufus and a potential date chosen at random from the crowd before they take the stage. Bass player: "So, we haven't met. I'm Mike, the bass player for Dufus." Audience member: "Buh-bye, Dufus." See what I mean? It's hard to put a good spin on that name. I think I might call a band meeting and politely request a snappier name, citing the bass player's bad experience transcribed above. Some alternate names might be The Studs. Or The Heartbreak Kids, or even Eddie from Ohio. So, let's try that scenario again, but using one of these new and improved names. Bass player: "So, we haven't met. I'm Mike, the bass player for Eddie from Ohio." Audience member: "Can you introduce me to Eddie?" Bass player: "Uh, I dunno, he's pretty busy." Audience member: "Leave me alone, you Dufus."

Quadtoning for Richer B&Ws

If you've ever wondered how the pros get those deep, rich-looking B&W photos, you might be surprised to learn that what you were looking at weren't just regular B&W photos, instead they were quadtones or tritones—B&W photos made up of three or four different grays and/or brown colors to make what appears to be a B&W photo, but with much greater depth. Luckily, Adobe has put a bunch of very slick preset quadtones, tritones, and duotones in your CS3 folder. Here's how to put them to use:

Step One:

Open the photo you want to apply your quadtoning effect to (the term quadtoning just means the final photo will use four different inks mixed together to achieve the effect. Tritones use three inks, and do I really have to mention how many duotones use?). Quadtoning effects seem to look best with (but are not limited to) two kinds of photos: (1) landscapes, and (2) people. Especially cowboys. I'm kidding. Kinda.

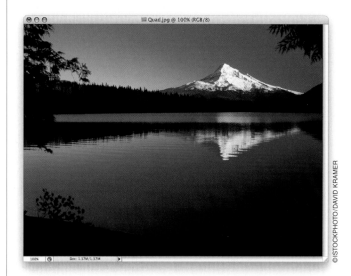

Step Two:

To create a quadtone, you'll have to convert to Grayscale mode first, but by now you know what a flat-looking B&W photo that creates, so instead use whichever method from the B&W chapter (Chapter 7) of this book you like best (in the example shown here, I used the simple Gradient Map adjustment layer method, which worked just great. In fact, I didn't even have to add a center stop under the gradient—it looked good "as is").

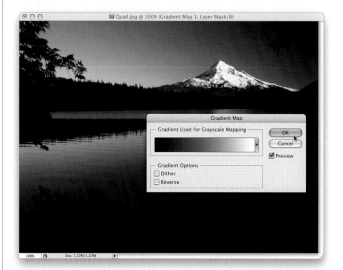

Step Three:

Now that your photo looks black and white, it's okay to convert to Grayscale mode. This won't change the look of the photo, it will just change the mode, and at this point (when the color's already gone), it's harmless. So, go under the Image menu, under Mode, and choose Grayscale (as shown here). When you do this, it will ask you if you want to flatten your layers (your only layer is that Gradient Map adjustment layer), so click on the Flatten button (if you keep the Gradient Map adjustment layer, it changes the look of your photo because the gradient map relies on the color channels to do its thing. Taking away those channels changes its effectiveness, so that's why you should go ahead and click the Flatten button in that warning dialog).

Step Four:

Of course, that's not the only warning dialog that appears (Adobe really doesn't want you to get into trouble. See, they care). The next one that appears asks you if you really want to discard the color information (as shown here). Then, it tells you that you should be using the Black & White control to make your conversion, because it doesn't know you've used a gradient map already. Since your color is already gone, you're safe to click the Discard button, but before you do, may I recommend turning on the Don't Show Again checkbox? If you don't click this, you'll become well acquainted with this well-meaning, yet incredibly annoying warning dialog. Unless you think you need more things popping up onscreen when you need them the least, I'd turn on that Don't Show Again checkbox. In fact, click it three times just for good measure.

Continued

Step Five:

Once your photo is in Grayscale mode, the Duotone menu item (which has been grayed out and unchoosable until this very moment) is now open for business. So, go under the Image menu, under Mode, and choose Duotone (if Duotone is still grayed out, you forgot Step Three—converting to grayscale).

Step Six:

When you choose Duotone, the Duotone Options dialog appears (shown here), and what do you think its default mode is? Duotone? Nope—that's too obvious. Even though you chose Duotone, and you're in the Duotone Options dialog, the default setting is for a one-color Monotone. (I'll bet some nights the Adobe engineers who designed this sit at a restaurant with glasses of wine and just laugh and laugh when they think about the look on our faces when we see Monotone as the default type. Aw, those rascals!) Anyway, your job here is to choose Quadtone from the Type pop-up menu (as shown here), but don't click OK yet.

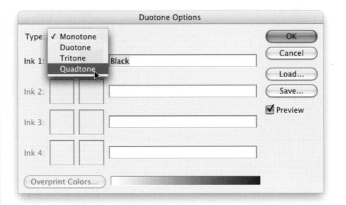

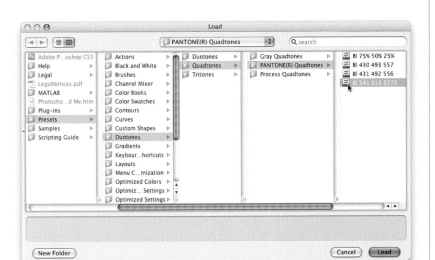

Step Seven:

Now, click the Load button in the Duotone Options dialog as it's time to start the search for those preset quadtones already on your hard drive (the ones I talked about in the introduction). By the way, did you see the movie *The DaVinci Code*? Cracking that was easier than finding these presets. I've shown the path to them here, but I'll break it down for you: Start by looking in your Adobe Photoshop CS3 Applications (PC: Program Files\Adobe\Adobe Photoshop CS3) folder, then inside that you'll find a Presets folder. Inside that find the Duotones folder and inside that are folders for Duotones, Quadtones, and Tritones. Open Quadtones, and inside that folder open PANTONE(R) Quadtones, and inside that click on the bottom file, named "BL 541 513 5773" to make it easy (listen closely, and you can hear those Adobe engineers giggling uncontrollably).

Step Eight:

Click the Load button and the quadtone you chose is applied to your B&W image, giving you the rich look you see here (compare this with the rather cold-looking original on the previous page, and you can really see the difference stacking up those four inks can make). For printing (or anything else for that matter), you'll need to go back to the Image menu, under Mode, and choose RGB color. Now, on the next two pages, I'm going to share some of my favorite quadtone, tritone, and duotone settings, and apply them to this same photo so you can see how they compare (they're all slightly different) and see if you'd like to try any of them.

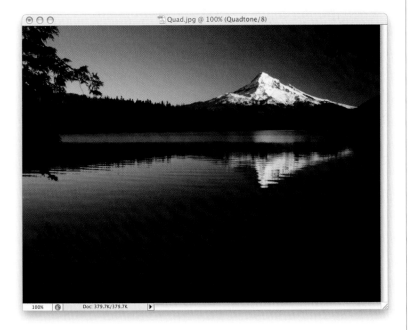

Continued

Step Nine:

This one is a tritone, so when you hit the Load button, you have to navigate your way back to the Tritones folder, then open the Gray Tritones folder, and inside of that choose the second tritone down, descriptively named "BL 409 WmGray 407 WmGray" for your convenience.

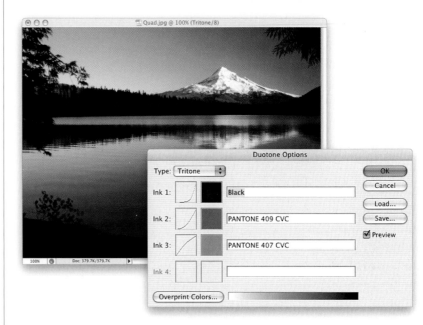

Step 10:

Here's another tritone, which has a somewhat similar look, but it's not quite as dark because of the tritone curve applied to the third ink, and because it uses a lighter combination of inks. This one is found in the same Gray Tritones folder as the previous tritone, but this one is the last one in the folder (the fourth one down on a PC), and it's named "BL WmGray 7 WmGray 2" (exactly what I would have named it. By the way, I did some research and learned that the "BL" stands for "Big Laugh." I should've known).

TIP: One thing about these multi-ink looks: they look different depending on the photo you apply them to, so make sure you give at least a few of them a try on different photos and you'll see what I mean.

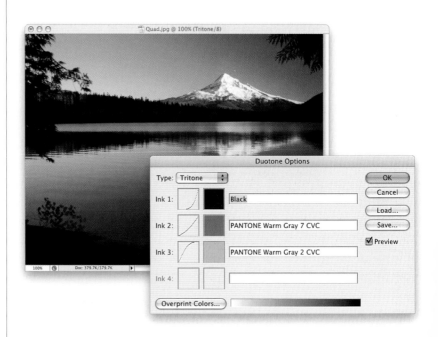

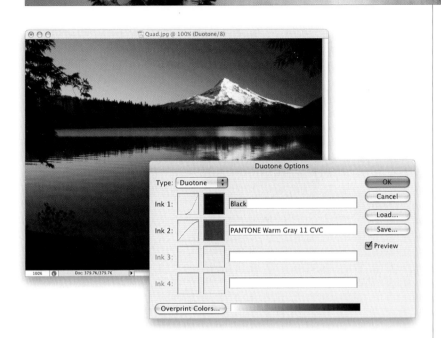

Step 11:

This one's just a simple duotone, but it's nice, so hit the Load button, go back to the Duotones folder, and inside the Duotones folder choose (you guessed it) Duotones. Inside that folder, look in the Gray/Black Duotones folder and scroll way down to choose the one called "Warm Gray 11 bl 2" to give you the effect shown here.

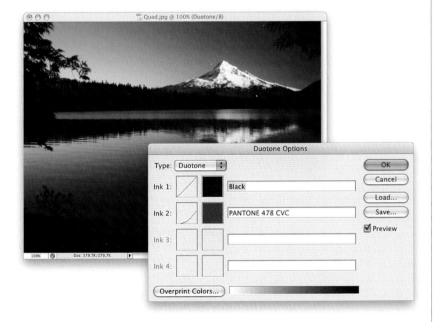

Step 12:

For one last look, try this duotone found in the Duotones folder, but in the PANTONE(R) Duotones folder. It's called "478 brown (100%) bl 4," and it adds a reddish brown to the mix that really works well for certain photos (that goes back to my "give at least a few of them a try on different photos" tip on the previous page. You'll be surprised at how different these same exact quadtones, tritones, and duotones will look when applied to different photos). Well, there you have it—four of my favorites (and don't forget, when you're done, convert back to RGB mode).

Taming Your Light

Sometimes the light falls where you don't want it, and sometimes you just mess up (like in the case here, where I didn't pay enough attention to the spread of the light, and both the bride's face and the bouquet she's holding share pretty much the same intensity of light. The subject really is the bride's face, and the flowers are just playing a supporting role, but I lit it like they're sharing the starring role). Luckily, it's pretty easy to tame and refocus the light in Photoshop (though I'd still rather have done it right when I shot it).

Step One:

As I mentioned above, here's the shot where the bride's face and the bouquet are both equally as bright, which is not a good thing (in fact, the bouquet may even be a little brighter, and is drawing your attention away from the bride, which is absolutely not what you, or the bride, want). So, we're going to tame our light using a very simple Levels move. Choose Levels from the Create New Adjustment Layer pop-up menu at the bottom of the Layers panel (as shown here).

Step Two:

The changes I make in the Levels dialog will affect the entire photo, but since adjustment layers come with their own built-in mask, we'll be able to tweak things very easily after the fact. At this point, you want to darken the bouquet, so drag the Input Levels middle slider to the right a bit to darken the midtones (and the bouquet), and then drag the bottom-right Output Levels slider to the left a little bit to darken the overall photo (as shown here), and click OK. One downside is that this oversaturates the colors quite a bit, which can also draw attention away from the face, but that's easy to fix.

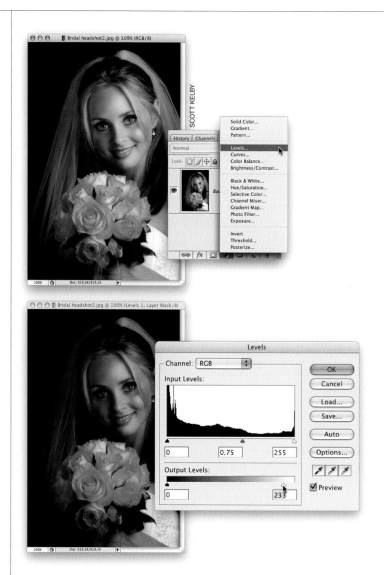

Step Three:
First, to reduce the oversaturation caused by our Levels move, go to the Layers panel and change the blend mode of the Levels adjustment layer from Normal to Luminosity. This keeps the darkening without oversaturating the color. Next, press Command-I (PC: Ctrl-I) to Invert the layer mask, which hides the darkening added by our Levels move behind a black mask. Now, get the Brush tool (B), make sure your Foreground color is set to white, then paint over everything in the photo except for her face and hair. As you paint, it darkens those areas (as shown here where I'm darkening the bouquet so now the bride's face is once again the focus).

Before (the bouquet has at least as much or more light than the bride's face)

After (everything else is darkened, leaving the bride's face nicely lit and making it the visual focus of the portrait)

Punching Up Drab Colors Using Lab Color

Okay, so why isn't this in the color correction chapter? It's because this isn't color correction. We're not trying to make colors look as they did, we're punching up the colors big time so they look better, more vibrant, and more contrasty than the scene really looked when the shot was taken. It's totally a color effect and what you're about to learn is a much simplified version of a Lab color technique I learned from Dan Margulis, master of all things color. The full-blown technique is found in Dan's amazing book *Photoshop LAB Color*.

Step One:

This technique works best on photos that are kind of flat and drab. If you apply this to an already colorful photo, it will pretty much take the color right over the top, so choose an appropriate photo whose color needs some serious pumping up (I'm going to totally resist the urge to use a *Saturday Night Live* reference, like "We're here to pump—you—up!" Oh rats, I just did it, didn't I? My bad).

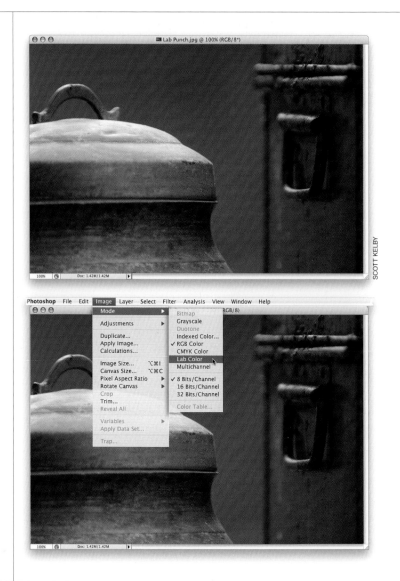

Step Two:

This is a Lab color move, so go under the Image menu, under Mode, and choose Lab Color (as shown here). This is a totally non-destructive move (moving from RGB to Lab color and back), so don't hesitate to jump over there whenever you feel the need.

Step Three:

There's no need to head over to the Channels panel, because you're going to be doing your work in the Apply Image dialog. So, go under the Image menu and choose Apply Image. Now, before we start working in Apply Image, here's a little background: You know how we have layer blend modes (like Multiply, Screen, Overlay, etc.)? Well, in the Channels panel, there is no channel blend mode pop-up menu like there is for layers in the Layers panel, so to get channels to blend using blend modes, you use Apply Image to apply a channel to itself. When the Apply Image dialog appears, by default the blend mode is set to Multiply (which always seems too dark), so to get to the starting place for our effect, change the Blending pop-up menu to Overlay, as shown here. As you can see, it looks pretty sweet! If anything, Overlay mode may make your photo look too vivid and contrasty, but we'll deal with that soon.

Step Four:

The nice thing about using Apply Image is that you get at least three different "looks," and you simply have to choose which one looks best to you (they look different depending on the photo, so you have to try all three). By default, you're seeing the full Lab color channel (that's seen back in Step Three), so once you've seen that channel, then click on the Channel pop-up menu and choose "a" (as shown here) to see how the "a" channel looks blended with an invisible copy of itself in Overlay mode. It certainly looks better than the original, but I don't think it looks as good as the Lab channel did in Step Three.

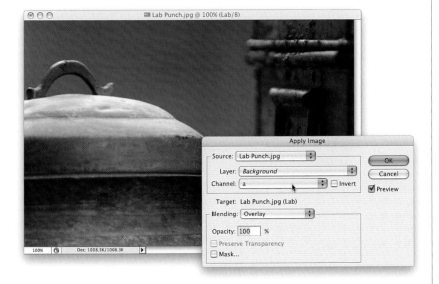

Continued

Step Five:

Now try the "b" channel by choosing "b" from the Channel pop-up menu (as shown here). This channel usually adds more yellow and warm tones to the photo (as seen in the example here). In fact, if you want to make an outdoor scene instantly look like a fall color scene somewhere in the Northeast, convert to Lab Color mode, choose Apply Image, switch to Overlay mode, and simply choose the "b" channel—voilá—instant fall colors. Now, back to our project: in the example shown here, it's very yellowish, and if you like that look— you're done—just click OK. If not, continue on with me.

Step Six:

So far, you've seen the photo blending in Overlay mode (which is a pretty punchy mode), using the Lab channel, the "a" channel, and the "b" channel. Personally, I like the Lab channel by far, and if you feel it's the best of the three, but think it might actually be a little too "punchy," then change the Blending pop-up menu to Soft Light (as shown here). This is a more mellow mode than Overlay (how's that for a New Age explanation), and if Overlay is too intense for you, you'll probably love Soft Light. I don't mind admitting that I probably use Soft Light more than Overlay. It's probably from burning incense and sitting in the Lotus position (by the way, I have no idea what the Lotus position is, but it sounds painful).

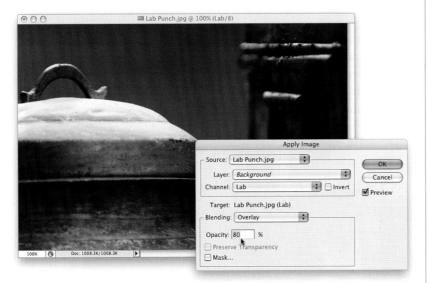

Step Seven:
There is another way to go if you think Overlay is too intense, and that's to use the volume knob. Well, I call it the volume knob, but it's actually the Opacity amount (which appears just below the Blending pop-up menu). The lower the opacity, the lower the amount of the effect. In the example shown here, I switched back to the Lab channel, chose Overlay in the Blending pop-up menu, but then lowered the Opacity to 80%. The After photo below was done using those same exact settings.

TIP: This Apply Image trick is a great thing to record as an action. But once you create it, go to the Actions panel and click in the second column beside the words "Apply Image" (a dialog icon will appear), and then when you run the action, the Apply Image dialog will appear onscreen for you to try your three choices. Once you make your choice, click OK, and the action will continue, and will convert you back to RGB.

Before

After (using the Lab channel in Overlay mode at 80%—no Curves, no Levels, no nuthin')

Step Five:

To knock the exact same hole out of the B&W layer (which means there will be "eye holes" knocked out of the top two layers, so you'll see the original eyes from the Background layer), just press-and-hold the Option (PC: Alt) key, click directly on the layer mask thumbnail itself on the top layer, and drag it to the middle layer (as shown here). This puts an exact copy of the top layer's layer mask on your middle layer. Now you're seeing the original full-color unretouched eyes from the Background layer. Pretty neat little trick, eh?

Step Six:

Now flatten the image by choosing Flatten Image from the Layers panel's flyout menu. The final step is to add some noise, so go under the Filter menu, under Noise, and choose Add Noise. When the Add Noise filter dialog appears (seen here), set the Distribution to Gaussian, and turn on the Monochromatic checkbox (otherwise, your noise will appear as little red, green, and blue specks, which looks really lame). Lastly, dial in an amount of noise that while visible, isn't overly noisy. I'm working on a very low-resolution version, so I only used 4%, but on a high-res digital camera photo, you'll probably have to use between 10% and 12% to see much of anything. You can see the before/after at the top of the next page. Beyond that, I gave you some other examples of how this effect looks on other portraits.

Before

After (applying the effect and revealing the eyes)

Before

After

©ISTOCKPHOTO/TYLER STALMAN

Step Seven:
Here's another example using the exact same technique (including the eyes trick), and you can see how different the effect looks on a completely different image. I particularly love the almost bronze skin tone it creates in this image. Very cool stuff. Turn the page for more examples.

TIP: Be careful not to add too much noise, because when you add an Unsharp Mask to the image (which you would do at the very end, right before you save the file), it enhances and brings out any noise (intentional or otherwise) in the photo.

ANOTHER TIP: I recently saw this effect used in a motorcycle print ad. They applied the effect to the background, and then masked (knocked out) the bike so it was in full color. It really looked very slick (almost eerie in a cool eerie way).

Continued

Step Eight:

Here's the same technique applied to a photo of a woman, however I didn't knock out the eyes because her eye color was pretty subtle. Instead I lowered the Brush tool's opacity to 50% and painted over her lips on the top layer, then copied that layer mask down to the B&W layer (just like before with the eyes—same technique with the mask). Without doing that, her lips looked pretty cold, and this way the subtle 50% red looks right with the rest of the photo.

Before   *After*

Step Nine:

Here's the final example, and there's a version of that bronze skin again. I love what it did to his skin (kind of blowing out the highlights in a cool way), and his hair. I did knock out the eye, so you're seeing his original eye color there.

TIP: Here are a couple of variations you can try with this effect: If the effect seems too subtle when you first apply it, of course you could try Overlay mode as I mentioned earlier, but before you try that, try duplicating the Soft Light layer once and watch how that pumps up the effect. Of course, you can lower the opacity of that layer if it's too much. Another trick to try is to lower the opacity of the original Soft Light layer to 70%, which brings back some color with almost a tinting effect. Give it a shot and see what you think. One last thing: wouldn't this be a great effect to apply as an action? Oh yeah—that's what I'm talkin' 'bout!

Before   *After*

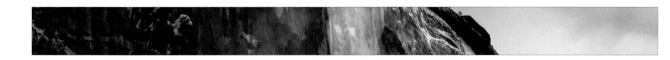

The duotone tinting look is all the rage right now, but creating a real two-color duotone, complete with curves that will separate in just two colors on press is a bit of a chore. However, if you're outputting to an inkjet printer, or to a printing press as a full-color job, then you don't need all that complicated stuff— you can create a fake duotone that looks at least as good (if not better).

Fake
Duotone

Step One:

Open the color RGB photo that you want to convert into a duotone (again, I'm calling it a duotone, but we're going to stay in RGB mode the whole time, so you can just treat this like any other color photo). Now, the hard part of this is choosing which color to make your duotone. I always see other people's duotones and think, "Yeah, that's the color I want!" but when I go to the Foreground color swatch and try to create a similar color in the Color Picker, it's always hit or miss (usually miss). That's why you'll want to know this next trick.

Step Two:

If you can find another duotone photo that has a color you like, you're set. So I usually go to a stock photo website (like iStockphoto.com) and search for "duotones." When I find one I like, I return to Photoshop, press I to get the Eyedropper tool, click-and-hold anywhere within my image area, and then (while keeping the mouse button held down) I drag my cursor outside Photoshop and onto the photo in my Web browser to sample the color I want. Now, mind you, I did not and would not take a single pixel from someone else's photo—I'm just sampling a color (take a look at your Foreground color swatch to see the sampled color).

Continued

Faking a Neutral Density Gradient Filter

One of the most popular lens filters for outdoor photographers is the Neutral Density filter, because often (especially when shooting scenery, like sunsets) you wind up with a bright sky and a dark foreground. A Neutral Density gradient lens filter reduces the exposure in the sky by a stop or two, while leaving the ground unchanged (the top of the filter is gray, and it graduates down to transparent at the bottom). Well, if you forgot to use your ND gradient filter when you took the shot, you can create your own ND effect in Photoshop.

Step One:
Open the photo (preferably a landscape) where you exposed for the ground, which left the sky too light. Press the letter D to set your Foreground color to black. Then, go to the Layers panel and choose Gradient from the Create New Adjustment Layer pop-up menu at the bottom of the panel (as shown here).

Step Two:
When the Gradient Fill dialog appears, it applies a Foreground to Transparent gradient to your photo (since you set your Foreground color to black first, it goes from black to transparent), but unfortunately this default gradient darkens the ground, as seen here (rather than the sky), which is exactly the opposite of what we need. Luckily, it's easy to fix.

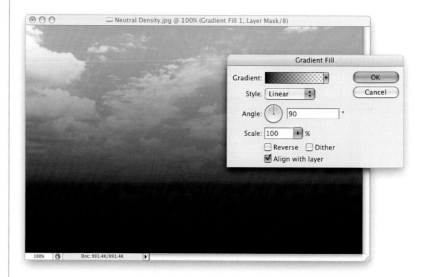

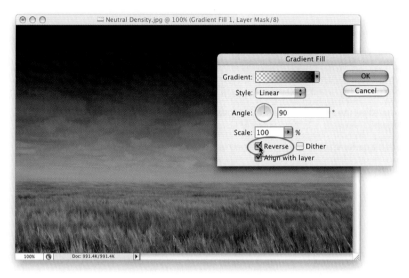

Step Three:
To fix this problem, just turn on the Reverse checkbox (shown circled here in red) to reverse the gradient, putting the dark area of your gradient over the sky and the transparent part over the land. Your image will look pretty awful at this point (with a black sky), but you'll fix that in the next step, so just click OK to apply the gradient.

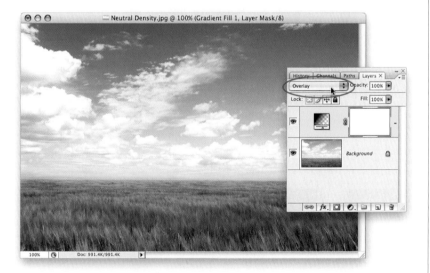

Step Four:
To make this gradient blend in with your photo, go to the Layers panel and change the blend mode of this adjustment layer from Normal to Overlay. This darkens the sky, but it gradually lightens until it reaches land, and then it slowly disappears. So, how does it know where the ground is? It doesn't. It puts a gradient across your entire photo, so in the next step, you'll basically show it where the ground is.

Continued

Step Seven:

Press Command-D (PC: Ctrl-D) to Deselect, and you'll see the effect is like a really soft spotlight aimed at your subjects. If the edge darkening actually is close enough to their faces to matter, get the Eraser tool (E), choose a soft-edged brush, and simply paint over the top of the head and hair (as shown here) to remove the edge vignetting in just that area. The final photo is seen below right. Notice the sharp eyes and hair, and general overall sharpness, but there's also a general overall softness, enhanced even more by that soft spotlight vignette you added at the end. Again, this is a perfect routine to turn into an action so it's always just one click away.

Before   *After (applying all three steps)*

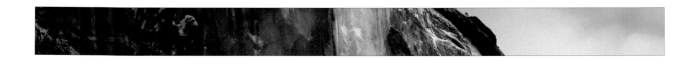

This is an incredibly popular effect with pro wedding photographers (in fact, I can't remember the last time I saw a wedding album without this effect in it). Basically, you're going to make a copy of the photo, remove all the color, and then just bring back color right where you want it (this is usually done on the bridal bouquet—I know, it's kind of an obvious choice). Anyway, although I'm showing it here in the context of a wedding, it's perfect for travel photography, product shots, and any instance where you want to lead the viewer using color.

Drawing the Viewer's Eye with Color

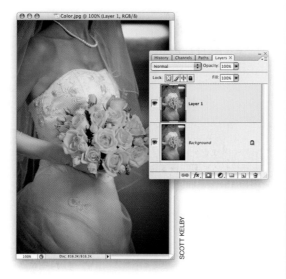

Step One:
Open the photo where you want to lead the viewer's eye with the use of color. As I mentioned in the intro above, the classic use of this technique in wedding photography is to make the photo black and white, and bring back the color in the bouquet. So, start by pressing Command-J (PC: Ctrl-J), which duplicates the Background layer.

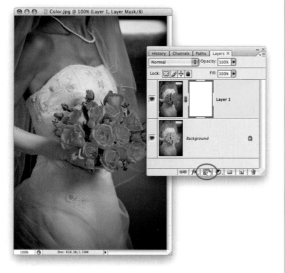

Step Two:
Next, to remove the color from this duplicate layer, press Command-Shift-U (PC: Ctrl-Shift-U), which is the shortcut for Desaturate (if you're charging by the hour, go under the Image menu, under Adjustments, and choose Desaturate). Once the layer is in black and white, click on the Add Layer Mask icon at the bottom of the Layers panel (as shown here).

Continued

Photo by Scott Kelby   Exposure: 1.3s   Focal Length: 24mm   Aperture Value: *f*/11

Look Sharp
sharpening techniques

For those of you who bought the CS2 version of this book, you might be looking up at that title "Look Sharp" and thinking, "Hey, that's the same title he used in the old book," and while that may be technically true, it's not the same song. The song I referenced in the CS2 book was from the band Roxette, but the song I'm referring to this time around is from Joe Jackson (the guy who had the '80s hit "Is She Really Going Out With Him?"). Now, you're probably wondering, with copyright laws being what they are today, how can two different songs have exactly the same name without creating an avalanche of lawsuits? Well, it's because of a special exemption within international trademark and copyright laws, which stipulates that the names of books or songs can't be copyrighted. It's because of this exemption that I nearly named this book *The DaVinci Code*, but beyond that, it's the only reason why Joe Jackson was allowed to not only name his song "Look Sharp" (like Roxette), but he was also allowed to have the same name as the father of the Jackson Five, which not coincidentally is (you guessed it) Joe Jackson. The more I thought about this, the more intrigued I became, and after months of intense research (most of which was conducted with the gracious help of a team at a small university about 30 kilometers outside of Gstaad), we learned that Joe Jackson isn't even his real name. It's David Ian Jackson. Worse yet, his original name for the song was actually "Unsharp Mask," but at the last minute, in the recording studio, he changed the name to "Look Sharp" to avoid creating confusion in the marketplace with the Beatles' #1 hit from 1968 "Lab Sharpen Man," from their classic album *Levels & Curves*.

Sharpening Essentials

After you've color corrected your photos and right before you save your file, you'll definitely want to sharpen your photos. I sharpen every digital camera photo, either to help bring back some of the original crispness that gets lost during the correction process, or to help fix a photo that's slightly out of focus. Either way, I haven't met a digital camera (or scanned) photo that I didn't think needed a little sharpening. Here's a basic technique for sharpening the entire photo:

Step One:

Open the photo you want to sharpen. Because Photoshop displays your photo differently at different magnifications, choosing the right magnification (also called the zoom amount) for sharpening is critical. Because today's digital cameras produce such large-sized files, it's now pretty much generally accepted that the proper magnification to view your photos during sharpening is 50%. If you look up in your image window's title bar, it displays the current percentage of zoom (shown circled here in red). The quickest way to get to a 50% magnification is to press-and-hold the Command (PC: Ctrl) key and then press the + (plus sign) key or – (minus sign) key to zoom the magnification in or out.

Step Two:

Once you're viewing your photo at 50% size, go under the Filter menu, under Sharpen, and choose Unsharp Mask. (If you're familiar with traditional darkroom techniques, you probably recognize the term "unsharp mask" from when you would make a blurred copy of the original photo and an "unsharp" version to use as a mask to create a new photo whose edges appeared sharper.)

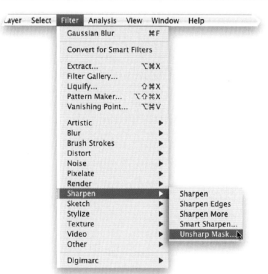

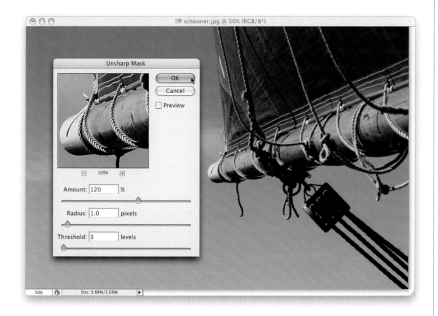

Step Three:
When the Unsharp Mask dialog appears, you'll see three sliders. The Amount slider determines the amount of sharpening applied to the photo; the Radius slider determines how many pixels out from the edge the sharpening will affect; and Threshold determines how different a pixel must be from the surrounding area before it's considered an edge pixel and sharpened by the filter (by the way, the Threshold slider works the opposite of what you might think—the lower the number, the more intense the sharpening effect). So what numbers do you enter? I'll give you some great starting points on the following pages, but for now, we'll just use these settings—Amount: 120%, Radius: 1, and Threshold: 3. Click OK and the sharpening is applied to the entire photo (see the After photo below).

Before

After

Continued

Sharpening soft subjects:

Here are Unsharp Mask settings—
Amount: 150%, Radius: 1, Threshold:
10—that work well for images where
the subject is of a softer nature (e.g.,
flowers, puppies, people, rainbows,
etc.). It's a subtle application of sharpening that is very well suited to these
types of subjects.

Sharpening portraits:

If you're sharpening close-up portraits,
try these settings—Amount: 75%,
Radius: 2, Threshold: 3—which apply
another form of subtle sharpening, but
with enough punch to make eyes sparkle
a little bit, and bring out highlights in
your subject's hair.

Moderate sharpening:

This is a moderate amount of sharpening that works nicely on everything from product shots, to photos of home interiors and exteriors, to landscapes (and in this case, a white tiger). These are my favorite settings when you need some nice snappy sharpening. Try applying these settings—Amount: 120%, Radius: 1, Threshold: 3—and see how you like it (my guess is you will). Take a look at how it added snap and detail to the tiger's whiskers and eyes.

Maximum sharpening:

I use these settings—Amount: 65%, Radius: 4, Threshold: 3—in only two situations: (1) The photo is visibly out of focus and it needs a heavy application of sharpening to try to bring it back into focus. (2) The photo contains lots of well-defined edges (e.g., rocks, buildings, coins, cars, machinery, etc.). In this photo, taken in Arizona's Antelope Canyon slots, the heavy amount of sharpening really brings out the detail in the rock walls.

Continued

All-purpose sharpening:

These are probably my all-around favorite sharpening settings—Amount: 85%, Radius: 1, Threshold: 4—and I use these most of the time. It's not a "knock-you-over-the-head" type of sharpening—maybe that's why I like it. It's subtle enough that you can apply it twice if your photo doesn't seem sharp enough the first time you run it, but once will usually do the trick.

Web sharpening:

I use these settings—Amount: 200%, Radius: 0.3, Threshold: 0—for Web graphics that look blurry. (When you drop the resolution from a high-res, 300-ppi photo down to 72 ppi for the Web, the photo often gets a bit blurry and soft.) If the sharpening doesn't seem sharp enough, try increasing the Amount to 400%. I also use this same setting (Amount: 400%) on out-of-focus photos. It adds some noise, but I've seen it rescue photos that I would otherwise have thrown away.

SCOTT KELBY

Coming up with your own settings:
If you want to experiment and come up with your own custom blend of sharpening, I'll give you some typical ranges for each adjustment so you can find your own sharpening "sweet spot."

Amount
Typical ranges run anywhere from 50% to 150%. This isn't a hard-and-fast rule—just a typical range for adjusting the Amount, where going below 50% won't have enough effect, and going above 150% might get you into sharpening trouble (depending on how you set the Radius and Threshold). You're fairly safe staying under 150%. (In the example here, I reset my Radius and Threshold to 1 and 4, respectively.)

Continued

Radius

Most of the time, you'll use just 1 pixel, but you can go as high as (get ready) 2 pixels. You saw one setting I gave you earlier for extreme situations, where you can take the Radius as high as 4 pixels. I once heard a tale of a man in Cincinnati who used 5, but I'm not sure I believe it. (Incidentally, Adobe allows you to raise the Radius amount to [get this] 250! If you ask me, anyone caught using 250 as their Radius setting should be incarcerated for a period not to exceed one year and a penalty not to exceed $2,500.)

Threshold

A pretty safe range for the Threshold setting is anywhere from 3 to around 20 (3 being the most intense, 20 being much more subtle. I know, shouldn't 3 be more subtle and 20 be more intense? Don't get me started). If you really need to increase the intensity of your sharpening, you can lower the Threshold to 0, but keep a good eye on what you're doing (watch for noise appearing in your photo).

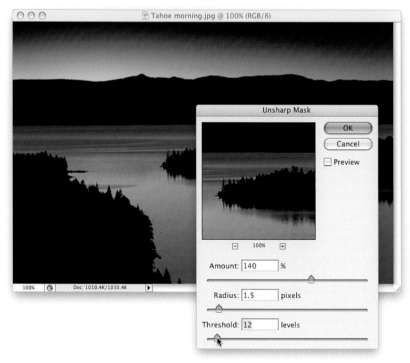

The Final Image

For the final sharpened image you see here, I used the Moderate Sharpening setting I gave earlier, and then I just dragged the Amount slider to the right (increasing the amount of sharpening), until it looked right to me (I wound up at around 140%, so I didn't have to drag too far). If you're uncomfortable with creating your own custom Unsharp Mask settings, then start with this: pick a starting point (one of the set of settings I gave on the previous pages), and then just move the Amount slider and nothing else (so, don't touch the Radius and Threshold sliders). Try that for a while, and it won't be long before you'll find a situation where you ask yourself, "I wonder if lowering the Threshold would help?" and by then, you'll be perfectly comfortable with it.

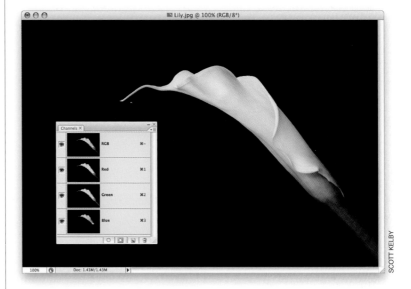

Lab Color Sharpening

This sharpening technique is probably the most popular technique with professional photographers because it helps to avoid the color halos and color artifacts (spots and noise) that appear when you add a lot of sharpening to a photo. And because it avoids those halos and other color problems, it allows you to apply more sharpening than you normally could get away with.

Step One:

Open the RGB photo you want to sharpen using Lab sharpening. Go to the Channels panel (found under the Window menu), and you can see that your RGB photo is made up of three channels—Red, Green, and Blue. Combining the data on these three channels creates a full-color RGB image (and you can see that represented in the RGB thumbnail at the top of the panel).

Step Two:

Go under the Image menu, under Mode, and choose Lab Color. In the Channels panel, you'll see that although your photo still looks the same onscreen, the channels have changed. There are still three channels (besides your full-color composite channel), but now there's a Lightness channel (the luminosity and detail of the photo) with "a" and "b" channels, which hold the color data.

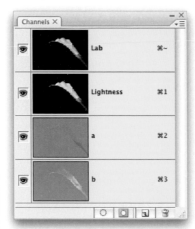

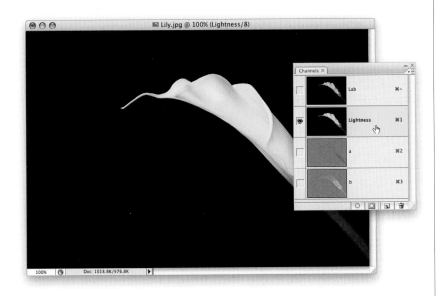

Step Three:

By switching to Lab color, you've separated the detail (Lightness channel) from the color info (the "a" and "b" channels), so click on the Lightness channel to select it. Now you'll go to the Filter menu, choose Sharpen, and apply the Unsharp Mask filter to just this black-and-white Lightness channel, thereby avoiding color halos because you're not sharpening the color (pretty tricky, eh?). *Note:* If you need some settings for using Unsharp Mask, look in the previous tutorial called "Sharpening Essentials"; however, I recommend these settings—Amount: 85%, Radius: 1, and Threshold: 4.

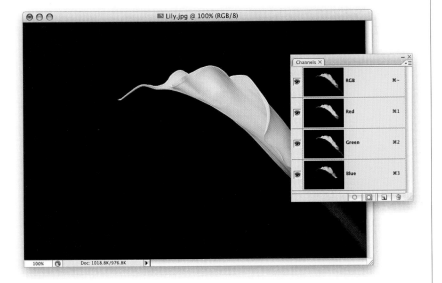

Step Four:

Once you've sharpened the Lightness channel, you may want to apply the sharpening again by pressing the keyboard shortcut Command-F (PC: Ctrl-F) for a crisper look. Then, go under the Image menu, under Mode, and choose RGB Color to switch your photo back to RGB. Now, should you apply this brand of sharpening to every digital camera photo you take? I would. In fact, I do, and since I perform this function quite often, I automate the process (as you'll see in the next step).

Continued

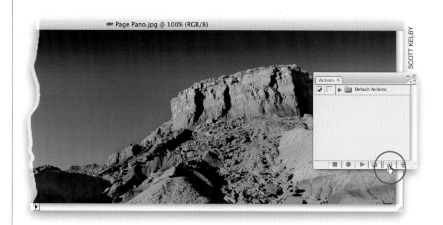

Step Five:

Open a different RGB photo, and let's do the whole Lab sharpening thing again, but this time before you start the process, go under the Window menu and choose Actions to bring up the Actions panel (seen here). The Actions panel is a "steps recorder" that records any set of repetitive steps and lets you instantly play them back (apply them to another photo) by simply pressing one button (you'll totally dig this). In the Actions panel, click on the Create New Action icon at the bottom of the panel (it looks just like the Create a New Layer icon from the Layers panel, and it's shown circled in red here).

Step Six:

Clicking that icon brings up the New Action dialog (shown here). The Name field is automatically highlighted, so go ahead and give this new action a name. (I named mine "Lab Sharpen." I know—how original!) Then, from the Function Key pop-up menu, choose the number of the Function key (F-key) on your keyboard that you want to assign to the action (this is the key you'll hit to make the action do its thing). I've assigned mine F11, but you can choose any open F-key that suits you (but everybody knows F11 is, in fact, the coolest of all F-keys—just ask anyone. On a Mac, you may need to turn off the OS keyboard shortcut for F11 first). You'll notice that the New Actions dialog has no OK button. Instead, there's a Record button, because once you exit this dialog, Photoshop CS3 starts recording your steps. So go ahead and click Record.

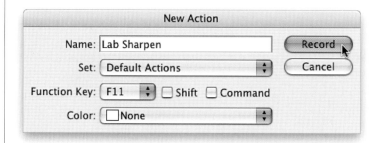

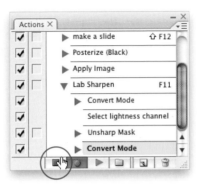

Step Seven:

With Photoshop recording every move you make, do the Lab sharpening technique you learned on the previous pages (convert to Lab color, click on the Lightness channel, and apply your favorite Unsharp Mask setting—basically repeat Steps 2–4. Also, if you generally like a second helping of sharpening, you can run the filter again, and then switch back to RGB mode). Now, in the Actions panel, click on the Stop icon at the bottom of the panel (it's the square icon, first from the left, shown circled here in red).

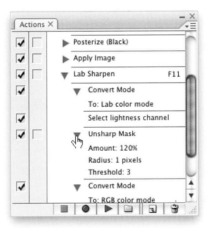

Step Eight:

This stops the recording process. If you look in the Actions panel, you'll see all your steps recorded in the order you did them. Also, if you expand the right-facing triangle beside each step (as shown here), you'll see more detail, including individual settings, for the steps it recorded. You can see here that I used the Amount: 120%, Radius: 1, and Threshold: 3 Unsharp Mask settings.

Continued

Step Nine:

Now, open a different RGB photo and let's test your action to see that it works (it's important to test it now before moving on to the next step). Press the F-key you assigned to your action (you chose F11, right? I knew it!). Photoshop immediately applies the sharpening to the Lightness channel for you (complete with conversions from Lab color back to RGB), and does it all faster than you could ever do it manually, because it takes place behind the scenes with no dialogs popping up.

Step 10:

Now that you've tested your action, we're going to put that baby to work. Of course, you could open more photos and then press F11 to have your action Lab sharpen them one at a time, but there's a better way. Once you've written an action, you can apply that action to an entire folder full of photos—and Photoshop will totally automate the whole process for you (it will literally open every photo in the folder and apply your Lab sharpening, and then save and close every photo—all automatically. How cool is that?). This is called batch processing, and here's how it works: Go under the File menu, under Automate, and choose Batch to bring up the Batch dialog (or you can choose Batch from the Tools menu's Photoshop submenu within Adobe Bridge CS3). At the top of the dialog, within the Play section, choose your Lab Sharpen action from the Action pop-up menu (if it's not already selected, as shown here).

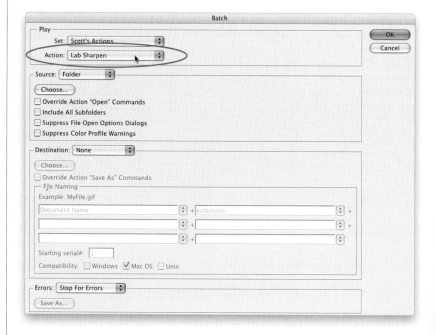

Step 11:
In the Source section of the Batch dialog, you tell Photoshop which folder of photos you want to Lab sharpen. So, choose Folder from the Source pop-up menu (you can also choose to run this batch action on selected photos from Bridge, or you can import photos from another source, or choose to run it on images that are already open in Photoshop). Then, click on the Choose button. A standard Open dialog will appear (shown here) so you can navigate to your folder of photos you want to sharpen. Once you find that folder, click on it (as shown), then click the Choose (PC: OK) button.

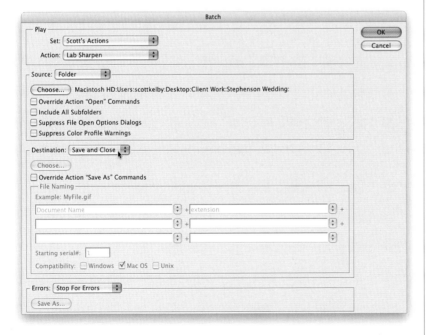

Step 12:
In the Destination section of the Batch dialog, you tell Photoshop where you want to put these photos once the action has done its thing. If you choose Save and Close from the Destination pop-up menu (as shown here), Photoshop will save the images in the same folder they're in. If you select Folder from the Destination pop-up menu, Photoshop will place your Lab-sharpened photos into a totally different folder. To do this, click on the Choose button in the Destination section, navigate to your target folder (or create a new one), and click Choose (PC: OK).

Continued

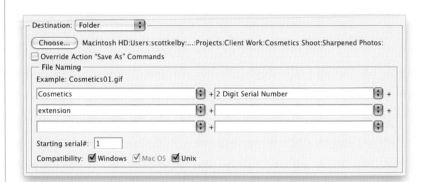

Step 13:

If you do choose to move them to a new folder, you can automatically rename your photos in the process. In short, here's how the file naming works: In the first field within the File Naming section, you type the basic name you want all the files to have. In the other fields, you can choose (from a pop-up menu) the automatic numbering scheme to use (adding a 1-digit number, 2-digit number, etc., and if you choose this, there's a field near the bottom where you can choose which number to start with). You can also choose to add the appropriate file extension (JPG, TIFF, etc.) in upper- or lowercase to the end of the new name. At the bottom of the dialog, there's a row of checkboxes for choosing compatibility with other operating systems. I generally turn all of these on, because ya never know. When you're finally done in the Batch dialog, click OK and Photoshop will automatically Lab Sharpen, rename, and save all your photos in a new folder for you. Nice!

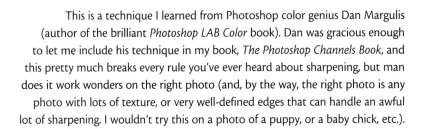

This is a technique I learned from Photoshop color genius Dan Margulis (author of the brilliant *Photoshop LAB Color* book). Dan was gracious enough to let me include his technique in my book, *The Photoshop Channels Book*, and this pretty much breaks every rule you've ever heard about sharpening, but man does it work wonders on the right photo (and, by the way, the right photo is any photo with lots of texture, or very well-defined edges that can handle an awful lot of sharpening. I wouldn't try this on a photo of a puppy, or a baby chick, etc.).

Two-Pass Super Sharpening

Step One:
The first step is to switch to Lab color mode, so go under the Image menu, under Mode, and choose Lab Color (as shown here).

Step Two:
Now you're going to load the Lightness channel as a selection (remember, we're in Lab color mode, so there's a Lightness channel, where all the detail is, and an "a" color channel and a "b" color channel, which hold the color). To load the Lightness channel as a selection, press Command-Option-1 (PC: Ctrl-Alt-1).

Continued

Step Three:

Once your selection is in place, you'll need to inverse it, so go under the Select menu and choose Inverse (or use the keyboard shortcut Command-Shift-I [PC: Ctrl-Shift-I]). Once your selection is inversed, we want to keep that selection in place, but hide it from view (so we can see how our sharpening looks without the distracting selection border), so press Command-H (PC: Ctrl-H).

Step Four:

Now that our selection is hidden from view, go to the Channels panel and click on the Lightness channel. We're going to apply our sharpening to the selected area on just this channel. This lets us avoid applying our sharpening to the color channels, which (as you now know) can cause a host of annoying problems. The big advantage of doing our sharpening this way is that since we're avoiding many of the problem areas of sharpening, we can actually get away with applying more sharpening without damaging our images.

Step Five:
Now you're going to apply your first round of sharpening using the Unsharp Mask filter (by now you know it's found under the Filter menu, under Sharpen). When the Unsharp Mask dialog appears, for Amount choose 500%, set the Radius at 1 pixel, set the Threshold to 2 levels, and click OK. This will apply a good, solid sharpening to the selected area of the Lightness channel.

Step Six:
Now you're going to add a second pass of sharpening, so bring up the Unsharp Mask filter once again. Start by leaving the Amount set to 500%, but then drag the Radius slider all the way to the left. Then slowly raise the radius by dragging the slider to the right, until the shape starts to come back. This two-pass sharpening is designed to be used on high-resolution images, and on a high-resolution image, your Radius setting will probably be somewhere between 25 and 35 pixels. I turned on the Preview checkbox in the example shown here, so you can see what this amount of sharpening does to your photo. Okay, I know it's not pretty, but you're going to fix that in the next step.

Continued

Step Seven:

Once you've dialed in that Radius amount (again, it will probably be between 25 and 35), lower the Amount to somewhere between 50% and 60% (just choose which looks best to you), and click OK to apply the final sharpening. Then go back under the Image menu, under Mode, and choose RGB Color to return to RGB. That's it—two different passes of the Unsharp Mask filter that make for some incredibly sharp photos (as seen below in the After photo).

Before

After

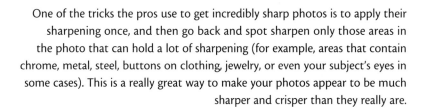

One of the tricks the pros use to get incredibly sharp photos is to apply their sharpening once, and then go back and spot sharpen only those areas in the photo that can hold a lot of sharpening (for example, areas that contain chrome, metal, steel, buttons on clothing, jewelry, or even your subject's eyes in some cases). This is a really great way to make your photos appear to be much sharper and crisper than they really are.

Making Photos Look Sharper Than They Really Are

Step One:
Open a photo you want to appear extra sharp. Go under the Filter menu, under Sharpen, and choose Unsharp Mask. For Amount, enter 120%; for Radius, enter 1; and for Threshold, enter 3 (as shown here). Then click OK to apply a moderate amount of sharpening to your entire photo.

Step Two:
Press Command-J (PC: Ctrl-J) to duplicate the Background layer. Now, on this duplicate layer, press Command-F (PC: Ctrl-F) to run the Unsharp Mask filter again, using the exact same settings. In fact, see if you can get away with applying it another time (or two). Unless you're working on a super-high-resolution photo, applying the filter three times in a row will oversharpen your photo enough to where it's pretty much trashed (as shown here, where the photo is totally oversharpened).

Continued

Step Three:

In the Layers panel, press-and-hold the Option (PC: Alt) key and click on the Add Layer Mask icon at the bottom of the Layers panel (as shown here). This adds a black mask to your super-sharp layer, and this mask totally hides that layer (so you're seeing the original Background layer with just one pass of the Unsharp Mask filter). Now your photo looks regular again.

Step Four:

Now press B to get the Brush tool, choose a medium-sized, soft-edged brush, and with your Foreground color set to white, paint over areas with lots of detail to bring out just those areas. In the example shown here, I painted over the parking light on the left-front fender of the red car (as shown here), along with the area of grill showing on the bumper. I also painted over the black rubber area connecting the side mirror, and over part of the mirror itself, as well as the window dividers on the passenger-side window. Revealing just these few sharper areas, which immediately draw the eye, makes the whole photo look much sharper (as seen on next page).

Before

After

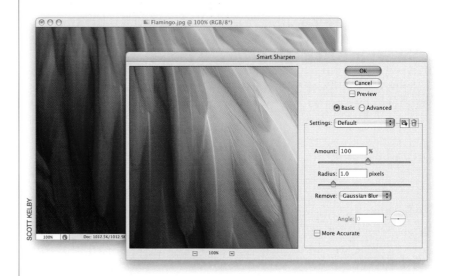

When to Use the Smart Sharpen Filter Instead

Count me as a fan of the Smart Sharpen filter (introduced back in Photoshop CS2), and although at the time I felt I would switch over to it for all my filter-based sharpening, I now pretty much find that I use it primarily when I run into a photo that is out of focus, or just needs some really serious sharpening. There are other advantages to Smart Sharpen, like being able to save your favorite settings in a pop-up menu, and there's a new sharpening algorithm that lets you avoid color halos, among others things, but here's how I'm using it today:

Step One:
Go under the Filter menu, under Sharpen, and choose Smart Sharpen. This filter is in Basic mode by default, so there are only two sliders: Amount (which controls the amount of sharpening—sorry, I had to explain that) and Radius (which determines how many pixels the sharpening will affect). The default settings are 100% for Amount (which I think is too high to use for just regular everyday sharpening), and the Radius is set at 1, which usually does the trick. You can see the first thing I like about the Smart Sharpen dialog, and that's the nice big preview window (shouldn't every Photoshop filter have a nice big preview like that? Don't get me started).

Step Two:
Below the Radius slider is the Remove pop-up menu (shown here), which lists the three types of blurs you can reduce using Smart Sharpen. Gaussian Blur (the default) applies a brand of sharpening that's pretty much like what you get using the regular Unsharp Mask filter (it uses a similar algorithm). Another choice is Motion Blur, but unless you can determine the angle of blur that appears in your image, it's tough to get really good results with this one.

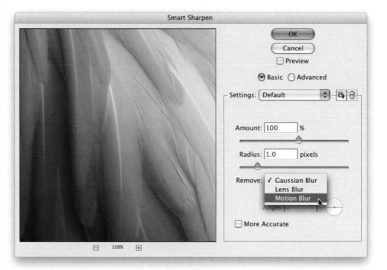

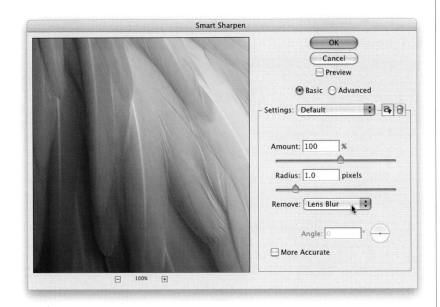

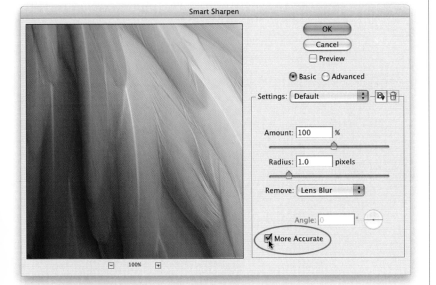

Step Three:

So, which one do I recommend? The third choice—Lens Blur. This is a sharpening algorithm created by Adobe's engineers that's better at detecting edges, so it creates fewer color halos than you'd get with the other choices, and overall I think it just gives you better sharpening for most images. The downside? Choosing Lens Blur makes the filter take a little longer to "do its thing." (That's why it's not the default choice, even though it provides better-quality sharpening.)

Step Four:

So, after you choose Lens Blur, go to the bottom of the dialog and you'll see a checkbox for More Accurate. It gives you (according to Adobe) more accurate sharpening by applying multiple iterations of the sharpening. I leave More Accurate turned on nearly all the time. (After all, who wants "less accurate" sharpening?) *Note:* If you're working on a large file, the More Accurate option can cause the filter to process slower, so it's up to you if it's worth the wait (I think it is). By the way, the use of the More Accurate checkbox is one of those topics that Photoshop users debate back and forth in online forums. For regular everyday sharpening it might be overkill, but again, the reason I use Smart Sharpen is because the photo is visibly blurry, slightly out of focus, or needs major sharpening to save. So I leave this on all the time. Please don't let anyone in the forums know I do that. They might slap me with some sort of fine. ;-)

Continued

Step Five:

I've found with the Smart Sharpen filter that I use a lower Amount setting than with the Unsharp Mask filter to get a similar amount of sharpening, so I usually find myself lowering the Amount to between 60% and 70%. However, the photo I'm working on here is so soft that I would actually go above 100% to…well…whatever it takes (in this case, around 170%, but again, that's only because the photo was a bit blurry from being hand-held in low light). So that's the extent of what I do with Smart Sharpen—I generally set the Amount to 60%–70%, I leave the Radius set at 1, I choose Lens Blur from the Remove pop-up menu, and I turn on the More Accurate checkbox. Take a look at the before and after on the bottom of the next page to see the results of using the Smart Sharpen filter.

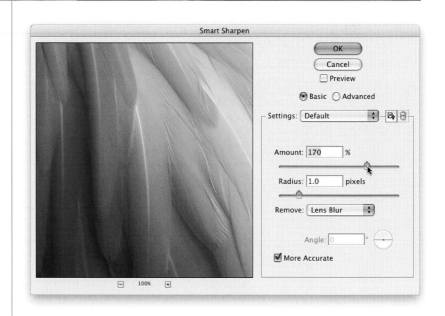

Step Six:

If you find yourself applying a setting such as this over and over again, you can save these settings and add them to the Settings pop-up menu at the top of the dialog by clicking on the floppy disk icon to the right of the pop-up menu. (Why a floppy disk icon? I have no idea.) This brings up a dialog for you to name your saved settings, so name your settings and click OK. Now, the next time you're in the Smart Sharpen filter dialog and you want to instantly call up your saved settings, just choose it from the Settings pop-up menu (as shown here).

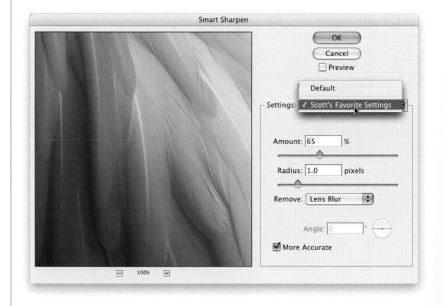

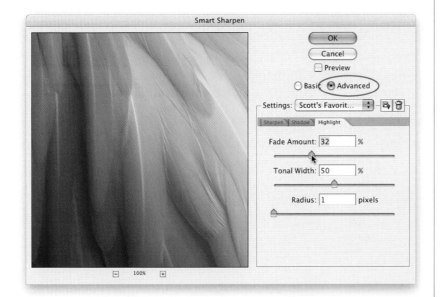

Step Seven:

If you click the Advanced radio button, it reveals two additional tabs with controls for reducing the sharpening in just the shadow or just the highlight areas that are applied to the settings you chose back in the Basic section. That's why in the Shadow and Highlight tabs, the top slider says "Fade Amount" rather than just "Amount." As you drag the Fade Amount slider to the right, you're reducing the amount of sharpening already applied, which can help reduce any halos in the highlights. (*Note:* Without increasing the amount of fade, you can't tweak the Tonal Width and Radius amounts. They only kick in when you increase the Fade Amount.) Thankfully, I rarely have had to use these Advanced controls, so 99% of my work in Smart Sharpen is done using the Basic controls.

Before

After

Edge-Sharpening Technique

This is a sharpening technique that doesn't use the Unsharp Mask filter, but still leaves you with a lot of control over the sharpening, even after the sharpening is applied. It's ideal to use when you have an image (with a lot of edges) that can hold a lot of sharpening or one that needs heavy sharpening to really make it snap.

Step One:
Open a photo that needs edge sharpening. Duplicate the Background layer by pressing Command-J (PC: Ctrl-J), as shown here.

Step Two:
Go under the Filter menu, under Stylize, and choose Emboss. You're going to use this filter to accentuate the edges in the photo. You can leave the Angle, Height, and Amount settings at their defaults (135°, 3, and 100%), but for low-res images, you'll want to lower the Height setting to 2 pixels (and for high-res 300-ppi images, try raising it to 4 pixels). Click OK to apply the filter, and your photo will turn gray with neon-colored highlights along the edges. To remove those neon-colored edges, press Command-Shift-U (PC: Ctrl-Shift-U) to Desaturate the color from this layer.

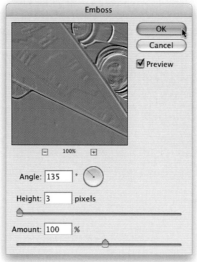

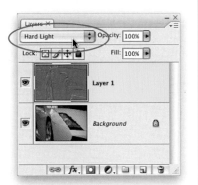

Step Three:

In the Layers panel, change the layer blend mode of this layer from Normal to Hard Light. This removes the gray color from the layer, but leaves the edges accentuated, making the entire photo appear much sharper.

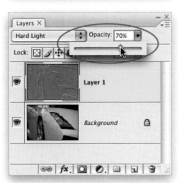

Step Four:

If the sharpening seems too intense, you can control the amount of the effect by simply lowering the Opacity of this layer in the Layers panel (in the After photo shown below, I lowered the layer's opacity to 70%, as shown here).

Before

After

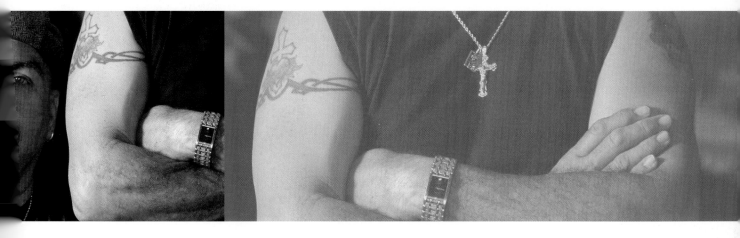

Best in Show
how to show your work

At some point in all of this, you're eventually going to want to show your client, or more likely a potential client, samples (or even finished products) of your work. Make sure you work on this part of the process long before your client is within 100 miles of your studio because (and this is a little-known fact), hardwired into your color inkjet printer is a small integrated chip that actually senses fear. That's right—if you're on a tight deadline, and you have to get your samples out of the printer right before your client arrives, the tiny electrodes in the chip sense your fear, and as a defense mechanism it releases millions of tiny silicon wafers into your printer's USB port, which causes your printer to basically go into sort of a prolonged hibernation mode which makes it just sit there and quietly hum. This auto-sleep or shut down mode is called "mocking mode" and is the digital equivalent of a small child giving you a raspberry. The more freaked out or rushed you get, the more of those tiny silicon wafers it releases, and the sleepier your printer becomes until it gets to the point that it has the operating functionality of a block of cheese. Now, you can fool your printer into printing again, but it's not easy. First, you have to continue to act freaked out, but when the printer's not paying attention you sneak out of the room and use your cell phone to call the studio phone nearest the printer. Once it starts ringing, you rush into the studio, and looking exasperated, you grab the phone and pretend it's the client on the line, and they're calling to cancel today's appointment. When your printer hears this (and trust me, this is true), it will instantly start outputting your prints. Try this—it works every time.

Watermarking & Adding Your Copyright Info

This two-part technique is particularly important if you're putting your proofs on the Web for client approval. In the first part of this technique, you'll add a see-through watermark so you can post larger proofs without fear of the client downloading and printing them; and second, you'll embed your personal copyright info, so if your photos are used anywhere on the Web, your copyright info will go right along with the file.

Step One:
Open the photo you want to add your copyright watermark to, then get the Custom Shape tool from the Toolbox (as shown here), or just press Shift-U until you have the tool (it looks like a star with rounded corners).

Step Two:
Once you have the Custom Shape tool, go up to the Options Bar and (1) click on the Fill Pixels icon (the third from the left), which makes your shape up of pixels (like normal), rather than as a Shape layer or path. Then, (2) click on the thumbnail to the right of the word "Shape" to bring up the Custom Shape Picker. When it pops down, (3) choose the copyright symbol, which is included in the default set of custom shapes (as shown here).

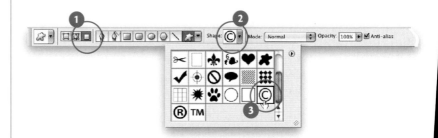

Step Three:
Create a new blank layer by clicking on the Create a New Layer icon at the bottom of the Layers panel. Click on the Foreground color swatch at the bottom of the Toolbox, and choose a light gray in the Color Picker for your Foreground color. Then, press-and-hold the Shift key (to keep things proportional), take your Custom Shape tool, and click-and-drag just above the center of your photo to add a large copyright symbol shape (seen here). Once it's drawn, click on the Add a Layer Style icon at the bottom of the Layers panel, and choose Bevel and Emboss from the pop-up menu (as shown here).

Step Four:
When the Layer Style dialog appears, you don't have to change any settings—just click OK to apply a beveled effect to your copyright symbol (seen here). Now, get the Type tool (T), make sure your Text color swatch in the Options Bar matches your Foreground color, type in "Copyright," followed by the current year, and lastly the name of your studio, then position it under the copyright symbol (as shown here).

Continued

Step Five:

Now you're going to duplicate your Bevel and Emboss layer style and apply it to your new Type layer. To do that, just press-and-hold the Option (PC: Alt) key, and in the Layers panel click directly on the word "Effects" on your copyright symbol layer, and drag-and-drop it onto your Type layer (as shown here). Holding that Option key down tells Photoshop CS3 to duplicate the effect. If you didn't hold the Option key, it wouldn't duplicate the effect on that layer—instead it would actually move it to that layer.

Step Six:

Go to the Layers panel, press-and-hold the Command (PC: Ctrl) key, and click on both layers to select them. Once they're both selected, press Command-E (PC: Ctrl-E) to merge these two layers into one single layer (don't worry—they will maintain the embossed effect look). Now, change the layer blend mode of this merged symbol layer from Normal to Hard Light (as shown here), which makes the watermark transparent. Now, you can lower the Opacity of this layer enough to where your clients can easily evaluate the photo, but there's enough watermark visible to keep them from using it as their final print (in the example shown here, I lowered the Opacity to 30%).

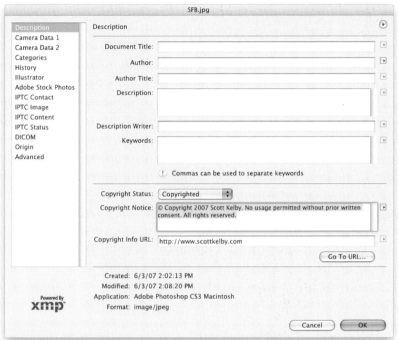

Step Seven:

Now that the watermarking is complete, let's embed your copyright info into the file itself. Go under the File menu and choose File Info to bring up the File Info dialog (seen here). In the left column, click on Description (if it doesn't come up by default). In the center section, choose Copyrighted from the Copyright Status pop-up menu. In the Copyright Notice field, enter your personal copy-right info, and then under Copyright Info URL, enter your full Web address (so if someone downloads your photo and opens it in Photoshop, they can click on the Go To URL button to go directly to your website). Lastly, click OK and this info is embedded into the file.

Step Eight:

When you click OK, Photoshop auto-matically adds a copyright symbol before your file's name in the title bar (shown circled in red here). Flatten your image by choosing Flatten Image from the Layers panel's flyout menu. Now you're going to create an action to automate this entire process. Start by opening a different photo, then go to the Actions panel (found under the Window menu) and click on the Create New Action icon at the bottom of the panel. When the dialog appears, name your action (as shown here) and click the Record button.

Continued

Step Nine:

Now repeat the whole process of adding the copyright symbol and copyright info (Photoshop will record all your steps as you're doing them, as seen here in the Actions panel). Start at Step One and stop after Step Seven (you stop after Step Seven, before flattening your file, because you may want to keep your layers intact so you can reposition your watermark, depending on the image).

Step 10:

When you're done, click on the Stop icon (it looks like a tiny square) at the bottom left of the Actions panel. Here's where it gets fun: you can apply this action to an entire folder full of photos. Go under the File menu, under Automate, and choose Batch. In the Play section, choose your action set and new watermark action from the pop-up menus. Under Source, choose Folder, then click the Choose button, navigate to your folder full of photos, and under Destination choose Save and Close. (If you want to save your watermarked photos to a different folder, choose Folder under the Destination section, click the Choose button, and navigate to the folder you want to save them to. You'll also need to add either a Flatten Image step or a Save and a Close step to your action.) Now, click OK and your watermark and copyright will be added to each photo in that folder automatically.

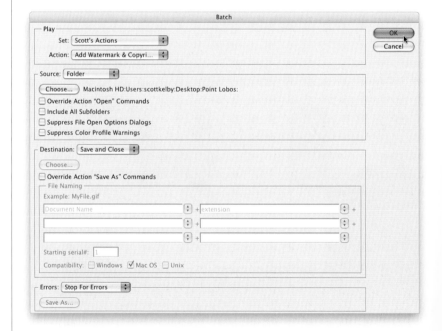

Artists always sign their work, and if you'd like to have your own signature so handy that you can add it to any finished piece with just one click, then you'll want to turn your signature into a brush. That way, you just grab the Brush tool, choose your signature brush, click once, and it's there. You can also do the same thing with your copyright watermark (if you download the bonus material from this book's companion website, I have a step-by-step tutorial for you on how to do just that). But for now, let's get on that signature project.

Turning Your Signature Into a Brush

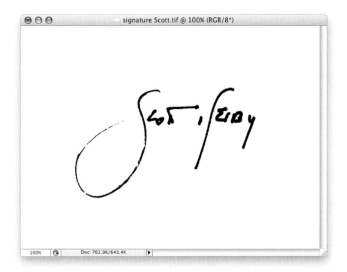

Step One:
The first step to all this is getting your signature into Photoshop CS3. There are basically two ways: (1) take a nice black writing pen, sign your name fairly large on a piece of paper, and then scan your signature (which is what I did here); or (2) if you have a Wacom tablet with its wireless pen, just open a new document (at a resolution of 300 ppi), press D to set your Foreground color to black, get the Brush tool (B), then choose a small, hard-edged brush from the Brush Picker, and sign your name at a fairly large size.

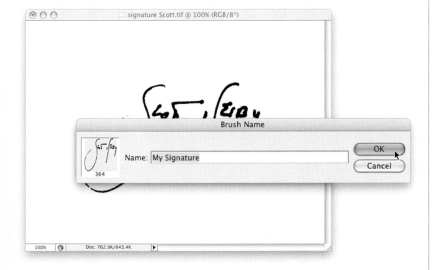

Step Two:
Now go under the Edit menu and choose Define Brush Preset. This brings up the Brush Name dialog (shown here), where you give your new signature brush a name (I named mine "My Signature," which is another carefully thought-out, highly original name) and click OK (as shown here). That's all there is to creating your signature brush, and the nice thing is—you only have to do this once—it's saved into Photoshop's Brush Presets for use in the future. Now let's put this new signature brush to use.

Continued

Step Three:

When you want to apply your signature to a photo, open that photo, get the Brush tool (B), Control-click (PC: Right-click) anywhere inside your image area, and the Brush Picker will appear right at the location of your cursor (as seen here). The new signature brush you just created in Step Two will appear as the last brush in the list of brushes, so scroll all the way down to the bottom, and click on that very last brush (you'll see a tiny version of your signature as the brush's thumbnail).

Step Four:

By default, the brush will be the size it was when you created your Brush Preset, so if you need to change the size of your brush, just drag the Master Diameter slider at the top of the Brush Picker (shown circled here in red). In my case, I needed to drag that slider to the left to make the brush much smaller, because if you look directly under the thumbnail, it shows your brush's size in pixels, and mine was 364 pixels. Kinda big, don'tcha think?

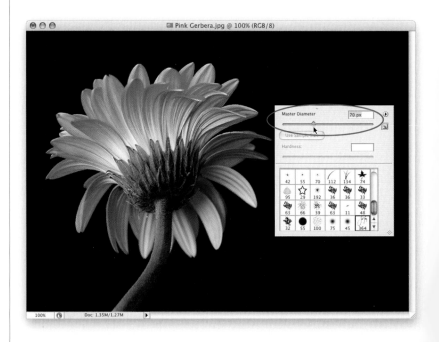

Step Five:
Now that you've got your signature brush, and have adjusted the size, go to the Layers panel and click on the Create a New Layer icon at the bottom. In our example here, the photo has a dark background so I'll have to change my Foreground color from black to something easily seen on a dark background (in this case, I just chose white). Then take the brush, and simply click once where you want the signature to appear (as shown here, where I clicked in the bottom-right corner).

Creating an Online Photo Gallery (Perfect for Client Proofing)

In Photoshop CS3, the Web Gallery function is still pretty limited, but Adobe has been developing something much better (and easier to use) for Adobe Bridge CS3 called the Adobe Media Gallery. AMG didn't initially ship with CS3, but Adobe released a free update for Bridge (version 2.1), and once you installed that update, you could then download the Adobe Media Gallery (from Adobe Labs at http://labs.adobe.com) and try this new feature before it's fully integrated into Bridge (which it could well be by the time you read this).

Step One:

First, make sure you read the intro above so you know to download the free Adobe Media Gallery (AMG) script from Adobe Labs. Now, by the time you read this, Adobe may have released it as a free update to Bridge CS3, so if you open Bridge and look under the Window menu, under Workspace, and see Adobe Media Gallery (as shown here), then you've already got AMG and you can continue on to Step Two. If not, then go download it (the download address is in the intro above), install it (it takes just 60 seconds), then choose Adobe Media Gallery from the Workspace menu (as shown here).

Step Two:

Once you choose AMG, an AMG Preview panel appears in the center, your photos appear in the Content panel in a filmstrip across the bottom of the Bridge window, and the Adobe Media Gallery panel now appears as the right-side panel (as seen here). That center preview area is where a preview of your Flash-based or HTML-based Web photo gallery will appear. Then, you customize your gallery using that AMG panel on the right. By the way, this is really easy stuff, so don't let the panel fool you—you need no Web experience to design a Web gallery.

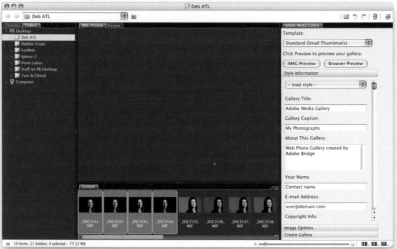

Step Three:

Press-and-hold the Command (PC: Ctrl) key and click on the photos in the Content panel you want in your Web gallery. Now, here's the weird thing: you won't see anything in the center AMG Preview panel until you press the AMG Preview button (as shown here). Once you do, after a few moments it displays a preview of your webpage (the default template is shown here), and sadly you have to press this button each time you want to see a change, or to see a different template layout.

Step Four:

You don't need that Folders panel on the left eating up all that space, so hide it from view by double-clicking directly on the vertical divider line on its right side. (See how much more room that gives you?) Next, you can customize the text that appears on your webpage using the fields in the Style Information section of the AMG panel. Just click on a field and start typing (as shown here). Now, remember: you can't see your new text until you press the AMG Preview button, but once you press it, in a few moments it builds the new preview (as seen in the next step).

Step Five:

If you scroll down further in the panel, you'll see a field for entering your Copyright Info (by the way, if you already added copyright info for this photo in Bridge, it uses that instead). You also can choose how long each photo appears onscreen when someone views your gallery as a slide show, and you can choose the style of transition you'd like (as shown here). Plus, there are color swatches you can click on to customize your page's colors.

Continued

Step Six:

At the bottom of the AMG panel, you'll see a title bar for Image Options. Click on it, and the Image Options section appears (seen here). This is where you choose how large you'd like the thumbnails, and how large you'd like the preview to appear when somebody clicks on one of the thumbnails. If you choose Extra Large as the preview size, it takes quite a bit longer to draw your preview because it creates the extra large previews from the original high-res file, so keep that in mind. And of course, to see any of your changes, you have to click the AMG Preview button once again, and wait until the preview draws.

Step Seven:

One nice feature is that if you decide to try a different template (by choosing it from the Template pop-up menu, as shown here, where I chose the Filmstrip template), it keeps all the custom text and the email link you added intact. The bad news: to see the new template, you have to (you guessed it) press the AMG Preview button again. Arrrggghh! Anyway, that's the way it works (at least, that's the way it worked when I wrote this book), and since it's one whole heck of a lot better than the Web Gallery back in CS2, I'm not going to gripe a lot.

Step Eight:

At the bottom of the AMG panel, there's one more section—Create Gallery (which is where you export your finished page). Click on its title bar, and you'll see a field to name your gallery, and if you click on the Save to Disk radio button (as I did here), you'll be able to choose where on your computer you want to save your exported page using the Browse button. Once selected, click the Save button, and your site is saved into that folder, ready for you to upload to the Web.

Step Nine:

If you're a little more Web savvy, and used to administering your own website, then you can use the built-in FTP function at the bottom of the Create Gallery section (by the way, if you're thinking something like, "What the heck is FTP?" then this isn't for you). You just enter your FTP Server info, username, password, and directory for uploading, then click the Upload button (shown here on the left) and away it goes—straight from Bridge to live online. Not too shabby! Now, regardless of which method you use, I strongly recommend that you go back up to the top of the AMG Panel and click the Browser Preview button (as shown here on the right). This launches your default Web browser, and displays the page in your browser just like your clients will see it, and it's fully functional, so test everything—the links, the email address, etc. The final previewed page is shown here.

So that's the process, and it's really simple (here's a quick recap): (1) Open Bridge and choose Adobe Media Gallery as your workspace. (2) Select the photos you want on your webpage (then hide the left-side Folders panel). (3) Choose a template from the AMG panel, and customize the text by simply typing in the fields, then press the AMG Preview button to see your text and photos previewed in the center AMG Preview panel. (4) In the Image Options section of the AMG panel, you can customize the size of your thumbnails and preview images from the pop-up menus. (5) Preview your finished page by clicking the Browser Preview button, and if all looks right, (6) use the Create Gallery section to export (or upload) your finished gallery.

The Trick to Putting High-Resolution Photos on the Web

When it comes to the Web, we live in a low-resolution world, which greatly limits how much detail our clients (or potential clients) can see in our work. You wouldn't think of uploading a high-res 100 MB+ photo, because it would take forever for the image to appear onscreen. Then came Zoomify. This clever technology (licensed by Adobe and included in CS3) lets you upload the full-res photo, but it loads as fast as a regular JPEG because only the area that appears in the smaller preview window displays at full resolution. As your clients pan and move around your image, each visible area (or tile) is then displayed at full res.

Step One:

You start by opening a high-resolution file in Photoshop (in this case, it's a 42" long panorama at a resolution of 240 ppi, which is made up of 29 individual photos stitched into one long pano). To get it to fit on my computer screen, I have to shrink the view to 8.33% (as seen here), so it's about impossible to see any real detail in the photo. The first step is to go under Photoshop CS3's File menu, under Export, and choose Zoomify (as shown here).

Step Two:

This brings up the Zoomify™ Export dialog (shown here), where you get to decide a number of options about how your high-resolution photo will be displayed on the Web. At the top of the dialog is a Template pop-up menu, and here's where you choose two things: (1) what color the background area surrounding your high-res photo will be, and (2) whether or not you want to have a mini-thumbnail appear in the upper-left corner that can be used for navigating around the full-sized image (kind of like a mini version of Photoshop's Navigator panel). Here, I chose a gray background with the Navigator.

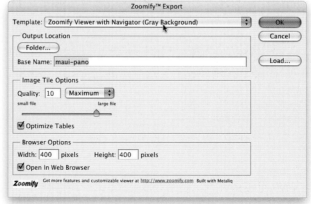

Step Three:

Next you need to pick a location for the final output that Zoomify creates, so under Output Location, click the Folder button and choose where you want it saved on your computer. The Image Tile Options lets you choose the quality of the final image (the default setting of 10 seems to work well). However, the default size in the Browser Options (which is how wide the preview area will appear on your web-page) seems pretty small at 400 pixels, so I usually increase mine to a Width setting of 800 pixels (as shown here). Be sure to leave the Open in Web Browser checkbox turned on so you can see what it's really going to look like on the Web.

Step Four:

Once you click OK, it launches your Web browser and you see your image just as your clients will see it (in our case, with that tiny Navigator in the top-left corner, and with a medium gray background behind your image, as seen here). At the bottom of the preview window is a slider your clients can use to increase the size of your preview, along with navigation buttons to move around (or they can click-and-drag right within the image area or the Navigator to move around).

Step Five:

If you're happy with the results, then look in the folder you chose to save your Zoomify image into (in our case, I saved it into a folder called Upload to Web, as seen here), and you'll need to upload both the folder (which contains the tiles of your high-res image) and the HTML file Zoomify created to your Web server, and you're good to go. Try this once—you'll be absolutely amazed.

TIP: If you want to add a white border around each photo (including the wallet-size photos), then before you open Picture Package, go under the Image menu and choose Canvas Size. Make sure the Relative checkbox is turned on and enter the amount of white border you'd like in the Width and Height fields (i.e., 0.25 inches for a quarter-inch border). Now, make sure your Background color is set to white (at the bottom of the dialog). When you click OK in the Canvas Size dialog, a white border will appear around your photo. Now you can choose Picture Package.

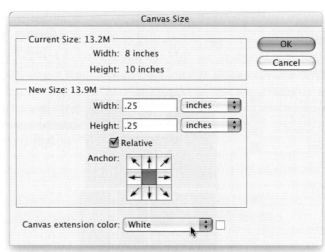

Step Five:
Another nice feature of Picture Package is that you can have two or more different photos on the same Picture Package page (say that three times fast). For example, to change just one of the 2.5x3.5" prints to a different photo, click on the preview of the image that you want to change in the Layout section (as shown here, where I'm clicking on the top one of the 2.5x3.5" photos).

Step Six:
This brings up the standard Open dialog so you can select a photo to replace the one you clicked on. Navigate your way to the photo you want to appear at this size and location on your printed sheet, and click Open. That photo will appear at the right size and position (as seen here).

SCOTT KELBY

Step Seven:

You can replace any other photo (or all the photos) using the same method (here I replaced two of the smaller photos with that same photo I just imported earlier by clicking on each one individually and choosing that same photo to replace it). When the Picture Package layout preview looks the way you want it to, click OK and Photoshop CS3 will create your final document.

Step Eight:

This is really an optional step, but if you decide that the layout you want doesn't appear in the built-in list of layouts, then you can create your own custom layout. You do that by clicking on the Edit Layout button, found just below the Layout preview area (and seen in the close-up of the Layout preview area shown in the previous step—Step Seven). This brings up the Picture Package Edit Layout dialog (shown here). Adobe calls each photo cell a "zone." To delete a zone just click on it, then click on the Delete Zone button. To add a new zone, click on the Add Zone button, and the same photo you currently have selected appears in the blank space. You can grab the corners to resize it to your liking. (*Note:* Drag the corners outward to rotate the photo.) Also, for step-by-step instructions, make sure you download my supplement to this chapter (the Web address is found in "An Unexpected Q&A Section" at the beginning of the book).

How to
Email Photos

Believe it or not, this is one of those most-asked questions, and I guess it's because there are no official guidelines for emailing photos. Perhaps there should be, because there are photographers who routinely send me high-res photos that either (a) get bounced back to them because of size restrictions, (b) take all day to download, or (c) never get here at all because "there are no official guidelines for emailing photos." In the absence of such rules, consider these the "official unofficial rules."

Step One:
Open the photo that you want to email. Before you go any further, you have some decisions to make based on whom you're sending the photo to. If you're sending it to friends and family, you want to make sure the file downloads fast, and (this is important) can be viewed within their email window. I run into people daily (clients) who have no idea how to download an attachment from an email. If it doesn't show up in their email window, they're stuck, and even if they could download it, they don't have a program that will open the file. So the goal: make it fit in their email browser.

Step Two:
Go under the Image menu and choose Image Size (or press Command-Option-I [PC: Ctrl-Alt-I]). Because they'll just be viewing this onscreen, you can lower the resolution to what's called "screen resolution," which is 72 ppi (no matter what kind of monitor or which kind of computer they have). Next, set the Width (in inches) to no wider than 8" (the height isn't the big concern, it's the width, so make sure you stay within the 8" width). By limiting your emailed photo to this size, you're pretty much ensuring that friends and family will be able to download it quickly, and it will fit comfortably within their email window.

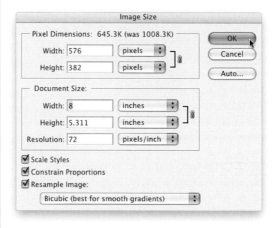

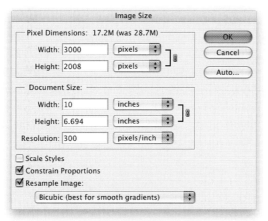

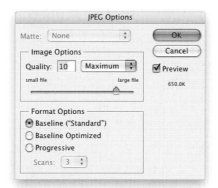

Step Three:

If you're sending this to a client or someone who you'll want to be able to print the photo out on their end, you'll need a bit more resolution. (Shoot for 240 ppi if they're printing to an inkjet printer, or 300 ppi, as shown here, if it will be printed on an actual printing press.) The photo's physical dimensions aren't a big concern now because the client will be downloading and printing out the file, rather than just viewing it onscreen in their email program.

Step Four:

JPEG is the most popular file format for sending photos by email. To save your photo as a JPEG, go under the Edit menu and choose Save As. In the Save As dialog, choose JPEG in the Format pop-up menu, and then click Save. This brings up the JPEG Options dialog (shown here), where you get to choose the amount of compression applied to your image (this compression shrinks the file size for email while maintaining as much of the quality as you choose using the Quality slider. I generally save all my JPEGs at a quality setting of 10, which I think gives great compression with no visible loss of quality).

Step Five:

Your goal is to email a photo that is small in file size (so it downloads quickly), yet still looks good. (Remember, the faster the download, the lower the quality, so you have to be realistic and flexible.) The chart shown here gives you a breakdown of how large the file size and download time would be for an image almost 13x9" saved with different resolutions and different amounts of JPEG compression. It's hard to beat that last one—with a 2-second download on a high-speed connection.

A.	10-megapixel photo (12.413x8.64" at 300 ppi resolution) Saved as a JPEG with **12 Quality setting** Approx. **3.5 MB** in file size · Download high speed: 38 seconds
B.	10-megapixel photo (12.413x8.64" at 300 ppi resolution) Saved as a JPEG with **10 Quality setting** Approx. **1.8 MB** in file size · Download high speed: 19 seconds
C.	10-megapixel photo (12.413x8.64" at 300 ppi resolution) Saved as a JPEG with **6 Quality setting** Approx. **710 KB** in file size · Download high speed: 7 seconds
D.	10-megapixel photo (12.413x8.64" at **72 ppi** resolution) Saved as a JPEG with **10 Quality setting** Approx. **256 KB** in file size · Download high speed: 2 seconds

Fine Art Poster Layout

This technique gives your work the layout of a professional poster, yet it's incredibly easy to do. In fact, once you learn how to do it, this is the perfect technique to turn into a Photoshop action. That way, anytime you want to give your image the poster look, you can do it at the press of a button.

Step One:

Press Command-N (PC: Ctrl-N) to create a new document in the size you want for your fine art poster layout (in our example here, I'm creating a standard-sized 11x14" print). Set your Resolution to 240 ppi (for color inkjet printing), then click OK to create your new blank document.

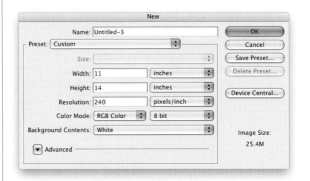

Step Two:

Open the photo you want to feature in your fine art poster layout. Get the Move tool (V) and click-and-drag that photo over into your fine art poster layout (as shown here). Press Command-T (PC: Ctrl-T) to bring up Free Transform. Press-and-hold the Shift key, grab a corner, and drag inward to size the photo down so it fits within your layout like the photo shown here. To perfectly center your photo within the document, click on the Background layer, press-and-hold the Command (PC: Ctrl) key, and click on the photo layer to select both layers. Then go up to the Options Bar, and click on the Align Horizontal Centers icon (circled here in red) to center the photo side-to-side (as shown here).

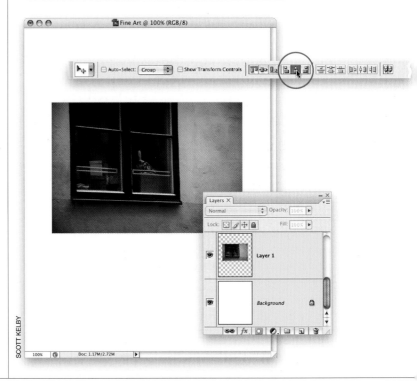

SCOTT KELBY

Step Three:

Go to the Layers panel, and click on the Background layer to select it. Now, click on the Create a New Layer icon at the bottom of the Layers panel to create a new blank layer, then get the Rectangular Marquee tool (M) and click-and-drag out a selection that is about 1/2" larger than your photo (as shown here). You're going to turn this selection into a fake mat. Press D, then X to make your Foreground color white, then fill this selected area with white by pressing Option-Delete (PC: Alt-Backspace).

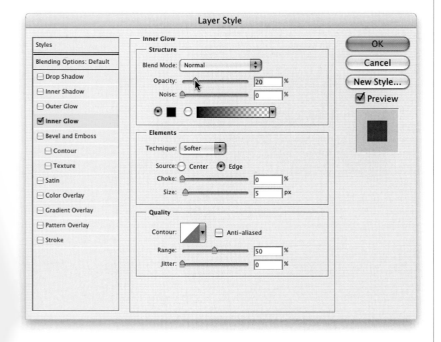

Step Four:

To create the mat effect, choose Inner Glow from the Add a Layer Style pop-up menu at the bottom of the Layers panel. This brings up the Inner Glow section of the Layer Style dialog. Click on the light yellow color swatch below the Noise slider and change the color of the glow to black. You won't be able to see the glow at this point, because the default blend mode for the Inner Glow is Screen, so to see your glow, change the Blend Mode pop-up menu (near the top of the dialog) to Normal. Increase the Size of the glow to 5 (try 10 for very high-res photos), then lower the Opacity of this glow to 20% (as shown here) to create the subtle shadow of a beveled mat (as seen in the next step), and click OK.

Continued

Step Five:

Press Command-D (PC: Ctrl-D) and you'll see the mat-like effect is in place around your photo. Although you want the photo centered side-to-side, you don't want the photo centered top-to-bottom. Fine art posters generally have the photo well above the center of the photo, at what is called the "optical center," which is the area just above the center. To move the photo up, go to the Layers panel, select both the photo layer and the mat layer beneath it, then get the Move tool (V), and use the Up Arrow key on your keyboard to nudge the photo and mat upward until it's well above the center top-to-bottom (as seen in the next step).

Step Six:

Now it's time to add your poster text. Press the letter T to get the Type tool to add your text (i.e., the name of your studio, the name of the poster, whatever you'd like). I chose the font Trajan Pro at 24 points, and I typed in upper- and lowercase (this font comes with the Creative Suite, so chances are you already have it installed. It actually doesn't have lowercase letters—instead, it uses large caps and smaller caps, as seen here). The extra space between the letters adds an elegant look to the type. To do that, highlight your type with the Type tool, then go to the Character panel (found under the Window menu), and in the Tracking field enter 120.

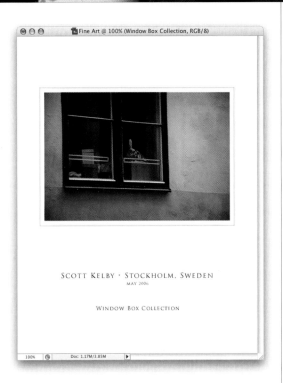

Step Seven:

The easiest way to add more type is to press Command-J (PC: Ctrl-J) to duplicate the Type layer. Then you can change the size of the type, and add additional lines of text (as I did here, where I added a line underneath the top line with the date the photo was taken. Then I duplicated the Type layer again and added the bottom line of text). To center all three lines of type side-to-side perfectly within your image area, click on the Background layer in the Layers panel, and then Command-click (PC: Ctrl-click) on each Type layer so all three layers are selected. Press V to get the Move tool, and in the Options Bar, you'll see four sets of alignment icons. In the second set from the left, click on the Align Horizontal Centers icon to center your text beneath your image.

Step Eight:

Lastly, you can add your signature (either after it's printed, or right within Photoshop CS3 itself if you have a scan of your signature or a Wacom tablet where you can just use the tablet's wireless pen to create a digital signature). Here's the final photo with my signature added under the right corner, and the letters "a/p" under the left corner, which stands for "Artist Print" indicating the print was output by the photographer him/herself.

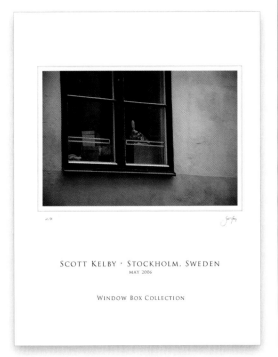

Simple Three-Photo Balanced Layout

This is just a simple layout that is very effective. It would work great as a template using Smart Objects, but since we've been down that road before (in Chapter 4), we'll just do it the old-fashioned way. Just don't forget that when it comes to bringing in the three photos for this layout, instead of opening them you could place them as Smart Objects. Hey, I'm just sayin'.

Step One:
Press Command-N (PC: Ctrl-N) and create a new document that is very wide (the one shown here is 11" wide by 3" deep). Go to the Layers panel, click on the Create a New Layer icon at the bottom of the panel, and then get the Rectangular Marquee tool (M). Press-and-hold the Shift key, and on the left side of the document, drag out a square selection (since you're holding the Shift key—don't worry—it will be perfectly square) that is almost as tall as the document itself (leave approximately ½" of white space all the way around). Press D to set your Foreground color to black, then press Option-Delete (PC: Alt-Backspace) to fill your selection with black. Don't Deselect.

Step Two:
Press V to get the Move tool from the Toolbox. Press-and-hold Option-Shift (PC: Alt-Shift), then click-and-drag yourself a copy of your selected black square. Drag it all the way over to approximately the same position on the right side of your document, as shown here. (Holding the Option key makes a duplicate of your square, and holding the Shift key keeps it perfectly aligned with the other square as you're dragging to the right.)

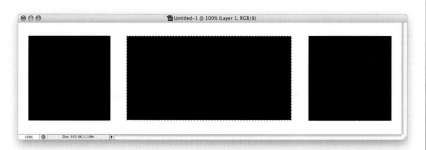

Step Three:

Deselect by pressing Command-D (PC: Ctrl-D). Switch back to the Rectangular Marquee tool, but this time don't hold the Shift key (that way, you can draw a rectangle). Now, draw a rectangular selection between the two squares, leaving approximately the same amount of space between your shapes (as shown here). Then fill that long rectangle with black. So, what you have is (from L to R): a black square, a long black rectangle, and another black square. Press Command-D (PC: Ctrl-D) to Deselect.

Step Four:

Open the photo you want to appear over the square on the left. Get the Move tool and drag-and-drop it into your three-square document. Once the photo appears, press Command-T (PC: Ctrl-T) to bring up Free Transform. Now you'll resize the photo (probably making it smaller) so it's slightly larger than the square on the left (as shown here), then press the Return (PC: Enter) key to lock in your resizing. *Note:* If you can't see the Free Transform handles, press Command-0 (zero; PC: Ctrl-0) to zoom out to where they will show.

Step Five:

Now press Command-Option-G (PC: Ctrl-Alt-G) to mask your rectangular photo into that black square (as shown here). You can get the Move tool and reposition your photo inside that black square by just clicking-and-dragging on it. Don't freak out if you see part of your photo appearing in the center rectangle (like you see here), because we'll cover that with a different photo layer.

Continued

Step Six:

Now repeat the last two steps, opening two other photos, and resizing them so that they're slightly larger than the boxes they're going to be masked into. Once one of them is sized, press Command-Option-G (PC: Ctrl-Alt-G) to mask it into the shape. Then do the same for the other photo. If, when you're done, any one of those photos extends into a different box, just go to the Layers panel and move that layer down one (or two) layers until that extra area is hidden behind one of the other masked photos.

Step Seven:

Now, unless the three photos were taken in almost the exact same light, chances are at least one of them is going to look a bit funky (colorwise), so you might want to consider creating a tint over all three (it's an easy way to ensure the colors match). Click on the top layer in your layer stack, then choose Hue/Saturation from the Create New Adjustment Layer pop-up menu at the bottom of the Layers panel (as shown here).

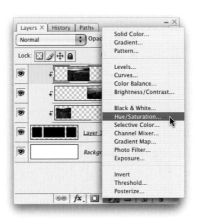

Step Eight:

When the Hue/Saturation dialog appears, turn on the Colorize checkbox, then set the Hue to 25, and the Saturation to 25, and click OK to add this slightly reddish-yellow sepia tone effect to all three photos at once. By the way, this is a great combination for instantly adding a sepia tone effect to wedding photos.

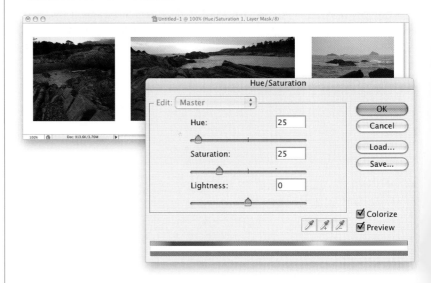

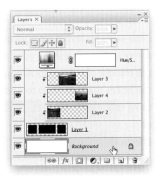

Step Nine:

The final step is to go to the Layers panel, click on the Background layer (as shown here), and press Option-Delete (PC: Alt-Backspace) to fill the Background layer with black.

Step 10:

Here's the final image, and I think what makes it work is the balance and visual interest between the two square shapes on the ends and the longer rectangle shape in the middle. Remember, this can be saved as a template, and then you can use Smart Objects to quickly change out the photos (as shown a couple of different times next in this chapter).

Exposure: 1/25s | Focal Length: 17mm | Aperture Value: ƒ/9.0

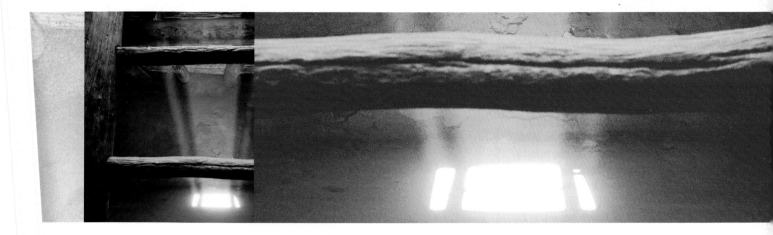

Working for a Livin'
my step-by-step workflow

This is the first time this chapter has appeared in any version of this book, and the only reason it's here is because I promised my assistant Kathy that I would find a way to include a Huey Lewis song as one of my chapter titles, but by the time the book was done, I didn't have one, and there's no way she was going to let this book go to press without one. (She has an unnatural obsession with '80s singer Huey Lewis. She's seen the movie *Duets* [where he plays a karaoke singer] 316 times as of the writing of this book. By the time it comes off press, she will have seen it 321 times, based on past experience. It's sad to see someone destroying her life like this, so I've been trying to focus her attention on something more positive like drinking or shoplifting, and she's making some progress there. Sadly though, one day she got pretty hammered, went into Walmart, shoved a copy of *Back to the Future* into her purse, ran out to the parking lot, jumped into her DeLorean, and nearly sideswiped a kid on a skateboard wearing a red sleeveless hunting vest.) Anyway, this chapter, an homage to the song "Working for a Livin'" by Huey Lewis & the News, is where I bring the whole process together, from importing the photos into Bridge, to correcting the images, sharpening, and printing—the whole thing, in the same workflow order I use everyday in my own work. So, this is the mini-chapter where it all comes together. It's where the rubber meets the road. Where the brick meets the pavement. Where the goose gets the gander. Where Bartles meets Jaymes. Where the roaster grinds the coffee (where the roaster grinds the coffee?), etc.

You Don't Have to be a Professional to Shoot Like One

Step-by-Step Secrets For How To Make Your Photos Look Like The Pros'

Scott Kelby, the man who changed the "digital darkroom" forever with his groundbreaking, #1 best-selling, award-winning book, *The Photoshop Book for Digital Photographers*, now tackles the most important side of digital photography—how to take pro-quality shots using the same tricks today's top digital pros use (and it's easier than you'd think). This isn't a book full of confusing jargon and detailed concepts. This is a book on which button to push, which setting to use, and nearly 200 of the most closely guarded "tricks of the trade" to get you shooting dramatically sharper, more colorful, more professional-looking photos with your digital camera. There's never been a book like it, and if you're tired of taking shots that look "okay," or if you're tired of looking in photography magazines and thinking, "Why don't my shots look like that?" then this is the book for you. *Cover Price: $19.99*

Available at a bookstore near you.